CW01080930

Moral Uncertainty

Moral Uncertainty

WILLIAM MACASKILL,
KRISTER BYKVIST, AND
TOBY ORD

OXFORD
UNIVERSITY PRESS

OXFORD

UNIVERSITY PRESS

Great Clarendon Street, Oxford, OX2 6DP,
United Kingdom

Oxford University Press is a department of the University of Oxford.
It furthers the University's objective of excellence in research, scholarship,
and education by publishing worldwide. Oxford is a registered trade mark of
Oxford University Press in the UK and in certain other countries

Published in the United States of America by Oxford University Press
198 Madison Avenue, New York, NY 10016, United States of America

British Library Cataloguing in Publication Data
Data available

Library of Congress Control Number: 2020932188

ISBN 978-0-19-872227-4

Printed and bound in Great Britain by
Clays Ltd, Elcograf S.p.A.

Links to third party websites are provided by Oxford in good faith and
for information only. Oxford disclaims any responsibility for the materials
contained in any third party website referenced in this work.

For Derek Parfit, a mentor and friend.

Acknowledgements

The authors would like to thank Ron Aboodi, Per Algander, Amanda Askell, Frank Arntzenius, Gustaf Arrhenius, Ralf Bader, Nick Bostrom, Richard Bradley, John Broome, Owen Cotton-Barratt, Erik Carlson, Sven Danielsson, Dan Deasy, Ben Eidelson, Anna Folland, Hilary Greaves, Johan Gustafsson, Anandi Hattiangadi, Iwao Hirose, Benjamin Kiesewetter, Jimmy Lenman, Jeff McMahan, Andreas Mogensen, Dan Moller, Graham Oddie, Jonas Olson, Jan Österberg, Mike Otsuka, Peter Pagin, Derek Parfit, Jessica Pepp, Filip Poignant, Wlodek Rabinowicz, Stefan Riedener, Michael Ridge, Olle Risberg, Simon Rosenqvist, Jacob Ross, Julian Savulescu, Andrew Sepielli, Peter Singer, Howard Sobel, Michael Smith, Bastian Stern, Folke Tersman, Torbjörn Tännsjö, Alex Voorhoeve, Ralph Wedgwood, Alex Worsnip, and Michael Zimmerman. For especially detailed comments, we would like to thank Christian Tarsney. We would also like to thank audiences at: the Rocky Mountain Ethics Congress, Boulder; the Stockholm Centre for Healthcare Ethics Workshop on Moral Uncertainty; the CRNAP workshops on moral epistemology at Princeton and Oxford; the Economics and Philosophy workshop at Princeton; the Centre de recherche en éthique de l'Université de Montréal; the Cumberland Lodge Weekend, organized by LSE; the British Society for Ethical Theory conference; and seminars at the Universities of Leeds, LSE, Oxford, and Princeton.

Some of the work in this book has been published before.

Chapters 1 (sections I–II), 2–6, and 8–9 are based in part on William MacAskill's DPhil thesis (though many passages within that thesis cited unpublished work by Toby Ord).

Chapter 1 (section III) draws, to some extent, on two papers by Krister Bykvist: 'Evaluative Uncertainty and Consequentialist Environmental Ethics' in: Leonard Kahn and Avram Hiller (eds), *Consequentialism and Environmental Ethics*, pp. 122–35, London: Routledge, doi: 10.4324/9780203379790, Copyright © 2014, and 'How to Do Wrong Knowingly and Get Away with it' in: Rysiek Sliwinski and Frans Svensson (eds.), *Neither/Nor: Philosophical Papers Dedicated to Erik Carlson on the Occasion of His Fiftieth Birthday*, Volume 58 in UPPSALA PHILOSOPHICAL STUDIES, pp. 31–47, Uppsala: Uppsala University, Copyright © 2011.

Chapter 2 is significantly based on William MacAskill and Toby Ord. 'Why Maximize Expected Choice-Worthiness', *Noûs* (July 2019), Copyright © 2019 by Wiley Periodicals, Inc.

The bulk of Chapter 3 is based on William MacAskill, 'Normative Uncertainty as a Voting Problem', *Mind*, Volume 125, Issue 500, pp. 967–1004, doi: 10.1093/mind/fzv169, Copyright © 2016, reprinted by permission of Oxford University Press: https://academic.oup.com/mind.

Chapter 4 is significantly based on Owen Cotton-Barratt, William MacAskill, and Toby Ord, 'Statistical Normalization Methods in Interpresonal and Intertheoretic Comparisons', *Journal of Philosophy* (forthcoming), Copyright © 2019.

Part of Chapter 6 is based on William MacAskill, 'The Infectiousness of Nihilism', *Ethics*, Volume 123, Issue 3, pp. 508–20, doi: 10.1086/669564, Copyright © 2013 by the University of Chicago Press. All rights reserved.

Chapter 7 is based on two papers co-authored by Krister Bykvist and Jonas Olson: 'Expressivism and Moral Certitude', *The Philosophical Quarterly*, Volume 59, Issue 235, pp. 202–15, doi: 10.1111/j.1467-9213.2008.580.x, Copyright © 2008 The Editors of *The Philosophical Quarterly*, reprinted by permission of Oxford University Press: https://academic.oup.com/pq, and 'Against the *Being For* Account of Normative Certitude', *Journal of Ethics and Social Philosophy*, Volume 6, Issue 2, pp. 1–8, doi: 10.26556/jesp.v6i2.63, Copyright © 2012.

Contents

Introduction

We are often uncertain about what we ought, morally, to do. Suppose that Alice has £20 to spend. With that money, she could eat out at a pleasant restaurant. Alternatively, she could pay for four long-lasting insecticide-treated bed nets that would protect eight children against malaria for two years.[1] Let's suppose that Alice knows all the morally relevant empirical facts about what that £20 could do. Even so, it might be that she still doesn't know whether she's obligated to donate that money or whether it's permissible for her to pay for the meal out, because she just doesn't know how strong her moral obligations to distant strangers are. If so, then even though Alice knows all the relevant empirical facts, she doesn't know what she ought to do.

Or suppose that the members of a government are making a decision about whether to tax carbon emissions. Let's assume that they know all the relevant facts about what would happen as a result of the tax: it would make presently existing people worse off, since they would consume less oil and coal, and would therefore be less economically productive; but it would slow down climate change, thereby on balance increasing the welfare of people living in the future. But the members of the government don't know how to weigh the interests of future people against the interests of presently existing people. So, again, the members of this government don't ultimately know what they ought to do.

These are instances of *moral uncertainty*: uncertainty that stems not from uncertainty about descriptive matters, but about moral or evaluative matters. Moral uncertainty is commonplace: given the difficulty of ethics and the widespread disagreement about ethical issues, moral uncertainty is not the exception, but the norm.

Moral uncertainty matters. If we don't know how to weigh the interests of future generations against the current generation, then we don't yet know

---

[1] For the relevant estimates, see GiveWell, 'Against Malaria Foundation', November 2016, http://www.givewell.org/charities/against-malaria-foundation/November-2016-version.

Moral Uncertainty. William MacAskill, Krister Bykvist, and Toby Ord, Oxford University Press (2020).
© William MacAskill, Krister Bykvist and Toby Ord.
DOI: 10.1093/oso/9780198722274.001.0001

how we ought to act in response to climate change. If we don't know how to weigh the interests of distant strangers against compatriots, then we don't yet know the extent of our duties to the global poor. We aren't going to resolve these difficult moral questions any time soon. But we still need to act now. So we need to know how to act, despite our uncertainty.

Given the prevalence and importance of moral uncertainty, one would expect ethicists to have devoted considerable research effort to the topic of how one ought to make decisions in the face of moral uncertainty. But this topic has been neglected. In modern times, only one book and fewer than twenty published articles deal with the topic at length.[2] The book you are reading attempts to begin to address this gap.

In this book, we address the questions of whether there are norms that are distinct from first-order moral norms that govern how one ought to act given one's fundamental moral uncertainty and, if so, what those norms are.

These questions raise many difficult theoretical issues, and we don't pretend to have comprehensive solutions to all of them. Our aim, instead, is to offer an up-to-date introduction to the topic, make a first pass at solving some of these issues, and to invite others to build on this work. Though we cover many topics, the core of our argument is to defend an information-sensitive approach to decision-making under moral uncertainty: accepting that different moral views provide different amounts of information regarding our reasons for action, and that the correct account of decision-making under moral uncertainty is sensitive to that. Ultimately, the default account we defend is a form of *maximizing expected choiceworthiness*. We defend various departures from this default position for cases in which expectation is not well-defined.

Before we begin, let us clarify some terms and delimit the scope of this book. When we refer to 'moral uncertainty', we use 'moral' in the broad sense, referring to uncertainty about what we all-things-considered morally ought to do. We can distinguish this from the even broader term 'normative uncertainty', which also applies to uncertainty about which

---

[2] We say 'modern times' because there was also extensive discussion of similar issues by Catholic theologians, such as Bartholomew Medina, Blaise Pascal, and Alphonsus Liguori. See Bartolomé de Medina, *Expositio in primam secundae angelici doctoris D. Thomæ Aquinatis*, 1577; Blaise Pascal, *Lettres Provinciales*, 1657; Alphonsus Liguori, *Theologia Moralis*, 2nd edn, 1755. For a summary of this discussion, see F. J. Connell, 'Probabilism', in Thomas Carson (ed.), *The New Catholic Encyclopedia*, 2nd edn, Detroit, MI: Thomson/Gale, 2002. For discussion of this debate and its relevance to the modern debate on moral uncertainty, see Andrew Sepielli, '"Along an Imperfectly Lighted Path": Practical Rationality and Normative Uncertainty', PhD thesis, Rutgers University, 2010, pp. 46–51.

theory of rational choice is correct,[3] and uncertainty about which theory of epistemology is correct. A full treatment of these additional issues would warrant a book of its own, so we have chosen to focus exclusively on moral uncertainty.

There are also issues relevant to moral uncertainty that, for reasons of focus, we do not address, except briefly. We do not thoroughly address the issue of whether moral ignorance is exculpatory in the same way that empirical ignorance is exculpatory, though we discuss this briefly in Chapter 1.[4] We do not significantly discuss the extent to which one should alter one's moral beliefs in light of moral disagreement, and, apart from a short discussion in the first chapter arguing that we ought to be at least reasonably unsure in our moral views, we do not discuss the question of what credences one ought to have in first-order moral theories. Finally, simply to remain focused, we do not attempt any significant discussion of the long-running debate within Catholic theology about what to do when different Church Fathers disagreed on some moral matter.[5]

Instead, the focus of this book is firmly on the question:

Given that we are morally uncertain, how ought we to act in light of that uncertainty?

We make the following structural assumptions about what a decision under moral uncertainty looks like. We consider a decision-maker choosing from a set of jointly exhaustive and mutually exclusive options (A, B, C, ...). These options could be acts, or they could be plans of action, or anything else that could be the subject of choice and moral assessment.

We suppose that the decision-maker has credence in each of a set of first-order moral theories (T_1, T_2, T_3, ...). We will normally talk about these theories as if they are complete stand-alone moral theories, such as a particular form of utilitarianism. However, they could often just as well represent partially specified theories, or particular moral considerations regarding the options at hand, such as whether killing is equivalent to letting die.

We will sometimes represent the credence in a given theory with a real number between zero and one. This is not to assume that we have precise

---

[3] For an introduction to this issue, see William MacAskill, 'Smokers, Psychos, and Decision-Theoretic Uncertainty', *The Journal of Philosophy*, vol. 113, no. 9 (September 2016), pp. 1–21.

[4] For a discussion of this issue, see Elizabeth Harman, 'Does Moral Ignorance Exculpate?', *Ratio*, vol. 24, no. 4 (December 2011), pp. 443–68.

[5] See footnote 2 for references to some of the literature on this topic.

credences in these theories. Nothing will turn upon the exact values of these credences, and we believe that everything we say could just as well be said if we were to use imprecise credences. In this book, we remain agnostic on whether theories of moral uncertainty should be specified with respect to decision-makers' actual credences or to their epistemic credences (that is, the credences they ought, epistemically, to have). Everything we say could apply given either choice.[6]

We will assume that the theories under consideration assess these options in terms of *choiceworthiness*, which represents the strength of the reasons for choosing an option. This need not be quantitative: it could just provide an ordering of which options are more choiceworthy than others. We will often consider theories which can make at least roughly quantitative judgments about choiceworthiness, such that one option might be slightly more choiceworthy than a second, but much more choiceworthy than a third. We will occasionally use numbers to represent these levels, and define a *choiceworthiness function* as a numerical representation of a theory's choiceworthiness ordering such that a higher number represents a more choiceworthy option. Apart from the subsection on supererogation in section IV of Chapter 2, where we discuss the issue of the relationship between choiceworthiness and deontic status, we'll call an option *permissible* (right) iff it is maximally choiceworthy (that is, iff there is no option that is more choiceworthy than it in the option set), and *impermissible* (wrong) if it is not maximally choiceworthy. Occasionally, where it is more natural to do so, we'll talk about 'severity of wrongness' or 'moral value' rather than choiceworthiness; we mean this to refer to the same concept.

Some decisions made under moral uncertainty are intuitively superior to others. For example, intuitively there is something important to be said against choosing option A when all theories in which you have credence consider it to be impermissible, and they all consider option B to be permissible— even if, according to the true moral theory, action A is the morally correct choice. We shall use the term *appropriate* to make such assessments of options under moral uncertainty, where A is more appropriate than B iff a rational and morally conscientious agent who had the same set of options and beliefs would prefer A to B.[7] As we use the term, to say that an act is

---

[6] For an argument that the theory should be specified in terms of epistemic credences, see Andrew Sepielli, 'How Moral Uncertaintism Can Be Both True and Interesting', *Oxford Studies in Normative Ethics*, vol. 7 (2017), pp. 98–116. https://www.oxfordscholarship.com/view/10.1093/oso/9780198808930.001.0001/oso-9780198808930-chapter-6

[7] We put aside cases where this account of appropriateness will give the wrong results, such as when a decision-maker who is not in fact morally conscientious faces a situation where an

appropriate is to say that no alternative option is more appropriate than it. More than one option can be appropriate, some options may be more appropriate than others, some may be *incomparable* in appropriateness, and there may be degrees of appropriateness.

This framework allows us to more precisely state the central question of this book:

For any given set of credences in moral theories and set of options that a decision-maker can have, what is the appropriateness ordering of the options within that option set?

We shall generally assume descriptive certainty, though it is of course possible to simultaneously have descriptive and moral uncertainty. This is just to simplify things.[8]

Our approach to answering the central question is as follows. We look at the different *informational situations* that decision-makers can find themselves in with respect to the theories they face, where an informational situation is determined by the way in which choiceworthiness can be compared both within each theory in which the decision-maker has credence, and across those theories.

In this book, the approach we take is 'divide and conquer'. We ask, for each of a number of different informational situations, what the correct theory of decision-making under moral uncertainty is given that informational situation. As an analogy for this approach: one might argue that, under empirical uncertainty, maximize expected value is the correct theory when one has determinate credences across all possible outcomes, but that maximin is the correct theory when one has no clue what credence to assign to different outcomes.

There is a wide range of possible informational situations, and in this book we will not be able to go through them all. We hope to demonstrate

---

evil demon has set things up such that a certain action is good only if the decision-maker is morally conscientious. Accommodating cases like this is not important for the project of this book.

[8] For an interesting argument that one cannot plausibly take both moral and empirical uncertainty into account at the same time, see Ittay Nissan-Rozen, 'Against Moral Hedging', *Economics and Philosophy*, vol. 31, no. 3 (November 2015), pp. 349–69. However, we don't find his argument compelling. If you are motivated to take moral uncertainty seriously, and you are genuinely unsure about how risk-averse you ought, morally, to be, then you should not find what Nissan-Rozen calls 'Standard Dominance' plausible; and if you don't find it plausible, then his argument has no bite.

Table 0.1

		Comparability Conditions			
		Full comparability	Unit-comparability	Level-comparability	Incomparability
Measurability Conditions	Ratio-scale	✓	✓	✗	✗
	Interval-scale	✓	✓	✗	✓
	Ordinal scale			✗	✓
	Preorder			✗	✓

the fruitfulness of the divide and conquer approach; we do not pretend to be comprehensive in its application. We therefore lay out the main possible informational situations in Table 0.1. We indicate with a tick which set-ups we consider, and shade out those informational conditions that are not possible:

The measurability of a theory describes which *intra*theoretic comparisons of choiceworthiness can be made, where the different measurability conditions we highlight are as follows.

First, a theory can give a preorder. If so, then the choiceworthiness relation is transitive (for all A, B, C, if A is at least as choiceworthy as B, and B is at least as choiceworthy as C, then A is at least as choiceworthy as C), and reflexive (for all A, A is at least as choiceworthy as A), but it is not complete (where completeness is the property that for all A, B, either A is at least as choiceworthy as B or vice-versa.) We therefore cannot represent the theory with a choiceworthiness function. A choiceworthiness preorder would naturally result from a theory on which some values are incomparable.

Second, a theory can give *ordinal scale measurable* choiceworthiness. On such theories, the choiceworthiness relation is transitive, reflexive and complete (therefore ranking options as 1st, 2nd, 3rd (etc.) in terms of choiceworthiness) and the relation can therefore be represented with a choiceworthiness function. However, such theories don't give any information about *how much* more choiceworthy the most choiceworthy option is, rather than the second most choiceworthy. More precisely: Let CW_i be a numerical representation of T_i's choiceworthiness ordering, such that

$CW_i(A) > CW_i(B)$ iff A is more choiceworthy than B on T_i. If T_i is ordinal scale measurable, then CW_j also represents T_i iff $CW_j = f(CW_i)$, where $f(x)$ is any strictly increasing transformation.

Third, theories that provide *interval-scale measurable* choiceworthiness give us not just ordinal information about choiceworthiness, but also tell us the ratio of differences in choiceworthiness between options. More precisely: If T_i gives interval-scale measurable choiceworthiness and CW_i is a numerical representation of T_i's choiceworthiness ordering, then CW_j also represents T_i iff $CW_j = kCW_i + c$, where k and c are real numbers with $k > 0$.

Fourth, theories could also potentially provide *ratio-scale* measurable choiceworthiness, in which case they would have a non-arbitrary zero point, and give meaning to ratios between the absolute levels of choiceworthiness of options. More precisely: If T_i gives ratio-scale measurable choiceworthiness and CW_i is a numerical representation of T_i's choiceworthiness ordering, then CW_j also represents T_i iff $CW_j = kCW_i$, where $k > 0$.

The comparability of two or more theories describes which *inter*theoretic comparisons of choiceworthiness can be made, where the different comparability conditions we highlight are as follows.

If two moral theories are *unit-comparable*, then we can meaningfully make claims about the ratio of differences in choiceworthiness between options across theories: we can say that the difference in choiceworthiness between A and B on T_i (where A is more choiceworthy than B on T_i) is k times as great as the difference in choiceworthiness between C and D on T_j (where C is more choiceworthy than D on T_j).

Whether or not they are unit-comparable, two theories might also be *level-comparable*. If two theories are level-comparable, then we can meaningfully say that the choiceworthiness of one option, on one theory, is greater than, equal to, or less than, the choiceworthiness of another option on the other theory.

If two moral theories are *fully comparable*, then the *intertheoretic* comparisons of choiceworthiness that can be made between theories are the same as the *intratheoretic* comparisons of choiceworthiness that can be made within each theory. So, for example, two interval-scale measurable theories that are fully comparable are both unit-comparable and level-comparable; two ratio-scale measurable theories that are fully comparable are both level-comparable and ratio-comparable (where we can compare the ratios of levels of choiceworthiness across both theories).

If two moral theories are *incomparable*, then they are neither unit- nor level-comparable. We cannot say that the difference in choiceworthiness between two options on one theory is larger, smaller or equally as great as the difference in choiceworthiness between two options on the other theory; nor can we say that the level of choiceworthiness of one option on one theory is greater, smaller, or equal to the level of choiceworthiness on the other theory.

We believe that Table 0.1 provides at least the primary informational situations of interest. But this table could be expanded. Though we doubt that such an idea is meaningful, one could potentially consider theories on which choiceworthiness is measured on an absolute scale (where no transformation of the theory's choiceworthiness function is permissible). More interestingly, one could also consider situations of ratio-scale or interval-scale measurability with intratheoretic incomparability; the meaningfulness of such a notion has been shown by Erik Carlson.[9]

Within those informational situations that we have listed above, we are able to investigate in depth only three, which we regard as particularly important: interval-scale measurability with unit-comparability, interval-scale measurability without unit or level-comparability, and ordinal scale measurability without level-comparability. Because we don't discuss conditions of level-comparability in this book, when we refer to *intertheoretic comparability* we are referring in every instance to unit-comparability.

We restrict ourselves to these informational conditions just to make things easier for ourselves: this is only the second modern book written on the topic of decision-making under moral uncertainty and we have to pick our battles if we are to make progress at all. However, in Chapter 6, we do briefly discuss how our account might be able to handle theories with incomplete choiceworthiness orderings. We do hope, though cannot argue here, that many other informational conditions can be treated in a similar way to how we treat the informational conditions we do consider.[10]

Of the informational situations that we don't discuss, one has been studied by other philosophers: Christian Tarnsey and Ron Aboodi have

---

[9] Erik Carlson, 'Extensive Measurement with Incomparability'. *Journal of Mathematical Psychology*, vol. 52, no. 4 (2008), pp. 250–9. We also note the possibility of multidimensional scales, and different scales to account for various infinite number systems (such as the extended reals, transfinite ordinals, infinite cardinals, hyperreals and surreals; we thank Christian Tarsney for emphasizing this.

[10] For example, Christian Tarsney ('Rationality and Moral Risk', dissertation, pp. 181–2) argues that binary structure (where a theory simply puts all options into two categories, 'permissible' and 'impermissible' and says nothing more) is importantly distinct from ordinal structure. Whether or not that is true, we are inclined to treat the two informational conditions in the same way, using the Borda method to aggregate both forms of uncertainty.

discussed what to do in conditions of ordinal measurability and level-comparability.[11] They argue in favour of stochastic dominance as a condition of adequacy on any theory of decision-making under such conditions. We find their approach promising—though there is much more work to be done in order to develop a complete theory—but simply for reasons of focus we are not able to discuss their work in this book. We don't know of work that addresses the other informational conditions. We believe that studying these informational conditions is a ripe area for further work.

As we will see, a decision-maker under moral uncertainty can face more than one of these informational situations at one and the same time, when theories in which the decision-maker has credence differ in how we can make choiceworthiness comparisons within or between them. We discuss this in Chapter 4.

With this terminology and these clarifications in hand, we can describe the structure of the book, as follows. In Chapter 1, we introduce the topic of moral uncertainty and argue that we should take moral uncertainty seriously, in particular arguing that there is a meaningful sense of 'ought' that is relative to moral uncertainty.

In Chapter 2, we will show that the problem of moral uncertainty cannot be solved by just saying that we should follow the moral theory we have most credence in, or by just saying that we should choose the option that is most likely to be morally right. Instead, we argue that one should treat empirical and normative uncertainty analogously and that, therefore, what we should do in cases of moral uncertainty depends upon both the decision-maker's credences over moral theories and the degrees of choiceworthiness that those theories assign to options. More specifically, we argue that, in conditions where all the moral views in which we have credence are both interval-scale measurable and intertheoretically comparable and we have well-defined credences, we should *maximize expected choiceworthiness*. We defend this idea against two objections: that the account is too demanding, and that it can't account for theories that allow for supererogation.

In Chapters 3–5, we discuss what we consider to be the most serious problems facing any account similar to *maximize expected choiceworthiness*: that sometimes choiceworthiness is not comparable across different moral

[11] Christian Tarsney, 'Moral Uncertainty for Deontologists', *Ethical Theory and Moral Practice*, (forthcoming); Ron Aboodi, 'Is There Still Room for Intertheoretic Choice-Worthiness Comparisons?', MS, University of Toronto.

theories and that sometimes theories do not even give meaningful quantities of choiceworthiness. In Chapter 3, we introduce an analogy between decision-making under moral uncertainty and the problem of social choice, and show how this allows us to develop principles for decision-making under moral uncertainty even when faced with theories that provide merely ordinal choiceworthiness and are non-comparable. In Chapter 4, we extend this work to address the situation where a decision-maker is faced with theories that do give meaningful quantities of choiceworthiness but are not comparable with each other, and then propose a general account of decision-making under moral uncertainty, which can be viewed as an extension of *maximize expected choiceworthiness*. In Chapter 5, we discuss the question of when, if ever, moral theories are comparable with each other, arguing against some accounts of intertheoretic comparisons that have been proposed in the literature and sketching our own novel account.

In Chapter 6, we discuss two key problems for any account of decision-making under moral uncertainty: the problems of fanaticism and infectious incomparability. We argue that the information-sensitive account defended in previous chapters allows us to give a satisfactory solution to these problems.

In Chapters 7–9, we discuss certain metaethical and practical implications of the idea that one ought to take moral uncertainty into account in one's decision-making. In Chapter 7, we discuss the apparent conflict between moral uncertainty and non-cognitivism, arguing that the existence of moral uncertainty poses a significant problem for non-cognitivists. In Chapter 8, we examine the implications of moral uncertainty for debates in practical ethics, and argue that in the literature so far the application of moral uncertainty to practical ethics has been simplistic. In Chapter 9, we introduce the concept of the value of moral information, and show how this has implications for the value of engaging in ethical reflection and study.

Let us now turn to our substantive arguments. We begin by arguing that we should take moral uncertainty seriously, and that our central question is a non-trivial one.

1
Why We Should Take Moral Uncertainty Seriously

Introduction

Our primary aim in this chapter is to introduce the topic of moral uncertainty, argue that moral uncertainty is a real and significant issue, and argue that there are non-trivial answers to the question, 'Given that we are morally uncertain, how ought we to act in light of that uncertainty?' We shall also consider and defend against some recent objections to the very project of trying to develop an account of decision-making under moral uncertainty: we'll call these the *fetishism objection*; the *regress objection*; the *blameworthiness objection*; the *conscientiousness objection*; and the *disanalogy with prudence objection*.

I. Why We Should Be Morally Uncertain

The theory of how to make decisions under moral uncertainty would be fairly uninteresting if it were the case that we should always be almost certain in one particular moral view. In this section, we'll give three arguments in favour of epistemic humility with respect to fundamental moral propositions: that, when it is contentious what the truth of a moral proposition is, we ought to be at least moderately uncertain in the truth of that moral proposition.

The Difficulty of Ethics

The first argument is simply that ethics is *hard*. As with other areas of philosophy, working out the correct moral view often involves being sensitive to subtle distinctions, being able to hold in mind many different arguments for different views, and paying attention to intuitions across many different

Moral Uncertainty. William MacAskill, Krister Bykvist, and Toby Ord, Oxford University Press (2020).
© William MacAskill, Krister Bykvist and Toby Ord.
DOI: 10.1093/oso/9780198722274.001.0001

thought experiments. It also involves difficult questions about how to weigh different theoretical virtues, such as simplicity and elegance against intuitive plausibility. Correctly balancing all these different considerations is extremely difficult, so even when we come to a firm stance about some ethical view, we should not always expect that our reasoning is error-free. But making a mistake concerning even just one of those considerations could result in a radical change of one's view.

Moreover, we can also be morally biased in many ways, such as through vested interests, influence from one's peers, one's culture, one's religion, one's upbringing, or influence from the status quo. One can be biased towards certain views because one finds them attractive on non-epistemic grounds: perhaps a desire to quantify everything biases one against the more qualitative nuances of morality; or perhaps, to go to the other extreme, an aversion to the coldness of numbers means that one is biased against moral theories that rely on them. We can be biased as a result of evolution, or as a result of general heuristics and biases in the brain's information processing.[1]

Typically, these biases are not transparent to us and, unless they've been pointed out to us, we don't know whether we suffer from them.[2] Moreover, these biases are generally also pernicious: even when we do know about them, we fail to adjust our beliefs adequately in response to them, and sometimes, in fact, knowledge of the bias makes the bias even worse.[3] So we should assume that we're biased in many ways even if we've tried our hardest not to be. The risk of bias combined with the difficulty of ethics means that it is very easy to make an ethical mistake.

Moral Disagreement

There are some moral issues about which there is widespread agreement. For example, most of us believe that, other things being equal, it's wrong to kill an innocent adult human being. In such cases, it seems reasonable to hold that view with high confidence, despite the general difficulty of ethics. But, on

[1] Amos Tversky and Daniel Kahneman, 'Judgement under Uncertainty: Heuristics and Biases', *Science*, vol. 185, no. 4157 (27 September 1974), pp. 1124–31.

[2] Emily Pronin, Daniel Lin and Lee Ross, 'The Bias Blind Spot: Perceptions of Bias in Self versus Others', *Personality and Social Psychology Bulletin*, vol. 28, no. 3 (March 2002), pp. 369–81.

[3] Emily Pronin, 'How We See Ourselves and How We See Others', *Science*, vol. 320, no. 5880 (30 May 2008), pp. 1177–80.

many moral issues, equally intelligent, well-read and reflective people disagree. Given this, it seems unreasonable to have very high confidence in your favoured moral view and you should think that there's at least a reasonable chance that other parties, who have thought about the issue as long as you have, have come to the correct view. This may be because these other parties have a different set of moral evidence (intuitions, life experiences, and knowledge of arguments) available to them, which, if it were available to you, would change your view. Or it may be because one of you is biased, or has made a mistake in their reasoning. Either way, given how difficult ethics is, this should reduce your confidence in your favoured moral view.

Note that the thought that one should become more uncertain in light of persistent disagreement about a difficult subject matter does not rely on any esoteric view of peer disagreement. It's a perfectly ordinary part of common-sense epistemological reasoning, and is captured by almost all views in the literature on peer disagreement.[4]

Overconfidence

The final argument is based on the fact that humans, in general, have a remarkable tendency towards overconfidence. In those cases where we can use a frequentist notion of probability, it has been repeatedly shown that we are far more confident in our views than we should be. When we give high probability estimates (above 75% likelihood of a particular event occurring or not occurring) about anything other than trivially easy matters, it's almost always true that we should have given a significantly lower estimate. This is a remarkably strong effect that is well supported by psychological evidence.[5] Consistently, research suggests that when subjects

[4] For example, the case of disagreement over difficult ethical issues is much more like Christensen's 'Mental Math' case, where two people quickly add up the items on a bill in their heads and each come to different totals, and therefore each person thinks it's quite likely that they might have made a mistake, than his 'Careful Checking' case, where two people have very carefully added up the items on the bill multiple times, and therefore each person thinks it's very unlikely that they have made a mistake. See David Christensen, 'Disagreement as Evidence: The Epistemology of Controversy', *Philosophy Compass*, vol. 4, no. 5 (September 2009), pp. 756–67. A view that might oppose the argument given is Thomas Kelly, 'The Epistemic Significance of Disagreement', *Oxford Studies in Epistemology*, vol. 1 (2005), pp. 167–96.

[5] For an overview, see Sarah Lichtenstein, Baruch Fischhoff and Lawrence D. Phillips, 'Calibration of Probabilities: The State of the Art to 1980', in Daniel Kahneman, Paul Slovic, and Amos Tversky (eds), *Judgment Under Uncertainty: Heuristics and Biases,* Cambridge: Cambridge University Press, 1982, pp. 306–34.

claim to be 98% certain about something, they are wrong about 30% of the time. As the degree of stated confidence gets higher, to one in a thousand probability of error, one in a million probability of error, or even '100% certainty', subjects are still wrong over 10% of the time.[6] Moreover, this effect holds just as strongly for most experts as it does for laypersons.[7]

Because fundamental moral truths are necessarily true, we can't directly use frequency of correctness to check whether people are morally over-confident or not.[8] But, given that we are overconfident in almost every other domain, we should expect ourselves to be overconfident in ethics, too.[9] So it's very likely that, when we are very confident in a particular moral view, we ought to be less confident in that moral view.

These three arguments convince us that, for at least very many moral issues, we should have at least some significant degree of belief in views other than the one we favour. So moral uncertainty is a real phenomenon. The next question is whether we ought to take this uncertainty into account in our decision-making.

II. The Motivation for Taking Moral Uncertainty Seriously

There are two main motivations for believing that there are facts about how one ought to act in the face of moral uncertainty. The first is an appeal to

---

[6] See Paul Slovic, Baruch Fischhoff, and Sarah Lichtenstein, 'Facts versus Fears: Understanding Perceived Risk', in Kahneman, Slovic, and Tversky (eds), *Judgment under Uncertainty*, pp. 463–90. When subjects estimated a one in a thousand probability of error, subjects were wrong 19% of the time; at one in a million odds, subjects were wrong 13% of the time. In another study, when subjects reported being '100% certain' that they were correct, they were wrong about 20% of the time. See Pauline Austin Adams and Joe K. Adams, 'Confidence in the Recognition and Reproduction of Words Difficult to Spell', *The American Journal of Psychology*, vol. 73, no. 4 (December 1960), pp. 544–52.

[7] Sarah Lichtenstein and Baruch Fischhoff, 'Do Those Who Know More Also Know More about How Much They Know?', *Organizational Behavior and Human Performance*, vol. 20, no. 2 (December 1977), pp. 159–83.

[8] We can still get at it through indirect means. For instance, one could use changing one's mind on an issue as a proxy for being proven wrong: if someone claims to be 99% confident in utilitarianism and then changes their mind to support egalitarianism a year later, this suggests they were overconfident.

[9] In fact, there are grounds for supposing that the bias would be stronger in ethics. For example, overconfidence has been found to be stronger on issues that are emotionally charged: see Charles S. Taber and Milton Lodge, 'Motivated Skepticism in the Evaluation of Political Beliefs', *American Journal of Political Science*, vol. 50, no. 3 (July 2006), pp. 755–69.

our intuitions about cases involving moral dominance. Consider the following example:

Moral Dominance

Jane is at dinner, and she can either choose the foie gras, or the vegetarian risotto. Jane would find either meal equally enjoyable, so she has no prudential reason for preferring one over the other. Let's suppose that Jane finds most plausible the view that animal welfare is not of moral value so there is no moral reason for choosing one meal over another. But she also finds plausible the view that animal welfare is of moral value, according to which the risotto is the more choiceworthy option.

In this situation, choosing the risotto over the foie gras is more choiceworthy according to one hypothesis and less choiceworthy according to none. In the language of decision theory, the risotto *dominates* the foie gras. It seems very clear to us that, in some sense, Jane would act inappropriately if she were to choose the foie gras, whether or not it is morally wrong to choose the foie gras. But, if this is true, then there must be norms that take into account Jane's moral uncertainty.

A second motivation is based on the analogy with empirical uncertainty. There has been a debate concerning whether there are norms that are relative to the decision-maker's empirical credences ('subjective' norms), in addition to norms that are not relative to the decision-maker's credences ('objective' norms).[10] Consider the following case developed by Frank Jackson:[11]

Susan and the Medicine—I

Susan is a doctor, who has a sick patient, Greg. Susan is unsure whether Greg has condition A or condition C: she thinks either possibility is equally likely. And it is impossible for her to gain any evidence that will help her improve her state of knowledge any further. She has a choice of three drugs that she can give Greg: drugs A, B, and C. If she gives him drug A, and he has condition A,

---

[10] See, for example, Frank Jackson, 'Decision-Theoretic Consequentialism and the Nearest and Dearest Objection', *Ethics*, vol. 101, no. 3 (April 1991), pp. 461–82; Michael Zimmerman, 'Is Moral Obligation Objective or Subjective?', *Utilitas*, vol. 18, no. 4 (December 2006), pp. 329–61; Peter Graham, 'In Defense of Objectivism about Moral Obligation', *Ethics*, vol. 121, no. 1 (October 2010), pp. 88–115.

[11] Cf. Jackson, 'Decision-Theoretic Consequentialism and the Nearest and Dearest Objection', pp. 462–3. Donald Regan gives a similar example in *Utilitarianism and Cooperation*, Oxford: Clarendon Press, 1980, pp. 264–5.

then he will be completely cured; but if she gives him drug *A*, and he has condition *C*, then he will die. If she gives him drug *C*, and he has condition *C*, then he will be completely cured; but if she gives him drug *C*, and he has condition *A*, then he will die. If she gives him drug *B*, then he will be almost completely cured, whichever condition he has, but not completely cured.

Finally, suppose that, as a matter of fact, Greg has condition *C*. So giving Greg drug *C* would completely cure him. What should Susan do? Her decision can be represented in Table 1.1.

In *some* sense, it seems that Susan ought to give Greg drug *C*: doing so is what will actually cure Greg. But given that her credence that Greg has condition *C* is only 0.5, it seems that it would be reckless for Susan to administer drug *C*. As far as she knows, in doing so she would be taking a 50% risk of Greg's death. And so it also seems that there are norms according to which the correct action for Susan is to administer drug *B*.

Similar considerations motivate the idea that there are norms that are relative to moral uncertainty. Just as one is very often uncertain about the consequences of one's actions, one is very often uncertain about which moral norms are true. Consider the following variant of the case:[12]

Susan and the Medicine—II

Susan is a doctor, who faces two sick individuals, Anne and Charlotte. Anne is a human patient, whereas Charlotte is a chimpanzee. They both suffer from the same condition and are about to die. Susan has a vial of a drug that can help. If she administers all of the drug to Anne, Anne will survive but with disability, at half the level of welfare she'd have if healthy. If Susan administers all of the drug to Charlotte, Charlotte would be completely

Table 1.1

	Greg has condition *A*—50%	Greg has condition *C*—50%
A	Completely cured	Dead
B	Almost completely cured	Almost completely cured
C	Dead	Completely cured

[12] This is a Jackson case under *moral* uncertainty. A similar case is given in Zimmerman, Michael. *Living with Uncertainty: The Moral Significance of Ignorance*. Cambridge: Cambridge University Press, 2008. See also, Krister Bykvist, 'Evaluative Uncertainty and Consequentialist Environmental Ethics' in Leonard Kahn and Avram Hiller (eds), *Environmental Ethics and Consequentialism*. London: Routledge, 2014, pp. 122–35 and 'How to Do Wrong Knowingly and Get Away with It' in Sliwinski Rysiek and Svensson Frans (eds), *Neither/Nor: Philosophical Papers Dedicated to Erik Carlson on the Occasion of His Fiftieth Birthday*. Uppsala: Uppsala University, 2011.

cured. If Susan splits the drug between the two, then they will both survive, but with slightly less than half the level of welfare they'd have if they were perfectly healthy. Susan is certain that the way to aggregate welfare is simply to sum it up, but is unsure about the value of the welfare of non-human animals. She thinks it is equally likely that chimpanzees' welfare has no moral value and that chimpanzees' welfare has the same moral value as human welfare. As she must act now, there is no way that she can improve her epistemic state with respect to the relative value of humans and chimpanzees.

Her three options are as follows:

A: Give all of the drug to Anne
B: Split the drug
C: Give all of the drug to Charlotte

Her decision can be represented in Table 1.2, using numbers to represent how choiceworthy each option is.

While the two theories disagree strongly about the relative choiceworthiness of options A and C, they both hold that option B is only slightly inferior to the best option. We can represent this in terms of choiceworthiness in Table 1.3.

Finally, suppose that, according to the true moral theory, chimpanzee welfare is of the same moral value as human welfare and that therefore the morally right option is to give all of the drug to Charlotte. What should Susan do?

Table 1.2

	Anne's welfare	Charlotte's welfare
A	50	0
B	49	49
C	0	100

Table 1.3

	Chimpanzee welfare is of no moral value—50%	Chimpanzee welfare is of full moral value—50%
A	Permissible	Extremely wrong
B	Slightly wrong	Slightly wrong
C	Extremely wrong	Permissible

In the first variant of this case, under empirical uncertainty, intuitively Susan would be reckless not to administer drug *B*. Analogously, in the case above, it seems it would be morally reckless for Susan not to choose option *B*: given her credences, she would be risking severe wrongdoing by choosing either option *A* or option *C*.[13] This motivates the idea that there are norms that take into account both one's empirical uncertainty and one's moral uncertainty.[14]

For these reasons, we think that there is a clear *prima facie* case in favour of the idea that there are norms that take first-order moral uncertainty into account. However, as we will see in section III, some detractors have recently expressed doubts about this idea.

III. Objections to Taking Moral Uncertainty Seriously

The worry we'll address in this section is that there is no distinctive 'ought' of decision-making under moral uncertainty. On this worry, the answer to the question of 'What ought you to do under moral uncertainty?' is just the same as the answer to the question, 'What ought you to do?', and this latter question is answered by the correct first-order moral theory, where a first-order moral theory (such as utilitarianism or Kantianism) orders options in terms of their moral choiceworthiness in a way that is not relative to moral uncertainty.[15]

---

[13] See Bykvist, 'Evaluative Uncertainty and Consequentialist Environmental Ethics' and 'How to Do Wrong Knowingly and Get Away with It'.

[14] We could strengthen this case further by considering the possibility that Susan could get more moral evidence. Suppose she knows that she will engage in sustained moral reflection in the future, and she knows that she could pay $5 to receive a letter from her future self, which would explain her views about human versus chimpanzee welfare, and give the reasons why she holds those views. Intuitively, she ought to pay the $5, update her moral views, and then take the best action in light of those new moral views. But, whatever the correct moral theory is, that course of action will not be the best option. On the 'human welfare only' view, giving all the drug to Anne and spending $5 is strictly worse than simply giving the drug to Anne; on the 'all animals are equal' view, giving all the drug to Charlotte and spending $5 is worse than simply giving all the drug to the chimpanzee. So the view on which one simply ought to do whatever is in fact morally right can't handle the intuition that, in at least some sense, it's clear that Susan ought to get more moral evidence if it's easy to do so before taking action. (Here we put aside issues of the intrinsic value of moral knowledge, or of the effects of better moral understanding on future decisions; we can assume that Susan is certain that some form of utilitarianism is correct, and that she knows that after the decision she will suffer a bout of amnesia and forget she ever made the decision or gained any moral evidence.)

[15] For a statement of this worry, see Brian Weatherson, 'Review of Ted Lockhart, *Moral Uncertainty and Its Consequences*', *Mind*, vol. 111, no. 443 (July 2002), pp. 693–6 and his 'Running Risks Morally', *Philosophical Studies*, vol. 167, no. 1 (January 2014), pp. 141–63.

There are five main objections that have been raised in the literature to motivate this worry: the *fetishism objection*; the *regress objection*; the *blameworthiness objection*; the *conscientiousness objection*; and the *disanalogy with prudence objection*. We will spend most time on the fetishism objection, in part because it is the strongest one, and in part because our answer to it will help us provide a more comprehensive view on the nature of the 'ought' of decision-making under moral uncertainty.[16]

Before we begin, we shall show why the 'ought' of moral uncertainty cannot be the same as the 'ought' of first-order moral theories. Consider, again, *Susan and the Medicine—II*. In this example, there's one sense in which option *B* is certainly not what Susan ought to do—it's an impermissible option on all moral views. But there's another, different, sense, in which option *B* is what Susan ought to do. We can see that the sense of 'ought' must be different because, after concluding that Susan ought to choose option *B*, we do not also think that Susan should revise her credences in her moral views. Whereas if we thought that there were just one sense of 'ought', then her belief that she ought to choose option *B* would be inconsistent with both moral views in which she has credence.

One way of making the idea of different senses of 'ought' more precise is by thinking about the different senses as different *levels* of moral ought. When we face a moral problem, we are asking what we morally ought to do, *at the first level*. Standard moral theories, such as utilitarianism, Kantianism, and virtue ethics provide answers to this question. In a case of moral uncertainty, we are moving up one level and asking about what we ought to do, at the second level, when we are not sure what we ought to do at the first level. At this second level, we take into account our credence in various hypotheses about what we ought to do at the first level and what these hypotheses say about the choiceworthiness of each action. That there is such a second level moral ought seems supported by the fact that agents are morally criticizable when they, knowing all the relevant empirical facts, do what they think is very likely to be morally wrong when there is another option that is known not to pose any risk of wrong-doing. (We will give a more detailed account of this kind of moral ought in 'The Fetishism Objection', and levels of ought will be discussed in 'The Regress Objection'.)

---

[16] For an independent set of arguments along similar lines, see Andrew Sepielli, 'Moral Uncertainty and Fetishistic Motivation', *Philosophical Studies*, vol. 173, no. 11 (November 2016), pp. 2951–68.

An alternative way to understand the 'ought' of moral uncertainty is in terms of *rationality*.[17] Rationality, in one important sense at least, has to do with what one should do or intend, *given one's beliefs and preferences*. This is the kind of rationality that decision theory is often seen as invoking. It can be spelled out in different ways. One is to see it as a matter of *coherence*: it is rational to do or intend what coheres with one's beliefs and preferences.[18] Another way to spell it out is to understand it as a matter of rational *processes*: it is rational to do or intend what would be the output of a rational process, which starts with one's beliefs and preferences.[19] To apply the general idea to moral uncertainty, we do not need to take a stand on which version is correct. We only need to consider agents who are morally conscientious in the following sense. They try their best to find out what is right and what is wrong. They care about doing right and refraining from doing wrong. They thus prefer doing right to doing wrong and are indifferent between different right-doings (when none of the right-doings are morally super-erogatory). They also care more about serious wrong-doings than minor wrong-doings. We take this to be a precisification of the ordinary notion of conscientiousness, loosely defined as 'governed by one's inner sense of what is right', or 'conforming to the dictates of conscience'.

The idea is then to apply traditional decision-theoretical principles, according to which rational choice is some function of the agent's preferences (utilities) and beliefs (credences). Of course, different decision-theories provide different principles (and require different kinds of utility information). But the plausible ones at least agree on cases where one option *dominates* another. Go back to the *Moral Dominance* case. Recall that Jane is considering only two moral theories: one that we may call 'business as usual', according to which it is permissible to eat foie gras and also permissible to eat vegetarian risotto, and another that we may call 'vegetarianism', according to which it is impermissible to eat foie gras but permissible to eat vegetarian risotto. The option of eating vegetarian risotto will dominate the option of eating foie gras in terms of her own preferences about right- and wrong-doings.

[17] See, for instance, Sepielli, 'What to Do When You Don't Know What to Do When You Don't Know What to Do…', *Noûs*, vol. 48, no. 3 (September 2014), pp. 521–44.

[18] See John Broome, *Rationality through Reasoning*, Chichester, West Sussex: Wiley-Blackwell, 2013. For a critic, see Nomy Arpaly, 'On Acting Rationally against One's Best Judgement', *Ethics*, vol. 110, no. 3 (April 2000), pp. 488–513.

[19] Niko Kolodny, 'State or Process Requirements?', *Mind*, vol. 116, no. 462 (April 2007), pp. 371–85.

No matter which moral theory is true, by eating vegetarian risotto she will ensure an outcome that she *weakly prefers* to the alternative outcome: if 'vegetarianism' is true, she prefers the outcome; if 'business as usual' is true, she is indifferent between the outcomes. The rational thing for her to do is thus to eat vegetarian risotto, given her beliefs and her preferences.

It is important to note that this decision-theoretical account of the 'ought' of moral uncertainty is only one of many ways of making sense of this 'ought'. The discussion in the following chapters does not hinge on this particular account. The reason we chose to develop this account further here is that it appeals to fairly uncontroversial notions that have significance outside the debate about moral uncertainty, namely decision theoretical rationality and moral conscientiousness.

The Fetishism Objection

One might object here that we have depicted the conscientious agent as a *moral fetishist*, someone who only cares about rightness and wrongness as such rather than what makes actions right or wrong. A conscientious agent should care about helping the needy, keeping promises, and not be concerned with doing the right thing as such.[20]

We do not think this objection is convincing, for a number of reasons. First of all, even if we concede that someone who cares about rightness and wrongness as such is a moral fetishist, it is still true that actions can be more or less rational for such agents. More generally, even immoral agents, with immoral preferences, can do what is rational, given their beliefs and immoral preferences. So, there is something these agents rationally should do when they are morally uncertain, which does not always coincide with what is in fact morally right. Hence, the fetishism objection, even if it shows

---

[20] This objection is presented in Weatherson, 'Running Risks Morally'. The general idea that it is fetishist to care about rightness and wrongness as such is presented in Michael Smith, *The Moral Problem*, London: Wiley-Blackwell, 1994, sect. 3.5. For a critical discussion of this idea, see Nomy Arpaly, *Unprincipled Virtue: An Inquiry into Moral Agency*, New York: Oxford University Press, 2003, ch. 2, and Julia Markovits, 'Acting for the Right Reasons', *The Philosophical Review*, vol. 119, no. 2 (April 2010), pp. 201–42. For a response to these criticisms, see Paulina Sliwa, 'Moral Worth and Moral Knowledge', *Philosophy and Phenomenological Research*, vol. 93, no. 2 (September 2016), pp. 393–418.

Table 1.4

	T_1	T_2
A	Right	Right
B	Right	Wrong

that agents concerned with moral rightness are unacceptably fetishistic, does not show that moral uncertainty should never be taken seriously.

Now, it is true that the relevance of taking moral uncertainty seriously would be weakened if only morally problematic agents could take moral uncertainty seriously. But we do not think we should concede that caring about rightness and wrongness is morally problematic. To see this, we only need to consider cases where the agent has *no clue* about the non-normative descriptive features of the outcomes of the feasible actions. Suppose the choice situation is simply the following, with no defined credences for the moral hypotheses under consideration (see Table 1.4).

Here we assume that the agent has only the information depicted in this diagram. This means that the agent does not have any clue about the non-normative descriptive features of the outcomes of the actions, except that they are not exactly identical (after all, one moral theory, T_2, deems the actions different in moral status, which precludes their outcomes being exactly similar in descriptive features). Suppose that A and B are in themselves obviously morally innocent actions, such as pressing different buttons. Under T_1, A and B have the same choiceworthiness (and assume that it is not a case of supererogation), but T_1 does not say why both A and B are right and also equally choiceworthy. Under T_2, A is right and B is wrong, but T_2 does not say why this is so. Even in such an informationally impoverished case, we still expect the morally conscientious agent to form preferences over the possible outcomes. More specifically, in this case, we expect a morally conscientious agent to be indifferent between right-doings and so be indifferent between (A, T_1) and (B, T_1), and prefer a right-doing to a wrong-doing and so prefer (A, T_2) to (B, T_2). The rational option, given this agent's belief and preferences, is thus to perform A. Performing B would be to risk doing wrong without any possible compensating expected gain. Now, this example is enough to show that it is simply a mistake to think that it is somehow necessarily wrong-headed, or meaningless, to ask what would be reasonable to do (in this case, rational to do) in a case of moral uncertainty.

Table 1.5

	T_1—50%	T_2—50%
A	Right	Major wrong
B	Minor wrong	Right

Obviously, we can go further and meaningfully ask what would be rational to do in cases where the agent lacks views about non-normative descriptive features of the relevant outcomes but has credences about various moral hypotheses. For example, take the case in Table 1.5.

A morally conscientious agent will prefer right-doings to wrong-doings and so prefer (T_1, A) to (T_1, B) and also prefer (T_2, B) to (T_2, A). The latter preference will be stronger, since her preference for a right-doing over a *major* wrong-doing should be stronger than her preference for a right-doing over a *minor* wrong-doing. But this means that it is rational for the agent to choose B, given his beliefs and preferences, since the possible loss, from right to minor wrong, is more than compensated for by the possible gain, from major wrong to right. More generally, as a rational person he prefers bringing about the prospect $(A, 0.5, B)$ rather than $(C, 0.5, D)$, if his preference for A over C is stronger than his preference for D over B. So, just by invoking standard decision-theoretic rationality, we can easily make sense of doing what is rational in a case of moral uncertainty.

In the above examples the agent had no views about right- or wrong-making features. Will the fetishism objection come back to haunt us if we consider cases where we do have such views? We do not think so, for the objection assumes a false dichotomy: either you care about moral rightness and moral wrongness, in which case you are a moral fetishist, or you care about right-makers and wrong-makers, in which you are morally commendable. However, it is both possible and morally commendable to care about both. An agent who cares only about moral rightness seems deficient: she should also care about what she believes makes actions right, e.g. the wellbeing of affected people, promise-keeping, and truth-telling. Similarly, she does not just care about moral wrongness, but also about what she thinks makes actions wrong, e.g. the suffering of affected people, promise-breaking, and lying. And she should care about these features *for their own sake*, not just because she thinks they are right- or wrong-making. To care about these features just because they are believed to be right- or wrong-making does indeed seem fetishist. But, equally, an agent who cares intrinsically only about these features, which she believes to make actions right or wrong, and not at all about whether her actions are right or wrong, would also be deficient as a moral agent. After all, coming to see an action as wrong should motivate a moral agent to change her intrinsic concerns so that she starts to care intrinsically about what makes actions right or wrong, according to her newly acquired moral beliefs.[21]

In the case of moral uncertainty, where the agent is uncertain about what makes actions right or wrong, it seems plausible to assume that the morally conscientious agent's intrinsic concern for the factors she believes to be right- or wrong-making will track her intrinsic concern for moral rightness and wrongness. To see what this means, consider the second example, now with added information about what the moral hypotheses say about right- and wrong-makers, which we assume are non-moral features of the options. We also assume that the agent is certain that the options have these features (see Table 1.6).

As pointed out above, a morally conscientious agent would prefer (T_1, A) to (T_1, B), and also prefer (T_2, B) to (T_2, A), since she prefers right-doings to wrong-doings. Furthermore, the latter preference will be stronger, since she cares more about avoiding major wrong-doings than about avoiding minor ones.

What about her intrinsic preference concerning the possible right-makers F and I, and the possible wrong-makers G and H? Since she is morally conscientious, her intrinsic preferences over these factors will perfectly track her intrinsic preferences concerning right- and wrong-doings. Thus, she will prefer F over G and prefer I over H, and the latter preference will be stronger.[22]

Table 1.6

	T_1—50%	T_2—50%
A	Right because of F	Major wrong because of H
B	Minor wrong because of G	Right because of I

---

[21] This point is clearly stated in James Dreier, 'Dispositions and Fetishes: Externalist Models of Moral Motivation', *Philosophy and Phenomenological Research*, vol. 61, no. 3 (November 2000), pp. 619–38.

[22] In the case of *radical* moral uncertainty (assuming it is possible), where the agent is uncertain about whether *one and the same* factor is either a right-maker or a wrong-maker, the intrinsic preferences concerning the right- and wrong-makers will simply match the preferences

Since it is stronger, her *overall* preference will in the end be for option B over option A.[23] Hence, there is no conflict between what is rational to prefer, given her intrinsic preferences concerning right- and wrong-makers, and what is rational to prefer, given her intrinsic preferences concerning rightness and wrongness.

What happens if the credence does not split evenly between the moral hypotheses? Again, the preferences concerning right-makers and wrong-makers will coincide with the preferences concerning rightness and wrongness. To see this, consider the case in Table 1.7.

Again, the morally conscientious person will prefer (T_1, A) to (T_1, B), and prefer (T_2, B) to (T_2, A), the latter preference being stronger than the former. However, since the credence speaks in favour of T_1, to decide which option it is rational to prefer, we need to make a *trade-off* between the degree of credence and the severity of wrongness. This is just an instance of the general problem of deciding to choose between the prospect (A, p_1, B) and (C, p_2, D), when p_1 is greater than p_2, which speaks in favour of the former prospect, and your preference for D over B is stronger than your preference for A over C, which speaks in favour of the latter prospect. Which prospect, and corresponding option, it is rational to prefer in the end depends on how great the difference in strength is between the preferences, and how great the difference in credence is between the two moral hypotheses. We will not take a stand on how to solve this more general

Table 1.7

	T_1—80%	T_2—20%
A	Right because of F	Major wrong because of H
B	Minor wrong because of G	Right because of I

concerning the corresponding prospects. Suppose that in the case above, $F = H$, and $G = I$. This means that the agent is uncertain whether F is a right-maker or a major wrong-maker, and also uncertain about whether G is a minor wrong-maker or a right-maker. Her preference concerning F and G will perfectly match her preferences concerning the prospects $((T_1, A), p_1, (T_2, A))$ and $((T_1, B), p_2, (T_2, B))$. Since she prefers $((T_1, B), p_2, (T_2, B))$ to $((T_1, A), p_1, (T_2, A))$, with a certain strength, she will also intrinsically prefer F to G, with the same strength.

---

[23] We assume here that there are no 'organic unities' to take into account: if the agent prefers A to B, and C to D, he also prefers the combination of A and C (if this combination is possible) to the combination of B and D (if this combination is possible). Furthermore, we assume that the strength of the overall preference over the combinations is simply the sum of the strengths of the preferences over the combined factors.

problem here, since it requires a fuller discussion of rational preference and comparisons of moral choiceworthiness across moral theories. Here it suffices to point out that no matter how we solve the trade-off problem, it is plausible to require that, at least for fully morally conscientious agents, the overall intrinsic preferences concerning right-makers and wrong-makers should match the rational preference concerning the prospects about right- and wrong-doings.

Even if we think that the agents we have considered are morally conscientious in a perfectly normal sense, one might still question whether they are conscientious in the right way. One contestable feature of the account is that whether or not the agent's credences concern what is *in fact* right-making or wrong-making is not relevant for assessing her moral conscientiousness. But do we not want to say that a person whose intrinsic concern lines up perfectly with what is in fact right-making and wrong-making but whose moral credences are completely off track would still be morally conscientious? Some argue that Huckleberry Finn would fit this description, since he frees his friend, the slave, out of a strong feeling of compassion, even though he seems to be convinced that it is morally wrong.[24]

Here we think it is important to distinguish between different kinds of moral appraisal. When we talk about moral conscientiousness, we have in mind a moral appraisal of the *internal* aspects of an agent, in particular, how well her preferences hang together with her moral beliefs and credences. This is not to rule out other kinds of assessments, which have more to do with external features, such as whether the agent's beliefs are true or whether her preferences line up with what is in fact morally important. We think both kinds of appraisal can live together peacefully and that there is no need to choose one over the other. Note that this kind of 'double perspective' appraisal is common in other domains. For example, a person who is deceived by an evil demon might be appraised epistemically for the way she organizes her beliefs and forms beliefs on the basis of perception, but she is still doing very poorly when it comes to truth and knowledge, two more external epistemic values.

So far, we have shown that moral uncertainty is a real issue not just for moral fetishists, but also for morally conscientious people. To this list we can also add people who are less than fully morally conscientious in the internal sense adopted above. For anyone who intrinsically cares, at least *to*

---

[24] This is argued in Weatherson, 'Review of Ted Lockhart, *Moral Uncertainty and Its Consequences*'.

some extent, about doing what is right and avoiding doing what is wrong will have to take moral uncertainty seriously. How much impact this will have depends on how strongly she cares about morality compared to other non-moral factors. But, since what is rational for her to do depends on her preferences, which in turn depend on her intrinsic concern for morality, what is rational for her to do will depend on her intrinsic concern for morality.[25] So, again, moral uncertainty needs to be taken seriously, for there is a non-trivial answer to the question of what the agent should do when faced with moral uncertainty.

It is important to add that, even if we were to concede that it is fetishistic to harbour any intrinsic attitude towards 'thin' moral considerations, such as rightness and wrongness, there is still room left to take moral uncertainty seriously.[26] Brian Weatherson, after having raised his fetishist objection, concedes that it is not fetishist to be moved by 'thick' moral considerations: 'one might not do something because there is a risk that it would be cowardly, or free riding, or violate the Golden Rule, or categorical imperative'.[27]

But this means that Weatherson has to concede that it would not be fetishistic to be guided by possible thick values when you are faced with a situation like the following: the agent is uncertain whether T_1, a virtue theory, or T_2, an alternative virtue theory, is correct. T_1 counts the character traits, compassion and machismo as virtues. T_2 also counts compassion as a virtue, but it counts machismo as a vice (see Table 1.8).

Table 1.8

	T_1	T_2
A	Right because A would express the virtue of compassion	Right because A would express the virtue of compassion
B	Right because B would express the virtue of machismo	Wrong because B would express the vice of machismo

---

[25] A more radical approach, which we will not pursue here, would be to drop the reference to preferences altogether and instead talk about what is rational to do, given one's descriptive and moral beliefs and credences. Even if the agent does not care much about morality, her moral beliefs and credences can still make it rational for her to take moral uncertainty seriously. On this approach, rationality has to do with coherence between moral and descriptive beliefs and credences, on the one hand, and intentions and actions, on the other. For more on this approach, see Christian Tarsney, 'Rationality and Moral Risk: A Defense of Moderate Hedging', PhD thesis, University of Maryland, 2017, ch. 2.

[26] A similar point is also made forcefully by Sepielli, 'Moral Uncertainty and Fetishistic Motivation', p. 2959.

[27] Weatherson, 'Running Risks Morally', p. 159.

Here Weatherson seems willing to concede that it would be unreasonable for the agent to choose *B*, since she would risk expressing a vice. This is to concede a lot. Instead of talking about the morally conscientious agent's preference for right-doings over wrong-doings, we could say that such an agent prefers doing something that has greater *'thick' value*: e.g. is more virtuous, satisfies rather than frustrates the Categorical Imperative, or is free-riding rather than not free-riding. The strength of her preference should match the difference in 'thick' value. With this at hand, we can again apply the standard machinery of decision theory, and determine what is rational to do for such an agent, given her preferences concerning 'thick' value.

Note that this approach will also work if one thinks that morally conscientious agents are never moved by credences in *obviously unreasonable* moral views, such as Nazi views, or fascist views.[28] For such agents can still be uncertain about which *reasonable* 'thick' value is weightier, e.g. whether kindness is more important than honesty. The rational choice approach can be applied to this restricted set of cases and identify what is the rational choice, given the agent's credences and preferences over reasonable 'thick' values.

Of course, one could still complain that a morally conscientious agent should only be guided by *true* 'thick' values, but, as pointed out above, that would be to completely ignore the internal aspect of agent assessment. Surely, all sides must at least agree that a morally conscientious agent can be uncertain about which *reasonable* 'thick' value is weightier and be moved by her credence about these value hypotheses.

So, we think we can conclude that moral uncertainty can be a real issue for fetishists and non-fetishists alike, and this is something that must be conceded even by people who think that only morally problematic fetishists can intrinsically care about moral rightness and wrongness. The fetishist objection to taking moral uncertainty seriously is not convincing.

One could try to resist this conclusion by arguing that, even though it is true that we can act rationally in cases of moral uncertainty without being fetishists, this is not enough to make moral uncertainty a *sufficiently* serious *moral* issue, for the following two reasons. First, since we are only talking

---

[28] Thanks to an anonymous reviewer for Oxford University Press, who pointed out that one could deny that morally conscientious agents are ever moved by moral views that are beyond the pale. Note that even if the agent tries as well as she can to find out what is right and wrong, she might still fail miserably because she has access only to very misleading evidence.

about rationality here, we seem not to be able to say that there is something *morally* problematic about risking a major moral wrong (or a major 'thick' disvalue).[29] Second, since we are talking about what is rational to do, *given* one's preferences and beliefs, these prescriptions will only apply to agents who have preferences concerning rightness and wrongness, or 'thick' moral values.[30] How can we say that this account takes moral uncertainty sufficiently seriously, if it has nothing to say to agents who lack such preferences?

In reply, we would say that this account does in fact imply that there is something morally problematic about risking a major wrong (or a major 'thick' disvalue) even when you do not care about the risk. After all, if you do not care about this risk, you lack a kind of motivation that a *morally* conscientious person would have, if she shared your moral credences. But this means that you lack a motivation that is morally commendable in one respect, since being morally conscientious is one of the moral ideals. So, the account can say that there is something morally problematic about your *motivation* in this case.

The account can also say that there is something morally problematic about your *action* of taking a great moral risk, even if you do not care about it. To take such a risk is to do something that a morally conscientious and rational person would not do in your situation, if she shared your credences in moral views. Hence, it is to do something that an agent, who has a certain *moral virtue*, would not do in your situation. But to do something that an agent with a certain virtue would not do is to act in a less than fully *virtuous* way with respect to this virtue.[31] Our account could thus be seen as providing a kind of (external) virtue assessment of actions, which is applicable even to agents who lack the preferences a virtuous agent would have.[32] More exactly, your action is virtuous in this respect just in case it would be done by a morally conscientious and rational agent, who shared your credences in

---

[29] Weatherson, 'Running Risks Morally', p. 147.

[30] Michael Zimmerman, *Ignorance and Moral Obligation*, Oxford: Oxford University Press, 2014, p. 46.

[31] This fits the standard virtue ethical formula, which can be traced back to Aristotle: an action is virtuous (in one respect) just in case a virtuous person (with a certain virtue) would do it. Another instance, famous from Kant's writings, is the shopkeeper who always gives correct change and thus acts honestly in the sense that he does what a fully honest person would do in the circumstances. He can act honestly in this external sense and still be an egoist, who only cares about his own economic gain but realizes that giving correct change will in fact promote his own financial good.

[32] This is not to deny that we can also make *internal* virtue assessments of both agents and acts. For example, an agent is kind only if she cares about other people. An act is caring only if the agent cares about others.

moral views. This account also gives us a kind of *moral ought*: what one ought to do in order to act virtuously in this respect.

It should be stressed that the relevance of the discussion to follow does not stand or fall with this virtue ethical extension of our account. Nor do we need to adopt the decision theoretical account presented above. As pointed out above, to have reason to take an interest in the discussion at all, you only need to think, with Weatherson, that there is a real issue about what to do when you are not certain which 'thick' values are the correct ones. Whether we should call the relevant prescriptions in cases of moral uncertainty moral (second-order), rational, virtue ethical or something else is less important. In order to signal this neutrality, we will use the term *appropriate* in the following chapters as a catch-all label for the particular normative status that is to be assigned to actions in cases of moral uncertainty.

The Regress Objection

No matter whether we see the 'ought' of moral uncertainty as a moral or a rational one, there seems to be a threat of an *infinite regress* of uncertainty.[33] It seems that if one can be uncertain about which first-order moral theory is correct, one can also be uncertain about how to deal with moral uncertainty itself. But it seems like this uncertainty can go even higher: one can be uncertain not only about how to deal with moral uncertainty, but also about how to deal with uncertainty about how to deal with moral uncertainty, and so on ad infinitum. We can spell this out more precisely in the following way.

Uncertainty at level 1: I am uncertain about first-order morality.

Uncertainty at level 2: I am uncertain about how to deal with uncertainty about first-order morality.

Uncertainty at level 3: I am uncertain about how to deal with uncertainty about how to deal with uncertainty about first-order morality.

---

[33] This kind of regress argument is stated in Weatherson, 'Running Risks Morally'. See also Elizabeth Harman, 'The Irrelevance of Moral Uncertainty', *Oxford Studies in Metaethics*, vol. 10 (2015), pp. 53–79 and Sepielli 'How Moral Uncertaintism Can be Both True and Interesting'.

Uncertainty at level 4: I am uncertain about how to deal with uncertainty about how to deal with uncertainty about how to deal with uncertainty about first-order morality.

We get an infinite regress if one's uncertainty shows up at all levels.

It is not clear that this poses a genuine threat of an *actual* infinite regress, however. First, even if we concede that for all levels i, it is possible to have uncertainty at level i, this does not show that it is possible to be in a situation in which one is uncertain at level 1, uncertain at level 2, uncertain at level 3, and so on ad infinitum. To make this inference would be to infer 'it is possible that, for all levels i, one is uncertain at level i' from 'for all levels i, it is possible that one is uncertain at level i'. But this is to commit a simple scope fallacy: to infer 'it is possible that, for all x, Fx' from 'for all x, it is possible that Fx'.

Second, it is not even clear that, for any level i, it is possible that one is uncertain at level i. Human agents have cognitive limitations, and therefore it is not true that they can express doubt at any level, no matter how high. There is, therefore, a natural limit on how many levels up we can go in our moral uncertainty. Indeed, just trying to figure out what uncertainty at level 4 means is tricky. In any case, it seems impossible for a human agent, in one and the same situation, to be uncertain 'all the way up' and thus have an infinite number of uncertainties.

How far should we go up in the levels of uncertainty in our theorizing? As we showed in the previous section, we cannot stay at the first level, the level of first-order morality. It is perfectly meaningful to ask about what to do in at least certain cases of moral uncertainty (minimally, the cases in which an agent is uncertain about which reasonable 'thick' value is more important). Our aim is to develop a theory for uncertainty about first-order morality.

We do not want to deny that there might be a need for a theory that can deal with *higher-order* uncertainty (higher than level 1). But our proposed theory can still fit into such a higher order theory, and this holds no matter whether the theory is 'bounded', i.e. sets a limit for the level of uncertainty that generates new prescriptions. Here is a sketchy recipe for an 'unbounded' higher order theory. Let T_1 be a first-order moral theory, such as utilitarianism, virtue ethics, or Kantianism; T_2 a theory that tells you what to do when you are uncertain about which first-order theory is correct; T_3 a theory that tells you what to do when you are uncertain about how to deal with uncertainty about which first order theory is correct; T_4 a theory that tells you what to do when you are uncertain about how to deal with uncertainty about how to deal with uncertainty about which first-order theory is correct; and so on. One way of making this more precise is the following:

0. If you are not uncertain about T_1, then follow T_1.
1. If you are uncertain about T_1 and you are not uncertain about T_2, then follow T_2.
2. If you are uncertain about T_2 and not uncertain about T_3, then follow T_3.
3. If you are uncertain about T_3 and not uncertain about T_4, then follow T_4.

And so on. If there is no infinite regress of uncertainty, i.e. in each situation, for some level i, the agent is not uncertain about T_i, which seems to be true of all human agents, then there is always a determinate answer about what the agent should do.[34]

Note that the theory does not require that you are *certain* that T_i is true for T_i to kick in and tell you what to do. It is enough that you fail to be certain because you do not consider T_i and thus are neither certain nor uncertain about T_i. Note also that this theory imposes *strict liability* constraints, to use Broome's apt phrase, namely the conditionals 0, 1, 2, 3,…(etc.).[35] So, it cannot take into account cases of uncertainty, where the agent doubts the whole metatheory itself. But no theory can avoid imposing some strict liability constraint. Even the principle 'Deal with moral uncertainty in whatever way you see fit' is itself a principle that imposes strict liability; it tells you to deal with moral uncertainty in the way you see fit even if you don't believe that you should deal with moral uncertainty in the way you see fit.[36]

It should be noted that the challenge of higher-order uncertainty is not just a challenge for those of us who take first-order moral uncertainty

---

[34] Obviously, for agents that are uncertain 'all the way up', there is no answer about what they should do. To take into account such unusual agents, the higher order theory needs to be revized. However, such revisions are simply beyond the scope of this book. Another bug in this theory (which we thank Christian Tarsney for alerting us to) is that it is impossible to act on a theory T_i while being less than fully certain that T_i is true. Again, revising the theory to avoid this unwelcome implication is simply beyond the scope of this book. For a more thorough discussion of different orders of normative prescriptions, see Sepielli, 'What to Do When You Don't Know What to Do When You Don't Know What to Do…' pp. 521–44.
[35] Broome, *Rationality through Reasoning*, p. 75.
[36] This argument is inspired by Broome, *Rationality through Reasoning*, p. 101.

seriously. This is a tricky question that anyone who believes in the notion of rational choice has to confront. Even if you reject our way of dealing with moral uncertainty, you still need to know what it is rational to choose given doubts about what makes a choice rational.[37]

To sum up, in this book, we will focus on how best to deal with uncertainty at level 1.[38] As pointed out above, we do not deny that there might be other levels to consider (perhaps an infinite number!), but no matter whether this is true, you need an answer about what to do when you are uncertain about which first-order moral theory is true.

The Blameworthiness Objection

Recall *Susan and the Medicine-II*. Splitting the drug between the human and the chimpanzee will guarantee that Susan performs an action that is slightly wrong. But it seems the sensible option, since the alternatives would involve risking a major wrong. If knowingly doing wrong implies blameworthiness, we have a problem, since then we then will have to say that Susan deserves blame for splitting the medicine. But we want to say that she deserves praise for not risking doing something that would have been a serious wrong.

In reply, we would maintain that the link between wrongness and blameworthiness is not this simple. There are many cases where knowingly doing wrong does not merit blame, namely, those cases in which you have a *valid excuse*.[39] In the Jackson cases under consideration, it seems obvious that Susan has a valid excuse; she is trying hard to figure out what is right to do but she can't tell which action is morally right. It would thus be unfair to blame her for knowingly doing wrong when she is being sensitive to her best-informed credence about degrees of wrongness and thus performing a minor wrong in order to avoid risking a major wrong. On the contrary, she

---

[37] For some discussion, see Holly Smith, 'Deciding How To Decide: Is There a Regress Problem?' in Michael Bacharach and Susan Hurley (eds), *Essays in the Foundations of Decision Theory*, Blackwell (1991), and Hanti Lin, 'On the Regress Problem of Deciding How to Decide', *Synthese* (2014).

[38] See MacAskill, 'Smokers, Psychos, and Decision-Theoretic Uncertainty', for a discussion of decision-making under uncertainty at level 2.

[39] See Cheshire Calhoun, 'Responsibility and Reproach', *Ethics*, vol. 99, no. 1 (January 1989), pp. 389–406; Gideon Rosen, 'Culpability and Ignorance', *Proceedings of the Aristotelian Society*, vol. 103, no. 1 (June 2003), pp. 61–84; Gideon Rosen, 'Skepticism about Moral Responsibility', *Philosophical Perspectives*, vol. 18, no. 1 (December 2004), pp. 295–313; and Michael Zimmerman, *Living with Uncertainty: The Moral Significance of Ignorance*, Cambridge: Cambridge University Press, 2008.

would be blameworthy if she only cared about avoiding wrong-doing and ignored morally relevant information about the differences in severity of different wrong-doings.

Some would argue that this reply is too complacent. By saying that the agent has a valid excuse because she does know not what is right, we seem also committed to the view that 'being caught in the grip of a false moral belief is exculpatory', as Elizabeth Harman puts it.[40] More precisely, we seem committed to the view that, if an agent is certain that an action is right, when in fact it is deeply wrong, she is not blameworthy for doing it. However, this view might seem wrong; surely, Hitler must be blameworthy for planning and executing the Holocaust even if he happened to be certain that it was morally right?

We agree that mere certainty cannot exculpate. But in the case of Susan, we were assuming that she did her best to decide what was right and what was wrong. Unlike Hitler, she took in all the relevant empirical information, and all the available information about moral views applicable to the situation. In the end, taking all relevant empirical and moral evidence into account, she still could not figure out which action was right. She knew which action was slightly wrong and, for each alternative action, she had 0.5 credence that it would be right and 0.5 credence that it would be deeply wrong. In order to avoid risking doing something deeply wrong, she decided to do the action she knew would be slightly wrong. This seems to be a morally commendable action and not something blameworthy. It would have been another story if she had just acted on blind faith and formed her credences about rightness and wrongness without trying her best to find out what was right and what was wrong. In this hypothetical case, we agree that it is plausible to say that Susan is not praiseworthy.

Harman seems to think that this is not enough to exculpate Susan, for she claims that:

> Believing that one's wrong action is morally required involves caring inadequately about the features of one's action that make it morally wrong, because believing that an action is morally wrong on the basis of the features that make it wrong is a way of caring about those features.[41]

[40] Harman, 'The Irrelevance of Moral Uncertainty'. See also Alexander A. Guerrero, 'Don't Know, Don't Kill: Moral Ignorance, Culpability, and Caution', *Philosophical Studies*, vol. 136, no. 1 (October 2007), pp. 59–97 and Miranda Fricker, 'The Relativism of Blame and Williams's Relativism of Distance', *The Aristotelian Society Supplementary Volume*, vol. 84, no. 1 (June 2010), pp. 151–77.
[41] Harman, 'The Irrelevance of Moral Uncertainty', p. 68.

We do not feel the force of this objection. Even if we agree that believing that an action is morally wrong on the basis of the features that make it wrong is a way of caring about those features, an agent who has done her best to identify those wrong-making features, but in the end failed, has done all we can expect from her given her unfortunate epistemic predicament. Of course, it would have been better if she could have identified the true wrong-makers. As pointed out earlier, there is always room for a more external appraisal of agents. But the fact that she could have done better in this external sense does not make her less praiseworthy.

The Conscientiousness Objection

A related objection to our account is that it violates the following constraint.

Constraint 1:   It is necessarily the case that, if one acts morally conscientiously, then one does not deliberatively do something that one believes to be morally wrong.

We agree that, at first sight, this constraint may sound plausible.[42] But it is easy to conflate it with the following constraint, which we think is the true one.

Constraint 2:   It is necessarily the case that, if one acts morally conscientiously, then one does not deliberatively do something that one believes to be morally wrong *rather than something one believes to be morally right.*

It is easy to conflate the two constraints, since, *typically*, if an agent believes an action to be morally wrong, he also believes an alternative action to be morally right. Jackson cases such as *Susan and the Medicine—II* would be an exception. In this case, the agent knows that, in order to avoid risking a major wrong, she has to perform the action that is slightly wrong, but she does not have a belief about which action is right because she does not know which alternative action is right. We think it is clear that Susan, if she is morally conscientious, should not risk the major wrong, and thus we are willing to reject Constraint 1 and stick to Constraint 2, which is uncontroversial.

---

[42] Michael Zimmerman defends this constraint under the label 'Constraint #2' (*Ignorance and Moral Obligation*, p. 33).

Disanalogy with Prudential Reasoning

One final line of objection comes from Weatherson.[43] The objection is that if there is an ought of moral uncertainty, then there is an ought of prudential uncertainty. But there is no ought of prudential uncertainty. Therefore, there is no ought of moral uncertainty.

We agree that if there is an ought of moral uncertainty, then there is an ought of prudential uncertainty. But we disagree with the second premise that there is no ought of prudential uncertainty. To argue for this premise, Weatherson gives the following case.

Bob and the Art Gallery

Bob has to decide whether to spend some time at an art gallery on his way home. He knows the art there will be beautiful, and he knows it will leave him cold. There isn't any cost to going, but there isn't anything else he'll gain by going either. He thinks it's unlikely that there's any prudential value in appreciating beauty, but he's not certain. As it happens, it really is true that there's no prudential value in appreciating beauty. What should Bob do?

Weatherson thinks that Bob makes no mistake in walking home. But, as is stipulated in the case, there's some chance that Bob will benefit, prudentially, from going to the art gallery, and there's no downside. This example, so the objection goes, therefore shows that there is no meaningful ought of prudential uncertainty.

We think, however, that the example is poorly chosen. Weatherson stipulates in the case that there's no cost to spending time in the art gallery. But it's difficult to imagine that to be the case: during the time that Bob would spend in the art gallery, having an experience that 'leaves him cold', could presumably have been doing something else more enjoyable instead.[44] In which case, depending on how exactly the example was specified, a plausible account of decision-making under prudential uncertainty would recommend that Bob goes home rather than to the art gallery. In order to correct for this, we could modify the case, and suppose that Bob has the choice of two routes home, A and B. Both will take him exactly the same length of time, and would require the same amount of physical effort. But route B passes by great works

---

[43] Weatherson, 'Running Risks Morally', pp. 148–9. For more discussion of this issue, see Christian Tarsney, 'Rationality and Moral Risk', dissertation (2017), pp. 79–83.
[44] We thank Amanda Askell for this point, and for the following example.

of architecture that Bob hasn't seen before, whereas route *A* does not. Bob knows these works are beautiful and he knows they will leave him cold. In this case, where there is some probability that viewing art has prudential value, any plausible view of decision-making under prudential uncertainty really would say it's appropriate to choose route *B* and not appropriate to choose route *A*. But that seems like the correct answer.

Other cases also suggest that there is a meaningful 'ought' of moral uncertainty in purely prudential cases. Consider the following case.[45]

Charlie and the Experience Machine

Charlie is a firm believer in hedonism, but he's not certain, and gives some significant credence to the objective list theory of wellbeing. He is offered the chance to plug into the experience machine. If he plugs in, his experienced life will be much the same as it would have been anyway, but just a little bit more pleasant. However, he would be living in a fiction, and so wouldn't realize the objective goods of achievement and friendship. As it happens, hedonism is true. Is there any sense in which Charlie should not plug in?

In this case, it seems clear that there's a sense in which Charlie should not plug in. Given his uncertainty, it would be too risky for him to plug in. That is, it would be appropriate for him to refrain from plugging in, even if hedonism were true, and even if he were fairly confident, but not sure, that hedonism were true.

Or consider the following prudential Jackson case.

Pleasure or Self-Realization

Rebecca is uncertain between two theories of wellbeing, assigning them equal credence. One is hedonism, which claims that a life is good to the degree to which it is pleasant. The other is a theory which claims that a life is good to the degree to which it involves Self-Realization. She is at a pivotal life choice and has three broad options available. Option *A* is a life optimized for pleasure: she would have a decadent life with a vast amount of pleasure, but little or no Self-Realization. Option *C* is a life aimed at perfect self-realization through seclusion, study, and extreme dedication. This life would contain almost no pleasure. Option *B* is a middle path, with very

---

[45] We thank Amanda Askell for this case.

nearly the height of pleasure of option *A* (just one less cocktail on the beach) and very nearly the extreme Self-Realization of option *C* (just one less morning of contemplation).

It seems clear to us that given her uncertainty, the appropriate choice is for Rebecca to hedge her bets and choose option *B*.[46] While it can be a bit harder to come up with clear examples concerning prudence (due to the much greater agreement on what in practice constitutes a good life than on how to act morally), we don't see any difference in the force of the arguments in favour of there being an 'ought' of moral uncertainty whether we're considering moral uncertainty or merely prudential uncertainty.

Conclusion

In this chapter, we have seen that there is a strong case for the position that there are norms (besides first-order moral norms) that govern what we ought to do under moral uncertainty. This position is intuitive and can be made sense of by identifying these norms either with higher-level moral norms or with norms of rationality for morally conscientious agents. Moreover, we have seen that objections on the basis of fetishism, regress, blameworthiness, conscientiousness and the alleged disanalogy with prudence are unconvincing.

Having established the substance and importance of our topic, we can now start developing our positive account of what to do under moral uncertainty.

---

[46] The contrasting of pleasure with Self-Realization is a reference to James L. Hudson, 'Subjectivization in Ethics', *American Philosophical Quarterly*, vol. 26, no. 3 (July 1989), p. 224, who listed these two goods as examples of values that obviously couldn't be compared. This example shows that, at least in an extreme enough case, we do have intuitions about how even these should be compared.

2
Maximizing Expected Choiceworthiness

Introduction

Our primary aim in this chapter is to argue that, in conditions of interval-scale measurability and unit-comparability, one should *maximize expected choiceworthiness*. Though this position has often been suggested in the literature, and is often taken to be the 'default' view, it has so far received little in the way of positive argument in its favour. We start, in section I, by providing new arguments against two rival theories that have been proposed in the literature—the accounts which we call 'My Favorite Theory' and 'My Favorite Option'.[1] Then we give a novel argument for the view that, under moral uncertainty, one should take into account both probabilities of different theories and magnitudes of choiceworthiness. Finally, we argue in favour of maximizing expected choiceworthiness (MEC).

I. Against My Favorite Theory

One might think that, under moral uncertainty, one should simply follow the moral view that one thinks is most likely. This has been suggested as the correct principle by Edward Gracely, in one of the earliest modern papers on moral uncertainty: 'the proper approach to uncertainty about the rightness of ethical theories is to determine the one most likely to be right, and

---

[1] We can distinguish between two versions of each of My Favorite Theory and My Favorite Option: a version which applies no matter what the informational situation of the decision-maker, and a version which applies only when theories are not comparable. We deal with the former version of these accounts here; in the next chapter we deal with the latter version. For those who are skeptical of the possibility of intertheoretic comparisons, the fact that MFT and MFO do not require intertheoretic comparisons could be considered a virtue.

Moral Uncertainty. William MacAskill, Krister Bykvist, and Toby Ord, Oxford University Press (2020).
© William MacAskill, Krister Bykvist and Toby Ord.
DOI: 10.1093/oso/9780198722274.001.0001

to act in accord with its dictates.[2] Making this view more precise, we could define it as follows.

My Favorite Theory (MFT):   *A* is an appropriate option iff *A* is a permissible option according to the theory that the decision-maker, *S*, has highest credence in.

This is an elegant and very simple view. But it has major problems. We'll first mention two fixable problems that need to be addressed, before moving on to a dilemma that we believe ultimately sinks the view.

The first fixable problem is that, sometimes, one will have equal highest credence in more than one moral theory. What is it appropriate to do then? Picking one theory at random seems arbitrary. So, instead, one could claim that if *A* is permissible according to *any* of the theories in which one has highest credence then *A* is appropriate. But that has odd results too. Suppose that John is 50:50 split between a pro-choice view and a radical pro-life view. According to this version of MFT, it would be appropriate for John to try to sabotage abortion clinics on Wednesday (because doing so is permissible according to the radical pro-life view) and appropriate for John to punish himself for doing so on Thursday (because doing so is permissible according to the pro-choice view). But that seems bizarre.

The second fixable problem is that the view violates the following principle, which we introduced in the previous chapter.

Dominance: If *A* is more choiceworthy than *B* according to some theories in which *S* has credence, and equally choiceworthy according to all other theories in which *S* has credence, then *A* is more appropriate than *B*.

MFT violates this in the case in Table 2.1.

That is, according to MFT it is equally appropriate to choose either *A* or *B*, even though *A* is certainly permissible, whereas *B* might be impermissible.

Table 2.1

	T_1—40%	T_2—60%
A	Permissible	Permissible
B	Impermissible	Permissible

---

[2] Edward J. Gracely, 'On the Noncomparability of Judgments Made by Different Ethical Theories', *Metaphilosophy*, vol. 27, no. 3 (July 1996), p. 331.

But there's no possible downside to choosing A, whereas there is a possible downside to choosing B. So it seems very plausible that it is appropriate to choose A and inappropriate to choose B.

These problems are bugs for the view, rather than fundamental objections. They can be overcome by modifying it slightly. This is what Johan Gustafsson and Olle Torpman do in a recent article.[3] Translating their proposal into our terminology, the version of MFT that they defend is as follows.

My Favorite Theory (Gustafsson and Torpman): An option A is appropriate for S if and only if:

1. A is permitted by a moral theory T_i such that
   a. T_i is in the set $\mathcal{T}$ of moral theories that are at least as credible as any moral theory for S, and
   b. S has not violated T_i more recently than any other moral theory in $\mathcal{T}$; and
2. There is no option B and no moral theory T_j such that
   a. T_j requires B and not A, and
   b. No moral theory that is at least as credible as T_j for S requires A and not B.

The first clause is designed to escape the problem of equal highest-credence theories. Clause 1(b) ensures that some bizarre courses of action are not regarded as appropriate; in the case above, if one sabotages the abortion clinic on Wednesday (following the radical pro-life view, but violating the pro-choice view), then it is not appropriate to punish oneself for doing so on Thursday (because one has violated the pro-choice view more recently than any other view). The second clause is designed to escape the problem of violating Dominance, generating a lexical version of MFT. If one's favorite theory regards all options as permissible, then one goes with the recommendation of one's second-favorite theory; if that regards all options as permissible, then one goes with the recommendation of one's third-favorite theory, and so on. This version of MFT no longer has the appeal of simplicity. But it avoids the counterintuitive results mentioned so far.

The much deeper issue with any version of MFT, however, is that it's going to run into what we'll call the *problem of theory-individuation*.

---

[3] Johan E. Gustafsson and Olle Torpman, 'In Defence of My Favourite Theory', *Pacific Philosophical Quarterly*, vol. 95, no. 2 (June 2014), pp. 159–74. Note that all of the revisions they make to their view that we discuss below are made in light of criticisms made by us in previously unpublished work or in discussion.

Consider the following case. Suppose that Sophie has credence in two different theories: a form of non-consequentialism and a form of hedonistic utilitarianism, and she's choosing between two options. *A* is the option of killing one person in order to save ten people. *B* is the option of refraining from doing so. So her decision situation is as in Table 2.2.

According to any version of MFT, *A* is the appropriate option. However, suppose that Sophie then learns of a subtle distinction between different forms of hedonistic utilitarianism. She realizes that the hedonistic theory she had credence in was actually an umbrella for two slightly different forms of hedonistic utilitarianism. So her decision situation instead looks as in Table 2.3.

In this new decision situation, according to MFT, *B* is the appropriate option. So MFT is sensitive to how exactly we choose to individuate moral theories. In order to use MFT to deliver determinate answers, we would need a canonical way in which to individuate ethical theories.

Gustafsson and Torpman respond to this with the following account of how to individuate moral theories.

Regard moral theories T_i and T_j as versions of the same moral theory if and only if you are certain that you will never face a situation where T_i and T_j yield different prescriptions.[4]

This avoids the arbitrariness problem, but doing so means that their view faces an even bigger problem, which is that any real-life decision-maker will

Table 2.2

	Non-consequentialism—40%	Utilitarianism—60%
A	Impermissible	Permissible
B	Permissible	Impermissible

Table 2.3

	Non-consequentialism—40%	Utilitarianism$_1$—30%	Utilitarianism$_2$—30%
A	Impermissible	Permissible	Permissible
B	Permissible	Impermissible	Impermissible

[4] Gustafsson and Torpman, 'In Defence of My Favourite Theory', p. 14.

Table 2.4

	U—2%	P_1—1%	P_2—1%	...	P_{98}—1%
A	Permissible	Impermissible	Impermissible	...	Impermissible
B	Impermissible	Permissible	Permissible	...	Permissible

have vanishingly small credence in their favorite theory. Suppose that Tracy is deciding whether to allocate resources in such a way as to provide a larger total benefit, but with an inegalitarian distribution (option A), or in such a way as to provide a slightly smaller total benefit, but with an egalitarian distribution (option B). She has some credence in utilitarianism (U), but is almost certain in prioritarianism (P). However, she's not sure exactly what shape the prioritarian weighting function should have. This uncertainty doesn't make any difference to the prioritarian recommendation in the case at hand; but it does make a small difference in some very rare cases. So her decision situation looks as in Table 2.4.

On Gustafsson and Torpman's version of MFT, the appropriate option for Tracy is A. But it seems intuitively obvious that it's appropriate to choose B, at least if we assume, as Gustafsson and Torpman do, that we cannot make choiceworthiness comparisons across theories and so we cannot appeal to the idea that there is much more at stake for the utilitarian theory than for all the prioritarian theories.

In unpublished work, Gustafsson responds to this argument. He suggests that in our argument we rely on the following principle.

The Principle of Unconscientiousness of Almost Certain Wrongdoing: If a morally conscientious person P faces a situation where options A and B are available and P is almost certain that A is wrong and almost certain that B is right, then P would not do A.[5]

Gustafsson then argues that this principle leads to choosing dominated sequences of actions.

However, our argument does not rely on this principle: indeed, this principle is inconsistent with the idea that what's appropriate is to maximize expected choiceworthiness. It is true that the account we ultimately defend can lead to intransitivity across choice-situations; we accept and defend this

---

[5] Gustafsson, 'Moral Uncertainty and the Problem of Theory Individuation' (unpublished).

implication in Chapter 4. But the issue of whether this means that one ought to choose dominated sequences of actions depends on whether a decision-maker should foresee the sequences of choices available to her and choose the *sequence* of actions that will result in the best outcome. This issue is independent from the account we defend.[6]

The true solution to the problem of theory individuation might seem obvious. Rather than focus on what *theory* the decision-maker has most credence in, we should instead think about what *option* is most likely to be right, in a given decision situation. That is, we should endorse something like the following.

My Favorite Option (MFO):   A is an appropriate option for S iff S thinks that A is the option, or one of the options, that is most likely to be permissible.[7]

MFO isn't sensitive to how we individuate theories. And it would get the right answer in the prioritarianism and utilitarianism case above. So it looks much more plausible than MFT. But it still has a serious problem (which MFT also suffers from): it doesn't allow us to make trade-offs between the degree of credence that one has in different moral views and the degree of choiceworthiness that those views assign to different options. We'll turn to this next.

II. In Favour of Trade-offs

We can construct examples to support the view that the correct theory of decision-making under moral uncertainty should consider trade-offs. First, suppose that your credence is split between two theories, with the second theory being just slightly more plausible. MFT and MFO both claim that you should do whatever this second theory recommends because it has the highest chance of being right. Suppose, however, that the theories disagree

---

[6] A further objection to Gustafsson and Torpman's version of *My Favorite Theory* is that the account loses the underlying motivation for thinking that there's an 'ought' that's relative to moral uncertainty in the first place. MFT, on their account, is not action-guiding. Nor can they draw support from the analogy with decision-making under empirical uncertainty. Given this, it's hard to see why we should endorse their view over the hard externalist position of Weatherson and Harman.

[7] Lockhart suggests this view, though ultimately rejects it (*Moral Uncertainty and Its Consequences*, p. 26).

not only on the right act but also on the magnitude of what is at stake. The slightly more plausible theory says it is a minor issue, while the less plausible one says that it is a matter of grave importance. We can represent this as in Table 2.5.

For vividness, suppose that the decision-maker is unsure about the acts/omissions distinction: T_1 is the view according to which there is no morally relevant distinction between acts and omissions; T_2 is the view according to which there is an important morally relevant distinction between acts and omissions. Let option B involve seriously harming many people in order to prevent a slightly greater harm to another group, while option A is keeping the status quo. Even if one is leaning slightly towards T_1, it seems morally reckless to choose B when A is almost as good on T_2's terms and much better on T_1's terms. Just as we can 'hedge our bets' in situations of descriptive uncertainty, so it seems that B would morally hedge our bets, allowing a small increase in the chance of acting wrongly in exchange for a greatly reduced degree of potential wrongdoing.

For a second example, consider again *Susan and the Medicine—II* (see Table 2.6).

According to MFT and MFO, both A and C are appropriate options, while B is inappropriate. But that seems wrong. B seems like the appropriate option, because, in choosing either A or C, Susan is risking grave wrongdoing. B seems like the best hedge between the two theories in which she has credence. But if so, then any view on which the appropriate option is always the maximally choiceworthy option according to some theory in which one has credence must be false. This includes MFT, MFO, and their variants.

Table 2.5

	T_1—51%	T_2—49%
A	Permissible	Gravely wrong
B	Slightly wrong	Permissible

Table 2.6

	Chimpanzee welfare is of no moral value—50%	Chimpanzee welfare is of significant moral value—50%
A	Permissible	Extremely wrong
B	Slightly wrong	Slightly wrong
C	Extremely wrong	Permissible

One might object that making trade-offs requires the possibility of intertheoretic choiceworthiness comparisons and argue that, since such comparisons are impossible, the above examples are spurious.[8] Our response is discussed at far greater length in Chapters 3–5: Chapter 5 argues that such comparisons are often meaningful; Chapter 4 argues that, even when they are not meaningful, we still have a principled method of placing those different moral theories on the same scale; and Chapter 3 argues that, even when the moral theories themselves provide a merely ordinal measure of choiceworthiness (and there are not meaningful ratios of choiceworthiness differences *within* a theory), we should still want to make trade-offs and MFT and MFO should be rejected. In the meantime, we will proceed on the assumption that such comparisons are meaningful.

An alternative response is suggested by Gustafsson.[9] Drawing on a suggestion from Tarsney,[10] he suggests a more coarse-grained form of My Favorite Theory: that, rather than acting in accordance with the individual moral theory in which one has the highest credence, one should instead act in accordance with the class of mutually comparable theories in which one has highest credence, and maximize expected choiceworthiness with respect to that class. Gustafsson suggests this is still a form of My Favorite Theory insofar as it is treating intertheoretically comparable theories as different specifications of the same theory.

In the next two chapters, we will argue in favour of an alternative account of what to do in varying informational conditions. For now we'll note that Gustafsson's suggestion still suffers from a grave problem for MFT that we noted earlier. Consider the utilitarianism vs prioritarianism case given above, and assume that none of the theories are comparable with each other. Coarse-grained MFT would recommend acting in accordance with utilitarianism: that is, it recommends acting in accordance with one's favorite theory even when one has vanishingly small credence in that theory, and even when all other theories oppose the recommendation of one's favorite theory.

Finally, as a side point, we note that *Susan and the Medicine—II* shows that one understanding of the central question for decision-making given moral uncertainty that has been presented in the literature by Jacob Ross, and which might lead one to find MFT or MFO attractive, is wrong. Ross seems to suggest that the central question is 'What ethical theories are

---

[8] See Gustafsson and Torpman, 'In Defence of My Favourite Theory', and Gustafsson, 'Moral Uncertainty and the Problem of Theory Individuation'.

[9] Gustafsson, 'Moral Uncertainty and the Problem of Theory Individuation'.

[10] Tarsney, 'Rationality and Moral Risk', pp. 215–19.

worthy of acceptance and what ethical theories should be rejected?', where acceptance is defined as follows.[11]

> to accept a theory is to aim to choose whatever option this theory would recommend, or in other words, to aim to choose the option that one would regard as best on the assumption that this theory is true. For example, to accept utilitarianism is to aim to act in such a way as to produce as much total welfare as possible, to accept Kantianism is to aim to act only on maxims that one could will as universal laws, and to accept the Mosaic Code is to aim to perform only actions that conform to its Ten Commandments.

The above case shows that this cannot be the right way of thinking about things. Option *B* is wrong, according to all theories in which Susan has credence: she is certain that it's wrong. The central question is therefore not about which first-order moral theory to accept: indeed, in cases like Susan's there is *no* moral theory that she should accept. Instead, it's about which *option* it is appropriate to choose.[12]

III. In Favour of Treating Moral and Empirical Uncertainty Analogously

In the previous section, we discussed an argument in favour of the view that appropriateness involves trade-offs between levels of credence in different theories and the degree of choiceworthiness that those theories assign to options. But this still leaves open exactly what account of decision-making under moral uncertainty is correct. In this section, we argue that, when choiceworthiness differences are comparable across theories, we should handle moral uncertainty in just the same way that we should handle empirical uncertainty. Expected utility theory is the standard account of how to handle empirical uncertainty probabilities.[13] So maximizing expected

---

[11] Jacob Ross, 'Rejecting Ethical Deflationism', *Ethics*, vol. 116, no. 4 (July 2006), p. 743.

[12] One could say that, in Susan's case, she should accept a theory that represents a hedge between the two theories in which she has credence (cf. Ross, 'Rejecting Ethical Deflationism', pp. 743–4). But why should she accept a theory that she knows to be false? This seems to be an unintuitive way of describing the situation, for no additional benefit.

[13] At least, expected utility theory is the correct account of how to handle empirical uncertainty when we have well-defined probabilities over states of nature. As we noted in the introduction, in this book we're assuming that we have well-defined credences over moral theories. If we had,

choiceworthiness should be the standard account of how to handle moral uncertainty.[14] This provides a further argument against MFT and MFO, which break from this standard approach.[15]

We can thus define the following rival to MFT and MFO:

Maximize Expected Choiceworthiness (MEC):   When we can determine the expected choiceworthiness of different options, *A* is an appropriate option iff *A* has the maximal expected choiceworthiness.

The argument for treating empirical and moral uncertainty analogously begins by considering that there are very many ways of distinguishing between proposition-types: we can divide propositions into the a priori and a posteriori, the necessary and contingent, or those that pertain to biology and those that do not.[16] These could all feature into uncertainty over states of nature. Yet, intuitively, in all these cases the nature of the propositions over which one is uncertain does not affect which normative theory we should use. So it would seem arbitrary to think that *only* in the case of normative propositions does the nature of the propositions believed affect which decision-theory is relevant. So it seems like the default view is that moral and empirical uncertainty should be treated in the same way.

One might think the fact that moral truths are *necessarily* true is a reason why it's wrong to take moral uncertainty into account using an analogue of expected utility theory. Under empirical uncertainty, one knows that there is some chance of one outcome, and some chance of another

for example, imprecise credences over moral theories, then we would need to depart from *maximize expected choiceworthiness*. However, our key argument in this chapter is that we should treat moral and empirical uncertainty analogously. So, if we try to accommodate imprecise credences over moral theories, the way in which we should depart from *maximize expected choiceworthiness* should mimic the way in which we should depart from expected utility theory more generally once we allow imprecise credences.

[14] The (risk-neutral) expected value of something (its 'expectation') is just the average of its value in the different cases under consideration weighted by the probability of each case. So the expected choiceworthiness of an option is the average of its choiceworthiness according to the different theories, weighted by the credence in those theories.

[15] One might claim, following Lara Buchak (*Risk and Rationality*, Oxford: Oxford University Press, 2013), that one ought, in general, to endorse a form of risk-weighted expected utility theory. We are perfectly open to this. Our primary claim is that one should endorse maximizing risk-weighted choiceworthiness if and only if risk-weighted expected utility theory is the correct way to accommodate empirical uncertainty. We don't wish to enter into this debate, so for clarity of exposition we assume that the risk-neutral version of expected utility theory is the correct formal framework for accommodating empirical uncertainty.

[16] For an argument of this sort, see Sepielli, ' "Along an Imperfectly Lighted Path" '.

outcome. But it doesn't make sense to speak of chances of different moral theories being true (apart from probabilities 1 or 0). And that, one might think, makes an important difference.

However, consider mathematical uncertainty. It is necessarily true whether or not the 1000th digit of the decimal expansion of π is a 7. But, unless we've sat down and worked out what the 1000th digit of π is, we should be uncertain about whether it's 7 or not. And when we need to take actions based on that uncertainty, expected utility theory seems to be the right account. Suppose that one is offered a bet that pays out $1 if the 1000th digit of π is a 7. How much should one be willing to pay to take that bet? Since there are ten possibilities and the limiting relative frequency of each of them in the decimal expansion of π is equal, it seems one's subjective credence that the 1000th digit of π is a 7 should be 0.1. If so, then, according to expected utility theory, one should be willing to pay 10 cents to take that bet (assuming that, over this range, money doesn't have diminishing marginal value). And that seems exactly right. Even if there's some, highly ideal, sense in which one ought to be certain of all mathematical truths, and act on that certainty, there's clearly a sense of 'ought' which is relative to real-life decision-makers' more impoverished epistemic situation; for that sense of 'ought', expected utility theory seems like the right account of how to make decisions in light of uncertainty. And if this is true in the case of mathematical uncertainty, then the same considerations apply in the case of moral uncertainty as well.[17]

This analogy between decision-making under empirical uncertainty and decision-making under moral uncertainty becomes considerably stronger when we consider that the decision-maker might not even *know* the nature of her uncertainty. Suppose, for example, that Sophie is deciding whether to eat chicken. She's certain that she ought not to eat an animal if that animal is a person, but she is uncertain about whether chickens are persons or not. And suppose that she has no idea whether her uncertainty stems from empirical uncertainty, about chickens' capacity for certain experiences, or from moral uncertainty, about what the sorts of attributes qualify one as a person in the morally relevant sense.

---

[17] Of course, this means departing from standard probability theory, which assigns probability 1 to all necessary propositions. How to create a formal theory of probability that can reject this idea is a problem that we will leave for another time; however, the fact that we *are* uncertain, and seem justifiably uncertain, in some necessary truths, means that we have to overcome this problem no matter what our view on moral uncertainty. See Michael G. Titelbaum, *Quitting Certainties: A Bayesian Framework Modeling Degrees of Belief*, Oxford: Oxford University Press, 2012.

It doesn't seem plausible to suppose that the nature of her uncertainty could make a difference as to what she should decide. It seems even less plausible to think that it could be extremely important for Sophie to find out the nature of her uncertainty before making her decision. But if we think that moral and empirical uncertainty should be treated in different ways, then this is what we're committed to. If her uncertainty stems from empirical uncertainty, then that uncertainty should be taken into account, and everyone would agree that she ought not (in the subjective sense of 'ought') to eat the chicken. If her uncertainty stems from moral uncertainty and moral and empirical uncertainty should be treated differently, then it might be that she should eat the chicken. But then, because finding out the nature of her uncertainty could potentially completely change her decision, she should potentially invest significant resources into finding out what the nature of her uncertainty is. This seems bizarre.

So, as well as pointing out the problems with alternative views, as we did in sections I–II, there seems to be a strong direct argument for the view that moral and empirical uncertainty should be treated in the same way. Under empirical uncertainty, expected utility theory is the standard formal framework. So we should take that as the default correct formal framework under moral uncertainty as well, and endorse maximizing expected choiceworthiness.[18]

IV. Two Objections to MEC

In this section we discuss two objections to MEC: that the view is *too demanding* and that it cannot handle the idea that some options are *supererogatory*.

---

[18] An argument for the risk-neutral version of MEC, in particular, could be made using the non-standard axiomatization of expected utility theory in Martin Peterson, 'From Outcomes to Acts: A Non-Standard Axiomatization of the Expected Utility Principle', *Journal of Philosophical Logic*, vol. 33, no. 4 (August 2004), pp. 361–78. Unlike standard axiomatizations (e.g. John Von Neumann and Oskar Morgenstern, *Theory of Games and Economic Behavior*, Princeton, NJ: Princeton University Press, 1953), which are given over *lotteries*, Peterson's is given over *outcomes*. This requires an independently motivated interval-scale structure of utility for outcomes, which is usually considered a problem. However, the analogue of utility of outcomes in our case is the choiceworthiness of options, according to a given theory, and we are already supposing this to be at least roughly interval-scale measurable and comparable between theories; so we are in a good position to use this axiomatization to argue for risk-neutral MEC. See also Stefan Riedener, 'Maximising Expected Value under Axiological Uncertainty', BPhil thesis, University of Oxford, 2013 for an axiomatic argument in support of maximizing expected value under evaluative uncertainty.

Demandingness

The first objection we'll consider is that MEC is too *demanding*: it has implications that require too great a personal sacrifice from us.[19] For example, Peter Singer has argued that members of affluent countries are obligated to give a large proportion of their income to those living in extreme poverty, and that failing to do so is as wrong, morally, as walking past a drowning child whose life one easily could save.[20] Many people who have heard the argument don't believe it to be sound; but even those who reject the argument should have at least some credence in its conclusion being true. And everyone agrees that it's at least permissible to donate the money. So isn't there a dominance argument for giving to fight extreme poverty? The decision situation seems to be as in Table 2.7.

If so, then it is appropriate for us, as citizens of affluent countries, to give a large proportion of our income to fight poverty in the developing world. But (the objection goes) that is too much to demand of us. So Dominance, and therefore MEC, should be rejected.

Our first response to this objection is that it is guilty of double-counting.[21] Considerations relating to demandingness *are* relevant to consideration of what it is appropriate to do under moral uncertainty. But they are relevant because they are relevant to what credences one ought to have across

Table 2.7

	Singer's conclusion is correct	Singer's conclusion is incorrect
Give	Permissible	Permissible
Don't Give	Impermissible	Permissible

[19] Weatherson hints at this objection in 'Review of Ted Lockhart, *Moral Uncertainty and Its Consequences*'; it is made at length in Christian Barry and Patrick Tomlin, 'Moral Uncertainty and Permissibility: Evaluating Option Sets', *Canadian Journal of Philosophy*, vol. 46, no. 6 (2016), pp. 898–923. For discussion, see Sepielli, '"Along an Imperfectly Lighted Path"', pp. 103–5.
[20] Peter Singer, 'Famine, Affluence, and Morality', *Philosophy & Public Affairs*, vol. 1, no. 3 (Spring 1972), pp. 229–43.
[21] For a response to this objection, see Christian Tarsney, 'Rejecting Supererogationism', *Pacific Philosophical Quarterly*, vol. 100, no. 2 (June 2019), pp. 599– 623, sect. 4. https://doi.org/10.1111/papq.12239. A separate, more deflationary, response would be to re-emphasize that we are not talking about permissibility under moral uncertainty, only about what the appropriateness ordering is, and to contend that demandingness is about what options are permissible under moral uncertainty. However, we think that there are interesting issues here, so we will assume that our objector finds even the fact that certain very self-sacrificial actions to be more appropriate than all other options to be implausibly demanding.

different moral theories. If they were *also* taken to be relevant to which theory of decision-making under moral uncertainty is true, then one has given demandingness considerations more weight than they should have. Consider an analogy: it would clearly be incorrect to argue against MEC because, in some cases, it claims that it is appropriate for one to refrain from eating meat, even though (so the objection goes) there's nothing wrong with eating meat. That would be double-counting the arguments against the view that it is impermissible to eat meat; in general, it seems illegitimate to move from claims about first-order moral theories to conclusions about which theory of decision-making under moral uncertainty is true.

However, we do think that it's reasonable to be suspicious of this dominance argument for giving a large proportion of one's income to fight global poverty. We think that a theory of decision-making under moral uncertainty should take into account uncertainty about what the *all-things-considered* choice-worthiness ordering is. And the decision-maker who rejects Singer's argument should have some credence in the view that, all things considered, the most choiceworthy option is to spend the money on herself (or on her family and friends). This would be true on the view according to which there is no moral reason to give, whereas there is a prudential reason to spend the money on herself (and on her friends). So the decision-situation for a typical decision-maker might look as in Table 2.8.

Given this, what it's appropriate to do depends on exactly how likely the decision-maker finds Singer's view. It costs approximately $3,200 to save the life of a child living in extreme poverty,[22] and it would clearly be wrong, on the common-sense view, for someone living in an affluent country not to

Table 2.8

	Singer's argument is correct	Singer's argument is mistaken + prudential reasons to benefit oneself	Singer's argument is mistaken + no prudential reasons to benefit oneself
Give	Permissible	Slightly wrong	Permissible
Don't Give	Gravely wrong	Permissible	Permissible

[22] GiveWell, 'Against Malaria Foundation'. Note that GiveWell's estimated cost per young life saved-*equivalent* is about $3,200. That is, GiveWell estimates that, if you give $3,200 to the Against Malaria Foundation, you will in expectation cause an outcome that, according to the values of the median GiveWell staff member, is morally equivalent to saving the life of one young child. For discussion, see Ajeya Cotra, 'AMF and Population Ethics', The GiveWell Blog, 12 December 2016. http://blog.givewell.org/2016/12/12/amf-population-ethics/

TWO OBJECTIONS TO MEC   53

save a drowning child even if it were at a personal cost of $3,200. It seems to us that this intuition still holds even if it cost $3,200 to prevent a one in ten chance of a child drowning. In which case, the difference in choice-worthiness between giving and not-giving, given that Singer's conclusion is true, is at least ten times as great as the difference in choiceworthiness between giving and not-giving, given that Singer's conclusion is false. So if one has at least 0.1 credence in Singer's view, then it would be inappropriate not to give. However, the intuition becomes much more shaky if the $3,200 only gave the drowning child an additional one in a hundred chance of living. So perhaps the difference in choiceworthiness between giving and not-giving, on the assumption that Singer's conclusion is true, is less than one hundred times as great as the difference in choiceworthiness between not-giving and giving, on the assumption that Singer's conclusion is false. In which case, it would be appropriate to spend the money on oneself if one has less than 1% credence that Singer's conclusion is true.

The above argument was very rough. But it at least shows that there is no two-line knockdown argument from moral uncertainty to the appropri-ateness of giving. Making that argument requires doing first-order moral philosophy, in order to determine how great a credence one should assign to the conclusion of Singer's view. And that, we think, should make us a lot less suspicious of MEC. The two-line argument seemed too easy to be sound. For example, Weatherson commented that: 'The principle has some rather striking consequences, so striking we might fear for its refutation by a quick modus tollens'[23] and

I'm arguing against philosophers who, like Pascal, think they can convince us to act as if they are right as soon as we agree there is a non-zero chance that they are right. I'm as a rule deeply sceptical of any such move, whether it be in ethics, theology, or anywhere else.[24]

We agree with him on these comments. But the error was not with MEC itself: the error was that MEC was being applied in too simple-minded a way.[25] We shall come back to the question of the practical implications of moral uncertainty in much more detail in Chapter 8.

---

[23] Weatherson, 'Review of Ted Lockhart, *Moral Uncertainty and Its Consequences*', p. 694.
[24] Weatherson, 'Running Risks Morally', p. 145.
[25] We think this reply is also effective against Barry and Tomlin, 'Moral Uncertainty and Permissibility: Evaluating Option Sets'. Barry and Tomlin present an alternative account, which is supposed to avoid the demandingness objection. However, it suffers from some significant

Supererogation

The second objection we'll consider is that MEC cannot properly accommodate the fact that theories include the idea of *supererogation*. That is, two options might both be permissible, but one may be, in some sense, morally superior to the other. Insofar as MEC is sensitive *only* to a theory's choiceworthiness function, and permissibility is defined as optimal choiceworthiness, it may seem to neglect this aspect of morality.[26]

In order to determine whether this is a good objection to MEC, we need to understand what supererogation is. Accounts of supererogation can be divided into three classes.[27]

The first and most popular type of account is the Reasons Plus type of account. On this type of account, the normative status of an option (in particular, whether it is obligatory or merely supererogatory) is determined by both the choiceworthiness of the option, and by some other factor, such as praiseworthiness.[28]

According to one account, for example, an option is permissible iff it's maximally choiceworthy; an option is supererogatory if it's permissible and if choosing that option is praiseworthy.

On this account, MEC has little trouble with supererogation. Different theories might label some options as supererogatory because of the reactive attitudes that it is appropriate for others to have towards people who choose those options. But that doesn't change the theory's choiceworthiness functions; so it doesn't affect how MEC should treat different theories.

If this account of supererogation were true, it would be true that there are elements of morality on which MEC is silent. If one regards praiseworthiness

---

unclarity. Moreover, it requires us to make sense of normative assessements of *sets* of options as well as *second-order* moral evaluations: it is morally bad that a moral theory is morally demanding. We find both of these requirements problematic.

[26] See Ted Lockhart, *Moral Uncertainty and Its Consequences*, New York: Oxford University Press, 2000.

[27] We take this classification, and the references below, from Sepielli, ' "Along an Imperfectly Lighted Path" ', pp. 238–45.

[28] For examples of this type of account, see Joseph Raz, 'Permissions and Supererogation', *American Philosophical Quarterly*, vol. 12, no. 2 (April, 1975), pp. 161–8; Bernard Williams, 'Persons, Character, and Morality', in Amélie Oksenberg Rorty (ed.), *The Identities of Persons*, Los Angeles: University of California Press, 1977, pp. 197–216; and Susan Wolf, 'Moral Obligations and Social Commands', in Samuel Newlands and Larry M. Jorgensen (eds), *Metaphysics and the Good: Themes from the Philosophy of Robert Merrihew Adams*, Oxford: Oxford University Press, 2009, pp. 343–67.

and blameworthiness as important moral concepts, then one might wish to extend our account: one might wish to develop an account of when one is blameworthy when acting under moral uncertainty, in addition to an account of what one ought to do under moral uncertainty. This is a major topic that we put aside in the book. But it doesn't pose a problem for MEC itself.

The second type of account of supererogation we may call the Kinds of Reasons accounts. On these accounts, options with the same level of choice-worthiness gain different normative statuses in virtue of their position in some other ordering.[29]

According to one possible account, for example, an option is permissible iff it's all-things considered maximally choiceworthy; an option is super-erogatory iff it's all-things-considered maximally choiceworthy and better in terms of other-regarding reasons (rather than prudential or esthetic reasons) than all other maximally choiceworthy options.

On this account, again, there seems to be little that is problematic for MEC, since it is a function from the all-things-considered choiceworthiness functions to an appropriateness ordering. Within this theory, we can accept that some maximally choiceworthy actions can be better in terms of other-regarding reasons than others.

The third type of account of supererogation we may call Strength of Reasons accounts. On this view, an option is obligatory iff it's maximally choiceworthy and the reasons in favour of it are sufficiently strong compared to other available options (that is, if the maximally choiceworthy option is only a little more choiceworthy than the other permissible options, in some sense of 'only a little' that would need to be defined).

This account poses some problems for MEC because, on this account, there is more reason to choose one option x than another option y even though both options are permissible. This leaves us with a decision. Are both options maximally choiceworthy (because both are maximally permissible)? Or is the one we have more reason to choose more choiceworthy?

We don't find this view particularly plausible. However, we suggest that, if you endorse such an account, you should regard option A as more choiceworthy than option B even if both options are permissible. If you

---

[29] For examples of this type of account, see Douglas W. Portmore, 'Position-Relative Consequentialism, Agent-Centered Options, and Supererogation', *Ethics*, vol. 113, no. 2 (January 2003), pp. 303–32; Michael Zimmerman, *The Concept of Moral Obligation*, Cambridge: Cambridge University Press, 1996; and Ruth Chang, 'Voluntarist Reasons and the Sources of Normativity', in David Sobel and Steven Wall (eds), *Reasons for Action*, Cambridge: Cambridge University Press, 2009, pp. 243–71.

were to endorse such a view, then you might wish to have a separate theory of how to aggregate deontic statuses under moral uncertainty; what it is rationally permissible to do under moral uncertainty might come apart from what the most appropriate option is.[30] However, we do not attempt that project here; our project is just about the strengths of reasons that we have, on different theories, and how to aggregate them in conditions of uncertainty.

Conclusion

In this chapter we have argued that, in conditions of interval-scale measurable and intertheoretically comparable choiceworthiness, moral and empirical uncertainty should be treated in the same way. Because we take expected utility theory to provide the default formal framework for taking empirical uncertainty into account, that means we think that *maximize expected choiceworthiness* is the default account for making decisions in the face of moral uncertainty. In the next chapter, we will discuss what the right theory is when moral theories are incomparable and provide merely ordinal choiceworthiness.

[30] To see that this is so, consider a decision-maker who is certain in a moral view on which this view of supererogation is correct. If one thought that only appropriate options were rationally permissible, then there would be situations in which the decision-maker would be certain that two options were morally permissible, but where only one option was rationally permissible (in the sense of rational permissibility that is relevant to decision-making under moral uncertainty). This seems problematic. We thank Christian Tarsney for this point.

3

Ordinal Theories and the Social Choice Analogy

Introduction

In the previous chapter, we argued that when the decision-maker has non-zero credence only in theories that are interval-scale measurable and intertheoretically comparable, it's appropriate to maximize expected choiceworthiness.

But when we try to apply MEC in general, a couple of problems immediately arise. First, what should you do if one of the theories in which you have credence doesn't give sense to the idea of interval-scale measurable choice-worthiness? Some theories will tell you that murder is more seriously wrong than lying, yet will not give any way of saying that the difference in choice-worthiness between murder and lying is greater, smaller, or equally as large as the difference in choice-worthiness between lying and telling the truth. But if it doesn't make sense to talk about ratios of differences of choice-worthiness between options, according to a particular theory, then we won't be able to take an expectation over that theory. We'll call this *the problem of merely ordinal theories*.

A second problem is that, even when all theories under consideration give sense to the idea of interval-scale choice-worthiness, we need to be able to compare the size of differences in choice-worthiness between options *across* different theories. But it seems that we can't always do this. A rights-based theory claims that it would be wrong to kill one person in order to save fifty; utilitarianism claims that it would be wrong not to do so. But for which theory is there more at stake? In line with the literature, we'll call this *the problem of intertheoretic comparisons*.[1]

Some philosophers have suggested that these problems are fatal to the project of developing a normative account of decision-making under moral

---

[1] E.g. Lockhart, *Moral Uncertainty and Its Consequences*; Ross, 'Rejecting Ethical Deflationism'; Sepielli, 'What to Do When You Don't Know What to Do'.

Moral Uncertainty. William MacAskill, Krister Bykvist, and Toby Ord, Oxford University Press (2020).
© William MacAskill, Krister Bykvist and Toby Ord.
DOI: 10.1093/oso/9780198722274.001.0001

uncertainty.[2] The primary purpose of this chapter and the next is to show that this is not the case.

We discuss these problems in more depth in section I. In section II, we introduce the analogy between decision-making under moral uncertainty and social choice, and explain how this analogy can help us to overcome these problems. The rest of the chapter is spent fleshing out how this idea can help us to develop a theory of decision-making under moral uncertainty that is applicable even when all theories under consideration are merely ordinal, and even when there is neither level- nor unit-comparability between those theories.[3] In section III, we show how the social choice analogy gives fertile ground for coming up with new accounts. We consider whether *My Favorite Theory* or *My Favorite Option* might be the right theory of decision-making under moral uncertainty in conditions of merely ordinal theories and incomparability, but reject both of these accounts. In section IV we defend the idea that, when maximizing choice-worthiness is not possible, one should use the Borda Rule instead.

Note that this chapter and the next chapter—which primarily discusses what to do in conditions of interval-scale measurability but incomparability— should ideally be considered together rather than read in isolation. The next chapter will discuss two objections to the Borda Rule—that it is sensitive to how one individuates options, and that it violates *Contraction Consistency*— and will also discuss what is the correct account of what to do in mixed informational conditions. We will suggest that the fact that the Borda Rule allows us to endorse a 'one-step' procedure for decision-making in varying informational conditions may be an additional benefit of the Borda Rule.

I. Intertheoretic Comparisons and Ordinal Theories

If you want to take an expectation over moral theories, two conditions need to hold. First, each moral theory in which you have credence needs to

---

[2] E.g. Gracely, 'On the Noncomparability of Judgments Made by Different Ethical Theories'; Hudson, 'Subjectivization in Ethics'; Ross, 'Rejecting Ethical Deflationism'; Gustafsson and Torpman, 'In Defence of My Favourite Theory'. In conversation with one of the authors, John Broome suggested that the problem is 'devastating' for accounts of decision-making under moral uncertainty; the late Derek Parfit described the problem as 'fatal'.

[3] For discussion of decision-making under moral uncertainty in conditions of merely ordinal theories and level-comparability, see Christian Tarsney, 'Moral Uncertainty for Deontologists', *Ethical Theory and Moral Practice*, vol. 21, no. 3 (2018), pp. 505–20. https://doi.org/10.1007/s10677-018-9924-4

provide a concept of choice-worthiness that is at least interval-scale measurable. That is, you need to be able to make sense, on every theory in which you have credence, of the idea that differences in choice-worthiness can be compared—that, for instance, the difference between the choice-worthiness of killing and that of lying is greater than the difference between the choice-worthiness of lying and that of withholding some insignificant truth.

Second, you need to be able to compare the magnitude of the difference in choice-worthiness across different moral theories. That is, you need to be able to tell whether the difference in choice-worthiness between A and B, on T_i, is greater than, smaller than, or equal to, the difference in choice-worthiness between C and D, on T_j. Moreover, you need to be able to tell, at least roughly, *how much* greater the choice-worthiness difference between A and B on T_i is than the choice-worthiness difference between C and D on T_j.

Many theories do provide interval-scale measurable choice-worthiness: in general, if a theory orders empirically uncertain prospects in terms of their choice-worthiness and the choice-worthiness relation satisfies the axioms of expected utility theory, then the theory provides interval-scale measurable choice-worthiness.[4] Many theories satisfy these axioms. Consider, for example, the version of utilitarianism according to which one should maximize expected wellbeing (and which therefore satisfies the axioms of expected utility theory[5]). If, according to this form of utilitarianism, a guarantee of saving person A is equal to a 50% chance of saving no one and a 50% chance of saving both persons B and C, then we would know that, according to this form of utilitarianism, the difference in choice-worthiness between saving person B and C, and saving person A, is the same as the difference in choice-worthiness between saving person A and saving no one. We give meaning to the idea of comparing differences in choice-worthiness by appealing to what the theory says in cases of uncertainty.

However, this method cannot be applied to all theories. Sometimes, the axioms of expected utility theory clash with common-sense intuition, such

---

[4] As shown in Von Neumann and Morgenstern, *Theory of Games and Economic Behavior*. The application of this idea to moral theories is discussed at length in John Broome, *Weighing Goods: Equality, Uncertainty, and Time*, Cambridge, MA: Basil Blackwell, 1991.

[5] For the purpose of this discussion, we assume away the possibility of infinite amounts of value (which would mean that the view violates the Archimidean axiom). Alternatively, one could replace the view we discuss with one on which moral value is bounded above and below.

as in the Allais paradox.[6] If a theory is designed to cohere closely with common-sense intuition, as many non-consequentialist theories are, then it may violate these axioms. And if the theory does violate these axioms, then, again, we cannot use probabilities in order to make sense of interval-scale measurable choice-worthiness.

Plausibly, Kant's ethical theory is an example of a merely ordinally measurable theory.[7] According to Kant, murder is less choiceworthy than lying, which is less choiceworthy than failing to aid someone in need. But we don't think it makes sense to say, even roughly, that on Kant's view the difference in choice-worthiness between murder and lying is greater than or less than the difference in choice-worthiness between lying and failing to aid someone in need. So someone who has non-zero credence in Kant's ethical theory simply can't use expected choice-worthiness maximization over all theories in which she has credence.

The second problem for the maximizing expected choice-worthiness account is the problem of intertheoretic comparisons. Even when theories do provide interval-scale measurable choice-worthiness, there is no guarantee that we will be able to compare magnitudes of choice-worthiness differences between one theory and another. Previously, we gave the example of comparing the difference in choice-worthiness between killing one person to save fifty and refraining from doing so, according to a rights-based moral theory and according to utilitarianism. In this case, there's no intuitive answer to the question of whether the situation is higher-stakes for the rights-based theory than it is for utilitarianism or vice versa. And in the absence of intuitions about the case, it's difficult to see how there could be any way of determining an answer. We'll discuss this issue more in Chapters 4 and 5.

The question of what to do when we cannot make intratheoretic comparisons of units of choice-worthiness (that is, those theories are merely ordinal), and when we can make neither unit nor level comparisons of choice-worthiness across theories, has not been discussed in the literature. At best, it has been assumed that, in the absence of intertheoretic comparisons, the only alternative to maximizing expected choice-worthiness is

---

[6] Maurice Allais, 'Allais Paradox', in John Eatwell, Murray Milgate, and Peter Newman (eds), *The New Palgrave: A Dictionary of Economics*, London: Macmillan, 1987, vol. 1, pp. 78–80.

[7] Kant's ethics violates at least the *continuity* assumption: that, for three options A, B, and C, such that A is at least as choiceworthy as B, which is at least as choiceworthy as C, there exists a probability p such that B is equally as choiceworthy as $p \times A + (1-p) \times C$.

the account according to which one should simply act in accordance with *My Favorite Theory* or *My Favorite Option*.[8] For that reason, it has been assumed that the lack of intertheoretic comparisons would have drastic consequences. For example, because intertheoretic incomparability entails that *maximize expected choice-worthiness* cannot be applied, Jacob Ross says: 'the denial of the possibility of intertheoretic value comparisons would imply that among most of our options there is no basis for rational choice. In other words, it would imply the near impotence of practical reason'.[9] In a similar vein, other commentators have regarded the problem of intertheoretic comparisons as fatal to the very idea of developing a normative account of decision-making under moral uncertainty. In one of the first modern articles to discuss decision-making under moral uncertainty,[10] James Hudson says:

> Hedging will be quite impossible for the ethically uncertain agent... Under the circumstances, the two units [of value, according to different theories] must be incomparable by the agent, and so there can be no way for her [moral] uncertainty to be taken into account in a reasonable decision procedure. Clearly this second-order hedging is impossible.[11]

Likewise, Edward Gracely argues, on the basis of intertheoretic incomparability, that:

> the proper approach to uncertainty about the rightness of ethical theories is to determine the one most likely to be right, and to act in accord with its dictates. Trying to weigh the importance attached by rival theories to a particular act is ultimately meaningless and fruitless.[12]

----

[8] E.g. Ross, 'Rejecting Ethical Deflationism', p. 762, fn.11.

[9] Note that Ross uses this purported impotence as a *reductio* of the idea that different theories' choice-worthiness rankings can be incomparable. However, if our argument in the preceding paragraphs is sound, then Ross's position is not tenable.

[10] The first modern article published on the topic of moral uncertainty appears to be Ted Lockhart, 'Another Moral Standard', *Mind*, vol. 86, no. 344 (October 1977), pp. 582–6, followed by James R. Greenwell, 'Abortion and Moral Safety', *Crítica*, vol. 9, no. 27 (December 1977), pp. 35–48 ad Raymond S. Pfeiffer, 'Abortion Policy and the Argument from Uncertainty', *Social Theory and Practice*, vol. 11, no. 3 (Fall 1985), pp. 371–86. We thank Christian Tarsney for bringing these articles to our attention.

[11] Hudson, 'Subjectivization in Ethics', p. 224.

[12] Gracely, 'On the Noncomparability of Judgments Made by Different Ethical Theories', pp. 331–2.

The above philosophers don't consider the idea that different criteria could apply depending on the informational situation of the agent. It is this assumption that leads to the thought that the problem of intertheoretic comparisons of value is fatal for accounts of decision-making under moral uncertainty. Against Ross and others, we'll argue that decision-making in conditions of moral uncertainty and intertheoretic incomparability is not at all hopeless. In this chapter, we focus on decision-making in conditions of merely ordinal theories. In the next chapter, we focus on decision-making when theories are interval-scale measurable but not comparable.[13] In both cases, we will exploit an analogy between decision-making under moral uncertainty and social choice. So let's turn to that now.

II. Moral Uncertainty and the Social Choice Analogy

Social choice theory, in the 'social welfare functional' framework developed by Amartya Sen,[14] studies how to aggregate individuals' utility functions (where each utility function is a numerical representation of that individual's preferences over social states) into a single 'social' utility function, which represents 'social' preferences over social states, i.e. which state is better than another. A *social welfare functional* is a function from sets of utility functions to a 'social' utility function. Familiar examples of social welfare functionals include: utilitarianism, according to which *A* has higher social utility than *B* iff the sum total of utility over all individuals is greater for *A* than for *B*; and maximin, according to which *A* has higher social utility than *B* iff *A* has more utility than *B* for the worst-off member of society.

Similarly, the theory of decision-making under moral uncertainty studies how to aggregate different theories' choice-worthiness functions into a single appropriateness ordering. The formal analogy between these two disciplines should be clear.[15] Instead of individuals we have theories; instead of

---

[13] For the purpose of these chapters, we put the issue of *intra*theoretic incomparability to the side, and only consider theories that have complete choice-worthiness orderings.

[14] Amartya Sen, *Collective Choice and Social Welfare*, San Francisco: Holden-Day, 1970.

[15] Note that this analogy is importantly different from other analogies between decision theory and social choice theory that have recently been drawn in the literature. Rachael Briggs's analogy ('Decision-Theoretic Paradoxes as Voting Paradoxes', *Philosophical Review*, vol. 119, no. 1 (January 2010), pp. 1–30) is quite different from ours: in her analogy, a decision theory is like a voting theory but where the voters are the decision-maker's future selves. Samir Okasha's analogy ('Theory Choice and Social Choice: Kuhn versus Arrow', *Mind*, vol. 120, no. 477 (January 2011), pp. 83–115) is formally similar to ours, but his analogy is between the problem

Table 3.1

Social Choice Theory	⇒	Moral Uncertainty
Individuals	⇒	First-order moral theories
Individual utility	⇒	Choice-worthiness function
Social welfare functional	⇒	Theory of decision-making under moral uncertainty
Utilitarianism	⇒	Maximize expected choice-worthiness

preferences we have choice-worthiness orderings; and rather than a social welfare functional we have a theory of decision-making under moral uncertainty. And, just as social choice theorists try to work out what the correct social welfare functional is, so we are trying to work out what the correct theory of decision-making under moral uncertainty is. Moreover, just as many social choice theorists tend to be attracted to weighted utilitarianism ('weighted' because the weights assigned to each individual's welfare need not be equal) when information permits,[16] so we are attracted to its analogue under moral uncertainty, *maximize expected choice-worthiness,* when information permits (see Table 3.1).

The formal structure of the two problems is very similar. But the two problems are similar on a more intuitive level as well. The problem of social choice is to find the best compromise in a situation where there are many people with competing preferences. The problem of moral uncertainty is to find the best compromise in a situation where there are many possible moral theories with competing recommendations about what to do.

What's particularly enticing about this analogy is that the literature on social choice theory is well developed, and results from social choice theory might be transferable to moral uncertainty, shedding light on that issue. In particular, since the publication of Amartya Sen's *Collective Choice and Social Welfare,*[17] social choice theory has studied how different social welfare functionals may be axiomatized under different *informational assumptions.* One can vary informational assumptions in one of two ways. First, one can vary the *measurability assumptions,* and, for example, assume that utility is

of social choice and the problem of aggregating different values within a pluralist epistemological theory, rather than the problem of aggregating different values under moral uncertainty.

[16] For the reasons why, given interval-scale measurable and interpersonally comparable utility, weighted utilitarianism is regarded as the most desirable social choice function see, for example, Charles Blackorby, David Donaldson, and John A. Weymark, 'Social Choice with Interpersonal Utility Comparisons: A Diagrammatic Introduction', *International Economic Review*, vol. 25, no. 2 (1984), pp. 327–56.

[17] Sen, *Collective Choice and Social Welfare.*

merely ordinally measurable, or assume that it is interval-scale measurable. Second, one can vary the *comparability assumptions*: one can assume that we can compare differences in utility between options across different individuals; or one can assume that such comparisons are meaningless. The problem of determining how such comparisons are possible is known as the problem of interpersonal comparisons of utility. As should be clear from the discussion in the previous section, exactly the same distinctions can be made for moral theories: choice-worthiness can be ordinally or interval-scale measurable; and it can be intertheoretically comparable or incomparable.

Very roughly, what is called voting theory is social choice theory in the context of preferences that are non-comparable and merely ordinally measurable. Similarly, the problem with which we're concerned in this chapter is how to aggregate individual theories' choice-worthiness functions into a single appropriateness ordering in conditions where choice-worthiness is merely ordinally measurable.[18] So we should explore the idea that voting theory will give us the resources to work out how to take normative uncertainty into account when the decision-maker has non-zero credence only in merely ordinal theories.

However, before we begin, we should note two important disanalogies between voting theory and decision-making under moral uncertainty. First, theories, unlike individuals, don't all count for the same: theories are objects of credences. The answer to this disanalogy is obvious. We treat each theory like an individual, but we weight each theory's choice-worthiness function in proportion with the credence the decision-maker has in that the theory. So the closer analogy is with weighted voting.[19]

The second and more important disanalogy is that, unlike in social choice, a decision-maker under moral uncertainty will face varying information from different theories at one and the same time. For a typical decision-maker under moral uncertainty, some of the theories in which she has credence will be interval-scale measurable and intertheoretically comparable; others will be interval-scale measurable but intertheoretically incomparable; others again will be merely ordinally measurable. In contrast, when social choice theorists study different informational set-ups, they generally assume that the same informational assumptions apply to all individuals.

---

[18]   And, as noted previously, we assume that comparisons of *levels* of choice-worthiness are not possible between theories.

[19]   An example of a weighted voting system is the European Council, where the number of votes available to each member state is proportional to that state's population.

We discuss this issue at the end of Chapter 3, providing a general theory of decision-making under moral uncertainty where the precise method of aggregating the decision-maker's uncertainty is sensitive to the information provided by the theories in which she has credence, but which can be applied even in cases of varying informational conditions. In this chapter, however, we assume that all theories in which the decision-maker has credence are merely ordinal. With these caveats, the obvious next question is: which voting system should we use as an analogy?

III. Some Voting Systems

In the previous chapter, we looked at *My Favorite Theory* and *My Favorite Option*. One key argument against them was that they are insensitive to magnitudes of choice-worthiness differences. But if we are considering how to take normative uncertainty into account given that a decision-maker only has non-zero credence in merely ordinal theories, then this objection does not apply. So one might think MFT or MFO gets it right in conditions of merely ordinal theories. However, even in this situation, we think we have good reason to reject these accounts. Consider the following case.[20]

Judge

Julia is a judge who is about to pass a verdict on whether Smith is guilty of murder. She is very confident that Smith is innocent. There is a crowd outside, who are desperate to see Smith convicted. Julia has three options:

A: Pass a verdict of 'guilty'.
B: Call for a retrial.
C: Pass a verdict of 'innocent'.

Julia knows that the crowd will riot if Smith is found innocent, causing mayhem on the streets and the deaths of several people. If she calls for a retrial, she knows that he will be found innocent at a later date, that the crowd will not riot today, and that it is much less likely that the crowd

---

[20] In the cases that follow, and in general when we are discussing merely ordinal theories, we will refer to a theory's choice-worthiness ordering directly, rather than its choice-worthiness function. We do this in order to make it clear which theories are to be understood as ordinal, and which are to be understood as interval-scale measurable. We use the symbol '>' to mean 'is more choiceworthy than'.

will riot at that later date. If she declares Smith guilty, the crowd will be appeased and go home peacefully. She has credence in three moral theories.

35% credence in a variant of utilitarianism, according to which $A>B>C$.

34% credence in a variant of common sense morality, according to which $B>C>A$.

31% credence in a deontological theory, according to which $C>B>A$.

MFT and MFO both regard A as most appropriate, because A is both most choiceworthy according to the theory in which the decision-maker has highest credence, and has the greatest probably of being right. But note that Julia thinks B is very nearly as likely to be right as is A; and she's 100% certain that B is at least second best. It seems highly plausible that this certainty in B being at least the second-best option should outweigh the slightly lower probability of B being maximally choiceworthy. So it seems, intuitively, that B is the most appropriate option: it is well supported in general by the theories in which the decision-maker has credence. But neither MFT nor MFO can take account of that fact. Indeed, MFT and MFO are completely insensitive to how theories rank options that are not maximally choiceworthy. But to be insensitive in this way, it seems, is simply to ignore decision-relevant information. So we should reject these theories.

If we turn to the literature on voting theory, can we do better? Within voting theory, the gold standard voting systems are *Condorcet extensions*.[21] The idea behind such voting systems is that we should think how candidates would perform in a round-robin head-to-head tournament—every candidate is compared against every other candidate in terms of how many voters prefer one candidate to the other. A voting system is a Condorcet extension if it satisfies the following condition: that, if, for every other option B, the majority of voters prefer A to B, then A is elected.

We can translate this idea into our moral uncertainty framework as follows. Let's say that A *beats* B (or B *is defeated by* A) iff it is true that, in a

---

[21] A brief comment on some voting systems we don't consider: we don't consider range voting because we're considering the situation where theories give us only ordinal choice-worthiness, whereas range voting requires interval-scale measurable choice-worthiness. We don't consider instant-runoff (or 'alternative vote') because it violates monotonicity: that is, one can cause A to win over B by choosing to vote for B over A rather than vice versa. This is seen to be a devastating flaw within voting theory (see, for example, Nicholas Tideman, *Collective Decisions and Voting*, Routledge (2017)), and we agree: none of the voting systems we consider violate this property.

pairwise comparison between *A* and *B*, the decision-maker thinks it more likely that *A* is more choiceworthy than *B* than that *B* is more choiceworthy than *A*. *A* is the *Condorcet winner* iff *A* beats every other option within the option-set. A theory of decision-making under moral uncertainty is a Condorcet extension if it elects a Condorcet winner whenever one exists. Condorcet extensions get the right answer in *Judge*, because *B* beats both *A* and *C*.

However, often Condorcet winners do not exist. Consider the following case.

Hiring Decision

Jason is a manager at a large sales company. He has to make a new hire, and he has three candidates to choose from. They each have very different attributes, and he's not sure what attributes are morally relevant to his decision. In terms of qualifications for the role, applicant *B* is best, then applicant *C*, then applicant *A*. However, he's not certain that that's the only relevant consideration. Applicant *A* is a single mother, with no other options for work. Applicant *B* is a recent university graduate with a strong CV from a privileged background. And applicant *C* is a young black male from a poor background, but with other work options. Jason has credence in three competing views.

30% credence in a form of virtue theory. On this view, hiring the single mother would be the compassionate thing to do, and hiring simply on the basis of positive discrimination would be disrespectful. So, according to this view, *A*>*B*>*C*.

30% credence in a form of non-consequentialism. On this view, Jason should just choose in accordance with qualification for the role. According to this view, *B*>*C*>*A*.

40% credence in a form of consequentialism. On this view, Jason should just choose so as to maximize societal benefit. According to this view, *C*>*A*>*B*.

In this case, no Condorcet winner exists: *B* beats *C*, *C* beats *A*, but *A* beats *B*. But, intuitively, *C* is more appropriate than *A* or *B*: *A*>*B*>*C*, *B*>*C*>*A*, and *C*>*A*>*B* are just 'rotated' versions of each other, with each option appearing in each position in the ranking exactly once. Given this, then the ranking with the highest credence should win out, and *C* should be the most appropriate option.

So Condorcet extensions need some way to determine a winner even when no Condorcet winner exists. Let us say that the *magnitude of a defeat* is the difference between the credence the decision-maker has that *A* is more choiceworthy than *B* and the credence the decision-maker has that *B* is more choiceworthy than *A*. A simple but popular Condorcet extension is the Simpson–Kramer method:

Simpson–Kramer Method: *A* is more appropriate than *B* iff *A* has a smaller biggest pairwise defeat than *B*; *A* is equally as appropriate as *B* iff *A* and *B*'s biggest defeats are equal in magnitude.

In *Hiring Decision*, the biggest pairwise defeat for *A* and *B* is 30% to 70%, whereas the biggest pairwise defeat for *C* is only 40% to 60%, so the magnitude of the biggest defeat is 40% for *A* and *B* and only 20% for *C*. So, according to the Simpson–Kramer method, *C* is the most appropriate option, which seems intuitively correct in this case (see Table 3.2).

In what follows, we'll use the Simpson–Kramer Method as a prototypical Condorcet extension.[22] Though Condorcet extensions are the gold standard within voting theory, they are not right for our purposes. Whereas voting systems rarely have to handle an electorate of variable size, theories of decision-making under moral uncertainty do: varying the size of the electorate is analogous to changing one's credences in different moral theories. It's obvious that our credences in different moral theories should often

Table 3.2

	A	*B*	*C*
A		30%:70%	70%:30%
B	70%:30%		40%:60%
C	30%:70%	60%:40%	

---

[22]   There are other Condorcet extensions that are, in our view, better than the Simpson–Kramer method, such as the Schulze method (Markus Schulze, 'A New Monotonic, Clone-Independent, Reversal Symmetric, and Condorcet-Consistent Single-Winner Election Method', *Social Choice and Welfare*, vol. 36, no. 2 (February 2011), pp. 267–303) and Tideman's Ranked Pairs (T. N. Tideman, 'Independence of Clones as a Criterion for Voting Rules', *Social Choice and Welfare*, vol. 4, no. 3 (September 1987), pp. 185–206), because they satisfy some other desirable properties that the Simpson–Kramer method fails to satisfy. However, these are considerably more complex than the Simpson–Kramer Method, and fail to be satisfactory for exactly the same reasons why the Simpson–Kramer method fails to be satisfactory. So in what follows we will just use the Simpson–Kramer method as our example of a Condorcet extension.

change. But Condorcet extensions handle that fact very poorly. A minimal condition of adequacy for handling variable electorates is as follows.[23]

Twin Condition: If an additional voter who has exactly the same preferences as a voter who is already part of the electorate joins the electorate and votes, that does not make the outcome of the vote worse by the lights of the additional voter.

The parallel condition in the case of decision-making under normative uncertainty is:

Updating Consistency: Increasing one's credence in some theory does not make the appropriateness ordering worse by the lights of that theory. More precisely: For all T_i, A, B, if A is more choiceworthy than B on T_i, and A is more appropriate than B, then if the decision-maker increases her credence in T_i, decreasing her credence in all other theories proportionally, it is still true that A is more appropriate than B.

Updating Consistency seems to us to be a necessary condition for any theory of decision-making under moral uncertainty. When all theories in which the decision-maker has non-zero credence are merely ordinally measurable, appropriateness should be determined by two things only: first, how highly ranked the option is, according to the theories in which the decision-maker has non-zero credence; and, second, how much credence the decision-maker has in those theories. It would be perverse, therefore, if increasing one's credence in a particular theory on which A is more choiceworthy than B makes A less appropriate than B.

However, all Condorcet extensions violate that condition. To see this, consider the following case.

Tactical Decisions

Jane is a military commander. She needs to take aid to a distant town, through enemy territory. She has four options available to her:

A: Bomb and destroy an enemy hospital in order to distract the enemy troops in the area. This kills 10 enemy civilians. All 100 of her soldiers and all 100 enemy soldiers survive.

---

[23] First given in Hervé Moulin, 'Condorcet's Principle Implies the No Show Paradox', *Journal of Economic Theory*, vol. 45, no. 1 (June 1988), pp. 53–64.

B: Bomb and destroy an enemy ammunitions factory, restricting the scale of the inevitable skirmish. This kills 10 enemy engineers, who help enemy soldiers, though they are not soldiers themselves. As a result, 90 of her soldiers and 90 enemy soldiers survive.

C: Status quo: don't make any pre-emptive attacks and go through the enemy territory only moderately well-armed. 75 of her soldiers and 75 enemy soldiers survive.

D: Equip her soldiers with much more extensive weaponry and explosives. 95 of her soldiers and none of the enemy soldiers survive.

Jane has credence in five different moral views.

She has 5/16 credence in T_1 (utilitarianism), according to which one should simply minimize the number of deaths. According to T_1, $A>B>C>D$.

She has 3/16 credence in T_2 (partialist consequentialism), according to which one should minimize the number of deaths of home soldiers and enemy civilians and engineers, but that deaths of enemy soldiers don't matter. According to T_2, $D>A>B>C$.

She has 3/16 credence in T_3 (mild non-consequentialism), according to which one should minimize the number of deaths of home soldiers and enemy civilians and engineers, that deaths of enemy soldiers don't matter, and that it's mildly worse to kill someone as a means to an end than it is to let them die in battle. According to T_3, $D>A>C>B$.

She has 4/16 credence in T_4 (moderate non-consequentialism), according to which one should minimize the number of deaths of all parties, but that there is a side-constraint against killing a civilian (but not an engineer or soldier) as a means to an end. According to T_4, $B>C>D>A$.

She has 1/16 credence in T_5 (thoroughgoing non-consequentialism), according to which one should minimize the number of deaths, but that there is a side-constraint against killing enemy civilians or engineers as a means to an end, and that killing enemy civilians as a means to an end is much worse than killing enemy engineers. According to T_5, $C>D>B>A$.

Given her credences, according to the Simpson–Kramer method D is the most appropriate option.[24] The above case is highly complicated, and we

---

[24] A's biggest pairwise defeat is to D, losing by 6/16. B's biggest pairwise defeat is to A, losing both by 6/16; C's biggest pairwise defeat is to B, losing by 8/16; D's biggest pairwise defeat is to C, losing by 4/16. So D is the most appropriate option according to the Simpson–Kramer method.

have no intuitions about what the most appropriate option is for Jane, so we don't question that answer. However, what's certain is that gaining new evidence in favour of one moral theory, and increasing one's credence in a moral theory, should not have the consequence of making an option which is *worse* by the lights of the theory in which one has increased one's credence *more appropriate*. But that's exactly what happens on the Simpson–Kramer method. Let us suppose that Jane hears new arguments, and increases her credence in T_5 so that now she has 5/20 credence in T_5. The ratios of her credences in all other theories stays the same: she has 5/20 in T_1, 3/20 in T_2, 3/20 in T_3 and 4/20 in T_4. After updating in favour of T_5, B becomes the most appropriate option, according to the Simpson–Kramer method.[25] But T_5 regards D as more choiceworthy than B. So the fact that Jane has updated in favour of T_5 has made the most appropriate option worse by T_5's lights. This is highly undesirable. So we should reject the Simpson–Kramer method.

In fact, it has been shown that *any* Condorcet extension will violate the *Twin Condition* described above;[26] and so any analogous theory of decision-making under moral uncertainty will violate *Updating Consistency*. So, rather than just a reason to reject the Simpson–Kramer method, violation of *Updating Consistency* gives us a reason to reject all Condorcet extensions as theories of decision-making under moral uncertainty.

Before moving on to a voting system that does better in the context of decision-making under moral uncertainty, we'll highlight one additional reason that is often advanced in favour of Condorcet extensions. This is that Condorcet extensions are particularly immune to strategic voting: that is, if a Condorcet extension voting system is used, there are not many situations in which a voter can lie about her preferences in order to bring about a more desirable outcome than if she had been honest about her preferences.

It should be clear that this consideration should bear no weight in the context of decision-making under moral uncertainty. We have no need to worry about theories 'lying' about their choice-worthiness function (whatever that would mean). The decision-maker knows what moral theories she

---

[25] A's biggest pairwise defeat is to D, losing by 10/20. B's biggest pairwise defeats are to A and D, losing both by 2/20; C's biggest pairwise defeat is to B, losing by 5/20; D's biggest pairwise defeat is to B, losing by 8/20. B has the smallest biggest defeat. So B is the most appropriate option according to the Simpson–Kramer method. The Schulze method and Ranked Pairs (mentioned in footnote 20 above) both give exactly the same answers in both versions of *Tactical Decisions*, so this case is a counterexample to them too.

[26] The proof of this is too complex to provide here, but can be found in Moulin, 'Condorcet's Principle Implies the No Show Paradox'.

has credence in, and she knows their choice-worthiness functions. So, unlike in the case of voting, there is no gap between an individual's stated preferences and an individual's true preferences.

IV. The Borda Rule

We have seen that MFT, MFO, and Condorcet extensions do not provide the basis for a plausible theory of decision-making under moral uncertainty. Let's now look at a voting system that does better: the Borda Rule. To see both the Borda Rule's similarity to, and difference from, Condorcet extensions, again we should imagine that all options compete against each other in a round-robin head-to-head tournament. Like the Simpson–Kramer method, the magnitudes of the victories and defeats in these pairwise comparisons matter (where the 'magnitude' of a victory is given by the number of votes in favour of the option minus the number of votes against that option). However, rather than focusing on the size of the biggest pairwise defeat, as the Simpson–Kramer method does, the Borda Rule regards the success of an option as equal to the sum of the magnitudes of its pairwise victories against all other options. The most appropriate option is the option whose sum total of magnitudes of victories is greatest.

To see the difference, imagine a round-robin tennis tournament, with players A–Z. Player A beats all other players, but in every case wins during a tiebreaker in the final set. Player B loses by only two points to A, but beats all other players in straight sets. Condorcet extensions care first and foremost about whether a player beats everyone else, and would regard Player A as the winner of the tournament. The Borda Rule cares about how many points a player wins in total, and would regard Player B as the winner of the tournament. It's not obvious to us which of these two approaches is correct when it comes to moral uncertainty: the arguments for choosing Player A or Player B both have something going for them. But the fact that it's not obvious shows that we shouldn't reject outright all theories of decision-making under moral uncertainty that aren't Condorcet extensions.

Defining the *Borda Rule* more precisely:

An option A's *Borda Score*, for any theory T_i, is equal to the number of options within the option-set that are less choiceworthy than A according to theory T_i's choice-worthiness function, minus the number of options within the option-set that are more choiceworthy than A according to T_i's choice-worthiness function.[27]

An option A's *Credence-Weighted Borda Score* is the sum, for all theories T_i, of the Borda Score of A according to theory T_i multiplied by the credence that the decision-maker has in theory T_i.

These definitions allow us to state the Borda Rule:

Borda Rule: An option A is more appropriate than an option B iff A has a higher Credence-Weighted Borda Score than B; A is equally as appropriate as B iff A and B have an equal Credence-Weighted Borda Score.

In this way, the Borda Rule generates not just a set of maximally appropriate actions, but also an appropriateness function.

We can argue for the Borda Rule in two ways. First, we can appeal to cases. Consider again the *Judge* case. We criticized MFT and MFO for not being sensitive to the entirety of the decision-maker's credence distribution, and for not being sensitive to the entire range of each theory's choice-worthiness ordering. The Borda Rule does not make the same error. In *Judge*, the Borda Rule ranks B as most appropriate, then C, then A.[28] This seemed to us to be the intuitively correct result: favouring an option that is generally well-supported rather than an option that is most choiceworthy according to one theory but least choiceworthy according to all others. In *Hiring*

---

[27] The reader might have seen an option's Borda Score defined as equal simply to the number of options below it. The addition of 'minus the number of options that rank higher' clause is the most common way of accounting for tied options. The motivation for this way of dealing with ties is that we want the sum total of Borda Scores over all options to be the same for each theory, whether or not that theory claims there are tied options; if we did not do this, we would be giving some moral theories greater voting power on arbitrary grounds. We will return to whether this account is accurate, suggesting that it should be slightly amended, in the next chapter. The reader may also have seen a Borda Score defined such that an option ranked *i*th receives $n - i$ points plus 0.5 for every option with which it is tied, where n is the total number of options in the option-set. This definition is equivalent to ours; however, ours will prove easier to use when it comes to extending the account in the next section.

[28] Because it doesn't affect the ranking when there are no ties, when giving working we will use a simpler definition of a Borda Score: that an option's Borda Score, for some theory T_i, is equal to the number of options below it on T_i's choice-worthiness ranking. Given this definition, option A receives a score of $35 \times 2 + 0 + 0 = 70$; option B receives a score of $35 + 34 \times 2 + 31 = 134$; option C receives a score of $0 + 34 + 31 \times 2 = 96$.

Decision, according to the Borda Rule, *C* is the most appropriate candidate, then *A* then *B*.[29] Again, this seems to us to be obviously the correct answer.

Finally, consider the *Tactical Decisions* case. In this case, according to the Borda Rule, before updating, the most appropriate option for Jane is *A*, followed by *B*, then *D*, then *C*.[30] As we said before, we don't have any intuitions in this case about which option is most appropriate. But we do know that Jane increasing her credence in T_5 (which ranks *C*>*D*>*B*>*A*) shouldn't make the most appropriate option worse by T_5's lights. Indeed, given that it seems unclear which option is most appropriate, we would expect a substantial increase in her credence in T_5 to improve the appropriateness ranking by T_5's lights. And that's what we find. After updating in favour of T_5, according to the Borda Rule, the appropriateness ranking is *D*, followed by *B*, then *C*, then *A*.[31]

However, appeal to cases is limited in its value because we can't know whether the cases we have come up with are representative, or whether there exist other cases that are highly damaging to our favoured proposal that we simply haven't thought of. A better method is to appeal to general desirable properties. One such property is *Updating Consistency*. In the context of voting theory, it has been shown that, among the commonly discussed and plausible voting systems, only *scoring rules* satisfy the equivalent property, where a scoring rule is a rule that gives a score to an option based on its position in an individual's preference ranking, and claims you should maximize the sum of that score across individuals.[32] The Borda Rule is an example of a scoring rule, as is MFO, whereas MFT and the Simpson–Kramer Method are not. But we rejected MFO on the grounds that it wasn't sensitive to the entirety of theories' choice-worthiness rankings. So we could add in another intuitively obvious condition that the score of each option in i^{th} position has to be strictly greater than the score given to an option in $(i+1)^{th}$ position. This wouldn't quite single out the Borda Rule, but it would come close.

---

[29] Option *A* receives a score of $30 \times 2 + 0 + 10 \times 1 = 100$. Option *B* receives a score of $30 \times 1 + 30 \times 2 + 0 = 90$. Option *C* receives a score of $0 + 30 \times 1 + 40 \times 2 = 110$. So, on the Borda Rule, *A*>*B*>*C*.

[30] Option *A* receives a score of $5 \times 3 + 3 \times 2 + 3 \times 2 + 0 + 0 = 27$. *B*'s score is $5 \times 2 + 3 \times 1 + 0 + 4 \times 3 + 1 \times 1 = 26$. *C*'s score is $5 \times 1 + 0 + 3 \times 1 + 4 \times 2 + 1 \times 3 = 19$. *D*'s score is $0 + 3 \times 3 + 3 \times 3 + 4 \times 1 + 1 \times 2 = 24$.

[31] Option *A* receives a score of $5 \times 3 + 3 \times 2 + 3 \times 2 + 0 + 0 = 27$. *B*'s score is $5 \times 2 + 3 \times 1 + 0 + 4 \times 3 + 4 \times 1 = 29$. *C*'s score is $5 \times 1 + 0 + 3 \times 1 + 4 \times 2 + 4 \times 3 = 28$. *D*'s score is $0 + 3 \times 3 + 3 \times 3 + 4 \times 1 + 4 \times 2 = 30$.

[32] See Moulin, 'Condorcet's Principle Implies the No Show Paradox'.

In order to fully axiomatize the Borda Rule, we need another condition, as follows.

Cancellation: If, for all pairs of options (A,B), S thinks it equally likely that $A>B$ as that $B>A$, then all options are equally appropriate.[33]

It has been shown that the only scoring function that satisfies the voting system analogue of *Cancellation* is the Borda Rule.[34]

One might question *Cancellation* on the following grounds. Consider a case where one has 50% credence in a theory according to which $A>B>C$, and 50% credence in a theory according to which $C>B>A$. One might think that B is the most appropriate option (even though, according to *Cancellation*, all three options are equally appropriate). The grounds for this might be the ordinal equivalent of risk-aversion, whereas the Borda Rule incorporates the equivalent of risk-neutrality. However, in Chapter 1, we endorsed risk-neutral MEC as a default view. If you should be risk-neutral when you can maximize expected choice-worthiness, then surely you should be risk neutral in the ordinal case as well. So for that reason we suggest that the Borda Rule should be the default theory of decision-making in the face of merely ordinal moral theories.

Conclusion

The problem of intertheoretic comparisons is generally considered to be *the* problem facing normative accounts of decision-making under moral uncertainty. It is often assumed that, if theories are intertheoretically incomparable, then all accounts of decision-making under moral uncertainty are doomed—we should just go back to ignoring moral uncertainty, or to assuming our favorite moral theory to be true when deciding what to do.

This chapter has shown the above assumption to be false. How to act in light of moral uncertainty should be sensitive to the information that theories give the decision-maker. And even in the situation in which choice-worthiness is merely ordinally measurable across all theories in

---

[33] The voting system analogue is: if for all pairs of alternative (x,y), the number of voters preferring x to y equals the number of voters preferring y to x, then a tie between all options should be declared. See H. P. Young, 'An Axiomatization of Borda's Rule', *Journal of Economic Theory*, vol. 9, no. 1 (September 1974), pp. 43–52.

[34] Young, 'An Axiomatization of Borda's Rule'.

which the decision-maker has non-zero credence, there is a plausible way to take decision-theoretic uncertainty into account, namely the Borda Rule.

However, even in conditions of intertheoretic incomparability we often have more information than merely ordinal information. Theories can give interval-scale measurable choice-worthiness, yet be incomparable with each other. How to take moral uncertainty into account in that informational condition is the subject of the next chapter.

4

Interval-Scale Theories and Variance Voting

Introduction

In Chapter 3, we discussed how to take into account moral uncertainty over merely ordinal and non-comparable theories. But, very often, theories will provide interval-scale measurable choice-worthiness functions. This chapter discusses how to take into account moral uncertainty over interval-scale measurable but non-comparable theories. Once again, we make use of the analogy between decision-making under moral uncertainty and voting.

In section I, we give examples of interval-scale theories where it's plausible to think that these theories are incomparable with each other. From section II onwards, we discuss what to do in such cases. In section II, we consider but reject the idea that one should use the Borda Rule in such situations. We then consider Ted Lockhart's idea that, in conditions of intertheoretic incomparability, one should treat each theory's maximum and minimum degree of choice-worthiness within a decision-situation as equal, and then aggregate using MEC. This is the analogue of *range voting*.

We consider Sepielli's objection that the principle is arbitrary, but argue that the idea of giving every theory 'equal say' has the potential to make the account non-arbitrary. However, in section III, we argue that Lockhart's suggestion fails by this principle, and that what we call *variance voting* is uniquely privileged as the account that gives incomparable theories equal say. We give intuitive examples in favour of this view, and then show, in section IV, that on either of two ways of making the principle of 'equal say' precise it is only variance voting that gives each theory 'equal say'.

In section V, we discuss what to do in conditions where one has positive credence in some merely ordinal theories, some interval-scale but non-comparable theories, and some theories that are both interval-scale measurable and comparable with each other. In section VI, we discuss whether

Moral Uncertainty. William MacAskill, Krister Bykvist and Toby Ord, Oxford University Press (2020).
© William MacAskill, Krister Bykvist and Toby Ord.
DOI: 10.1093/oso/9780198722274.001.0001

the normalization used by this account should be done only within the decision-situation at hand, or whether it should be done over all possible decision-situations.

I. Intertheoretic Incomparability

As described in Chapter 3, a problem that has dogged accounts of decision-making under moral uncertainty is how to make intertheoretic comparisons of choice-worthiness differences.[1] Describing this more fully, the problem is as follows. All a moral theory needs to provide, one might suppose, is all the true statements of the form, 'A is at least as choiceworthy as B', where A and B represent possible options.[2]

If the choice-worthiness relation of the moral theory orders all options (including lotteries) and satisfies the von Neumann–Morgenstern axioms, then we can construct an interval-scale measure of choice-worthiness.[3] This means that we can represent this choice-worthiness relation using a choice-worthiness function so that it's meaningful to say that the difference in choice-worthiness between two options A and B, according to the theory, is greater than, less than, or equal to, the difference in choice-worthiness between two other options C and D.[4] But, importantly, the choice-worthiness function is only unique up to a positive affine transformation: if you multiply that numerical representation by a positive constant or add any constant, the resulting function still represents the same choice-worthiness ordering. Thus, from the moral theories alone, even though we can meaningfully compare differences of choice-worthiness *within* a moral theory, we just don't have enough information to enable us to compare differences of choice-worthiness *across* moral theories.[5] But if so, then we cannot apply MEC.

---

[1] The problem is normally called the 'problem of intertheoretic comparisons of value'. But this is somewhat misleading. What we and the others who have explored decision-making under moral uncertainty are primarily interested in is comparing *choice-worthiness* across moral theories, rather than comparing *value* across theories.

[2] We deny this supposition in the following chapter; but assuming it provides a particularly clear way of understanding of where the problem comes from.

[3] Namely: Transitivity, Completeness, Continuity, and Independence. For discussion of these axioms in relation to moral theory, see Broome, *Weighing Goods*.

[4] In fact, it even allows us to talk about the ratio between two such differences.

[5] A similar problem arises in the study of social welfare in economics: it is desirable to be able to compare the strength of preferences of different people, but even if you represent

There are really (at least) two questions that fall under the label of 'the problem of intertheoretic choice-worthiness comparisons'. The first question is:

When, if ever, are intertheoretic choice-worthiness comparisons (of differences) possible, and in virtue of what are true intertheoretic comparisons true?

We address this question in Chapter 5. The second question is:

Given that choice-worthiness (of differences) is sometimes incomparable across first-order moral theories, what is it appropriate to do in conditions of moral uncertainty?

We focus on this second question in this chapter, addressing the situation where the non-comparable theories are interval-scale measurable.

To show that it's at least plausible that theories are sometimes interval-scale measurable but incomparable, let's consider two consequentialist theories, prioritarianism and utilitarianism. Prioritarianism gives more weight to gains in wellbeing to the worse-off than it does to gains in wellbeing to the better-off. But does it give more weight to gains in wellbeing to the worse-off than utilitarianism does? That is, is prioritarianism like utilitarianism but with additional concern for the worse-off; or is prioritarianism like utilitarianism but with *less* concern for the better-off? We could represent the prioritarian's idea of favouring the worse-off over the better-off equally well either way. And there seems, at least, to be no information that could let us determine which of these two ideas is the 'correct' way to represent prioritarianism vis-à-vis utilitarianism.

Now, one might think that there is an easy solution, relying on the fact that both of these views make the same recommendations in situations that involve saving identical lives under uncertainty. On both views, a 50% chance of saving two lives with the same lifetime wellbeing and a guarantee of saving one of those lives are equally choiceworthy. So, according to both of these theories, saving two identical lives is twice as good as saving one. One might think that one can use this 'agreement' between the two theories on the

preferences by interval-scale measurable utility functions, you need more information to make them comparable.

difference in choice-worthiness between saving one life and saving two as a common measure.[6]

To see that this doesn't work, consider Annie and Betty. For each of these people, if you administer a certain drug they'll each live for nine more years. Both utilitarianism and prioritarianism agree that the difference in choice-worthiness between doing nothing and saving both Annie and Betty is exactly twice as great as the difference in choice-worthiness between doing nothing and saving Annie alone. For concreteness, we'll assume that the prioritarian's concave function is the square root function. And we'll begin by assuming that Annie and Betty have lived for sixteen years so far. If so, then the prioritarian claims that the choice-worthiness difference between saving both Betty and Annie's lives and saving Annie's life alone is $\sqrt{25} - \sqrt{16}$, which equals 1. The utilitarian claims that this difference is $25 - 16$, which equals 9. So if we are normalizing the two theories at the difference between saving one life and saving two, then 1 unit of choice-worthiness, on prioritarianism, equals 9 units of choice-worthiness, on utilitarianism.

But now suppose that both Annie and Betty had lived much longer. Suppose they had lived for sixty-four years each. In this case, the difference in choice-worthiness, on prioritarianism, between saving both Betty and Annie's lives, and saving Annie's life alone is $\sqrt{73} - \sqrt{64}$, which is approximately 0.5. The utilitarian, in contrast, claims that this difference is $73 - 64$, which equals 9. So, if we are normalizing the two theories at the difference between saving one life and saving two lives in this case, then 1 unit of choice-worthiness, on prioritarianism, equals approximately 18 units of choice-worthiness, on utilitarianism. But this is inconsistent with our previous conclusion. Applying the 'normalize at the difference between saving one life and saving two' rule gives different answers depending on which two lives we're talking about.

So we cannot consistently normalize utilitarianism and prioritarianism at the difference ratio between saving one life and saving two lives, and saving two lives and saving no lives. With this possibility ruled out, it thus seems very difficult to see how there could be any principled way of claiming that there is a unit of value that is shared between utilitarianism and prioritarianism. So one might reasonably think that they cannot be placed on a common scale.

---

[6] Both Ross, 'Rejecting Ethical Deflationism', p. 764 and Sepielli, 'What to Do When You Don't Know What to Do' make suggestions along these lines. We discuss this idea more thoroughly in the next chapter.

This gives at least one case where choice-worthiness differences seem, on their face, to be incomparable between different theories. But if we have no way of making the intertheoretic comparison, then we cannot take an expectation over those moral theories. Given this, it's unclear what a decision-maker under moral uncertainty should do if she faces theories that are interval-scale measurable but intertheoretically incomparable. So we need an account of what it's appropriate to do in conditions where we cannot put two different moral theories on a common scale. Let us now look at some contenders.

II. Two Unsatisfactory Proposals

One might initially think that our work in Chapter 3 gives a solution. When theories are intertheoretically incomparable, one should aggregate those theories' choice-worthiness orderings using the Borda Rule.

The problem with this proposal should be obvious. Consider the decision-situation in Table 4.1.

In this case, the difference between B and C, on T_1, is far greater than the difference between A and B. Similarly, the difference between A and B, on T_2, is far greater than the difference between B and C. Yet the difference between the Borda Scores of A and B is the same as the difference in the Borda Scores between B and C, on both theories. The Borda Rule therefore seems to misrepresent the theories themselves, throwing away interval-scale information when we have it. The voting analogy might prove useful, but ignoring interval-scale information when we have it is not the way to proceed.

Lockhart has suggested a different account: what he calls the 'Principle of Equity among Moral Theories'. He defines it as follows:

> The maximum degrees of moral rightness of all possible actions in a situation according to competing moral theories should be considered equal. The minimum degrees of moral rightness of possible actions in a situation according to competing theories should be considered equal unless all possible actions are equally right according to one of the theories (in which case all of the actions should be considered to be maximally right according to that theory).[7]

---

[7] Lockhart, *Moral Uncertainty and Its Consequences*, p. 84.

Table 4.1

	T_1—50%	T_2—50%
A	10	0
B	9	90
C	0	100

It's ambiguous whether Lockhart thinks that the PEMT is giving an account of how two theories actually compare, or whether he is giving an account of what to do, given that all theories are incomparable. In the above quote it sounds like the latter, because he says, 'should be considered' rather than 'is', and this is how we'll understand it in this chapter. (In Chapter 5 we will consider whether accounts similar to Lockhart's are plausible as accounts of how choice-worthiness actually compares intertheoretically, and argue that they are not.)

Lockhart's account is analogous to range voting.[8] On range voting, every voter can give each candidate a score, which is a real number from, say, 0 to 10. The elected candidate is the candidate whose sum total of scores across all voters is highest.

To illustrate Lockhart's account, let's look again at the previous table. If we were to take the numbers in the table at face value, then we would suppose that the difference between B and C, on T_2, is ten times as great as the difference between A and B, on T_1. But to do so would be to forget that each theory's choice-worthiness function is unique up to its own positive affine transformation. According to Lockhart's proposal, we should treat the best and worst options as equally choiceworthy. So we should treat the choice-worthiness of $CW_1(A)$ as the same as the choice-worthiness of $CW_2(C)$ and we should treat the choice-worthiness of $CW_1(C)$ as the same as the choice-worthiness of $CW_2(A)$ (using '$CW_n(A)$' to refer to the number assigned to option A by theory n's choice-worthiness function). One way of representing the theories, therefore, in accordance with the PEMT is as in Table 4.2.

What seems promising about Lockhart's account is that it provides a way of taking into account moral uncertainty across interval-scale theories that are incomparable. However, Lockhart's account has come under fire

[8] Claude Hillinger, 'The Case for Utilitarian Voting', *Homo Oeconomicus*, vol. 22, no. 3 (2005), pp. 295–321.

Table 4.2

	T_1—50%	T_2—0.5%
A	10	0
B	9	9
C	0	10

in a recent article by Andrew Sepielli.[9] Most of the problems with his account arise from the fact that it treats maximum and minimum degrees of choice-worthiness as the same *within a decision-situation* rather than *across all possible decision-situations*. We discuss those criticisms in section VI; in the meantime, we'll stick with the *within a decision-situation* formulation.

For now, we want to discuss a different problem that Sepielli raises. As he puts it, 'perhaps the most telling problem with the PEMT is that it is arbitrary'.[10]

There is a wide array of alternatives to Lockhart's view. Why, one might ask, should one treat the maximum and minimum choiceworthiness as the same, rather than the difference between the most choiceworthy option and the mean option, or between the least choice worthy option and the mean option? Or why not treat the mean difference in choiceworthiness between options as the same for all theories?

Lockhart anticipates this objection, stating: 'It may appear that I have, in an ad hoc manner, concocted the PEMT for the sole purpose of defending the otherwise indefensible claim that moral hedging is possible'.[11] However, he responds as follows.

The PEMT might be thought of as a principle of fair competition among moral theories, analogous to democratic principles that support the equal counting of the votes of all qualified voters in an election regardless of any actual differences in preference intensity among the voters...PEMT appears not to play favorites among moral theories or to give some type(s) of moral theories unfair advantages over others.[12]

[9] Andrew Sepielli, 'Moral Uncertainty and the Principle of Equity among Moral Theories', *Philosophy and Phenomenological Research* 86, no. 3 (2013), pp. 580–9.
[10] Sepielli, 'Moral Uncertainty and the Principle of Equity among Moral Theories', p. 587.
[11] Lockhart, *Moral Uncertainty and Its Consequences*, p. 86.
[12] Lockhart, *Moral Uncertainty and Its Consequences*, p. 86.

That is, he appeals to what we'll call the *principle of 'equal say'*: the idea, stated imprecisely for now, that we want to give equally likely incomparable moral theories equal weight when considering what it's appropriate to do, and that the degree of influence that a moral theory has over the appropriateness of options across a wide variety of different decision-situations should be only in proportion to the degree of credence assigned to that theory.

As Sepielli points out, this idea doesn't seem at all plausible if we're trying to use the PEMT as a way of actually making intertheoretic comparisons. Considerations of fairness are relevant to issues about how to treat *people*: one can be unfair to a person. But one cannot be unfair to a theory. Perhaps by saying that one was being 'unfair' to Kantianism, one could mean that one's degree of belief was too low in it. But one can't be unfair to it insofar as it 'loses out' in the calculation of what it's appropriate to do. If a theory thinks that a situation is low stakes, we should represent it as such.

But the idea of 'equal say' has more plausibility if we are talking about how to come to a decision in the face of genuine intertheoretic incomparability. In developing an account of decision-making under moral uncertainty, we want to remain neutral on what the correct moral theory is: we do not want to bias the outcome of the decision-making in favour of some theories over others. Against this one could argue that some theories are simply higher stakes in general than other theories. But if, as we assume in this chapter, we are in a condition where there really is no fact of the matter about how two theories compare, then we cannot make sense of the idea that things might be higher stakes in general for one theory rather than the other. So we need a way of taking uncertainty over those theories into account that is not biased towards one theory rather than another.

To see a specific case of how this could go awry, consider average and total utilitarianism, and assume that they are indeed incomparable. Suppose that, in order to take an expectation over those theories, we choose to treat them as agreeing on the choice-worthiness of differences between options in worlds where the only person that exists is the decision-maker, and therefore only their welfare is at stake. If we do this, then, for almost all practical decisions about population ethics, the appropriate action will be in line with what total utilitarianism regards as most choiceworthy because, for almost all decisions (which involve a world with billions of people), the stakes would be large for total utilitarianism, but tiny for average utilitarianism. So it is plausible that, if we treat the theories in this way, we are being partisan towards total utilitarianism.

In contrast, if we chose to treat the two theories as agreeing on the choice-worthiness differences between options with worlds involving some extremely large number of people (say 10^{100}), then for almost all real-world decisions, what it is appropriate to do will be the same as what average utilitarianism regards as most choiceworthy. This is because we are representing average utilitarianism as claiming that, for almost all decisions, the stakes are much higher than for total utilitarianism. In which case, it seems that we are being partisan to average utilitarianism. What we really want is to have a way of treating the theories such that each theory gets equal influence.

Lockhart states that the PEMT is the best way to give every theory 'equal say'. But he doesn't argue for that conclusion, as Sepielli notes:[13]

> But even granting that some 'equalization' of moral theories is appropriate, Lockhart's proposal seems arbitrary. Why equalize the maximum and minimum value, rather than, say, the mean value and the maximum value? [...] It seems as though we could find other ways to treat theories equally, while still acknowledging that the moral significance of a situation can be different for different theories. Thus, even if we accept Lockhart's voting analogy, there is no particularly good reason for us to use PEMT rather than any of the other available methods.

In a very similar vein, Amartya Sen has argued against an analogue of the PEMT within social choice theory, the 'zero-one' rule:[14]

> It may be argued that some systems, e. g., assigning in each person's scale the value 0 to the worst alternative and the value 1 to his best alternative are interpersonally 'fair' but such an argument is dubious. First, there are other systems with comparable symmetry, e.g., the system we discussed earlier of assigning 0 to the worst alternative and the value 1 to the sum of utilities from all alternatives.

We think both Sen and Sepielli are right that principled reasons for endorsing the PEMT over its rivals have not been given. But, further to that, we will argue in the following two sections that it's demonstrably *false* that the PEMT is the best way of giving each theory 'equal say'. Instead, we think

---

[13] Sepielli, 'Normative Uncertainty for Non-Cognitivists', pp. 587–8.
[14] Sen, *Collective Choice and Social Welfare*, p. 98.

that what we'll call variance voting is the best way to take moral uncertainty into account across theories that are interval-scale and incomparable, because it is the best way of giving each theory 'equal say'.

III. Variance Voting

We'll call Lockhart's view and its rivals interval-scale *voting systems*. To develop an intuitive sense of how different interval-scale voting systems can differ in how they apportion 'say' between theories, let's consider some examples. Let's consider four different interval-scale voting systems using the 'across all decision-situations' formulation of each:

(i)   Lockhart's PEMT, which treats the range of the choice-worthiness function (i.e. the difference between minimum and maximum assigned values) as the same across all interval-scale and incomparable theories;

(ii) what we'll call max-mean, which treats the difference between the mean choice-worthiness and the maximum choice-worthiness as the same across all interval-scale and incomparable theories;

(iii) what we'll call mean-min, which treats the difference between the mean choice-worthiness and the minimum choice-worthiness of all interval-scale and incomparable theories as the same (this is the account that Sen suggests in the above quote);

(iv) variance voting, which treats the variance (i.e. the average of the squared differences in choice-worthiness from the mean choice-worthiness) as the same across all theories.

Variance is a very important statistical property, measuring how spread out choice-worthiness is over different options. While its formula is a bit more complex, it is typically seen as the most natural measure of spread. Since the variance is the square of the standard deviation, normalizing at variance is the same as normalizing at the size of the standard deviation.[15] One can

---

[15] In order to make sense of the variance of a choice-worthiness function, we need a notion of *measure* over possibility space. This is discussed in section V, in relation to the Borda Rule. We assume that we should use the same choice of measure when using variance voting as we do when using the Borda Rule. Having a measure over the option-set allows variance normalization to apply to many unbounded moral theories: we take this to be yet another advantage of variance voting over the PEMT.

compute the normalized choice-worthiness for an option by subtracting the mean choice-worthiness, then dividing by the standard deviation.

Note that like Lockhart's original statement of PEMT, we should, for each of these normalization methods, also specify that if a theory ranks all options as exactly equally choiceworthy, all of these four methods leave its choice-worthiness function alone: the normalized choice-worthiness function is just equal to the original one. To do otherwise would involve dividing by zero.

We shall apply these four different structural normalization methods to four types of first-order moral theory. We'll call the first type *Bipolar* theories. According to Bipolar theories, the differences in choice-worthiness among the most choiceworthy options, and among the least choiceworthy options, are zero or tiny compared to the differences in choiceworthiness between the most choiceworthy options and the least choiceworthy options. For example, a view according to which violating rights is impermissible, everything else is permissible, and where there is very little difference in the severity of wrongness between different wrong actions, would be a Bipolar theory.

We'll call the second type of theory *outlier* theories. According to this view, most options are roughly similar in choiceworthiness, but there are some options that are extremely choiceworthy, and some options that are extremely un-choiceworthy. A bounded total utilitarian view with a very high and very low bounds might be like this: the differences in value between most options are about the same, but there are some possible worlds which, though unlikely, are very good indeed, and some other worlds which, though unlikely, are very bad indeed.

We'll call the third type of theory *Top-Heavy*. According to this type of theory, there are a small number of outliers in choice-worthiness, but they are only on one side of the spectrum: there are just a small number of extremely un-choiceworthy possible options. Any consequentialist theory that has a low upper bound on value, but a very low lower bound on value, such that most options are close to the upper bound and far away from the lower bound, would count as a Top-Heavy moral theory.

The fourth type of theory is *Bottom-Heavy*. These are simply the reverse of Top-Heavy theories.

We can represent these theories visually, where horizontal lines represent different options, which are connected by a vertical line, representing the choice-worthiness function. The greater the distance between the two horizontal lines, the greater the difference in choice-worthiness between those

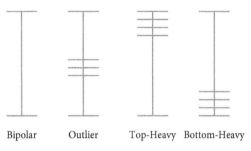

Bipolar   Outlier   Top-Heavy Bottom-Heavy

Figure 4.1

two options. If we used PEMT, the four theories would look as follows (see Figure 4.1).

When comparing Top-Heavy and Bottom-Heavy, the PEMT yields the intuitively right result. Top-Heavy and Bottom-Heavy are simply inversions of each other, so it seems very plausible that one should treat the size of choice-worthiness differences as the same according to both theories, just of opposite sign.

For Bipolar and outlier, however, the PEMT does not yield the intuitively right result. Because it *only* cares about the maximal and minimal values of choice-worthiness, it is insensitive to how choice-worthiness is distributed among options that are not maximally or minimally choiceworthy. This means that Bipolar theories have much more power, relative to outlier theories, than they should.

This might not be immediately obvious, so let us consider a concrete case. Suppose that Sophie is uncertain between an absolutist moral theory (Bipolar), and a form of utilitarianism that has an upper limit of value of saving 10 billion lives, and a lower limit of forcing 10 billion people to live lives of agony (outlier), and suppose that those views are incomparable with each other. She has 1% credence in the absolutist theory, and 99% credence in bounded utilitarianism. If the PEMT normalization is correct, then in almost every decision-situation she faces she ought to side with the absolutist theory. Let's suppose she is confronted with a murderer at her door, and she could lie in order to save her family: an action required by utilitarianism, but absolutely wrong according to the absolutist view. Given the PEMT, it's as bad to lie, according to the absolutist view, as it is to force 10 billion people to live lives of agony, according to utilitarianism. So her 1% credence in the absolutist view means that she shouldn't lie to the murderer at the door. In fact, she shouldn't lie even if her credence was as low as 0.000001%. That seems incredible. The PEMT is supposed to be motivated by the idea of giving each moral theory 'equal say', but it fails to do this in cases where some theories put almost all options into just two categories.

For a second illustration of how other accounts can fail to respect the principle of 'equal say', giving undue influence to some theories over others, consider the max-mean principle. Taking our four theories described above, it would normalize them such that they would be represented as follows (see Figure 4.2), where to 'normalize' two theories is to give them a shared fixed unit of choice-worthiness.

That is, max-mean favours Top-Heavy theories and punishes bottom-heavy theories. It's clear, therefore, that max-mean does not deal even-handedly between these two classes of theories. Exactly analogous arguments apply to mean-min.

What, though, of variance voting If we treat the variance of choice-wor-thiness as the same across all four theories, they would be represented as follows (see Figure 4.3).

Because Top-Heavy and Bottom-Heavy are inverses of one another, they have the same variance. So, on variance voting, the magnitudes of choice-worthiness differences between options are treated as the same, only opposite in sign. This is the result we wanted, doing better than max-mean or mean-min. But it also does better than the PEMT in terms of how it treats Bipolar compared with outlier: because Bipolar places most of its options at

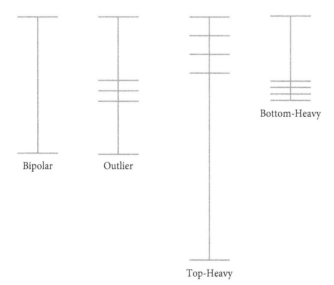

Figure 4.2

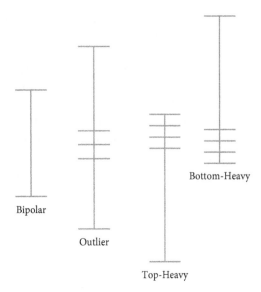

Bottom-Heavy

Bipolar

Outlier

Top-Heavy

Figure 4.3

the top or bottom of its choice-worthiness function, in order to make the variance equal with outlier, its range must be comparatively smaller than outlier. Again, that was the result we wanted. So the consideration of particular cases seems to motivate variance over its rivals.

These examples are suggestive, but hardly constitute a knockdown argument. Perhaps there are other voting methods that do as well as variance does on the cases above. Perhaps there are other cases in which variance does worse than the other methods we've mentioned. So it would be nice to provide a more rigorous argument in favour of variance. The next two sections do exactly that. We'll suggest two different ways of making the idea of 'equal say' formally precise. We find the second precisification more compelling, but we show that, either way, normalizing at 'equal say' means normalizing at variance. In so doing, we thereby produce a non-arbitrary justification for normalizing at variance rather than the range or any other features of a theory's choice-worthiness functions: variance voting is the normalization that best captures the principle of 'equal say'.[16]

---

[16] The following two sections draw very heavily on two results within social choice theory that can be found in Owen Cotton-Barratt, 'Geometric Reasons for Normalising Variance to Aggregate Preferences', unpublished MS, http://users.ox.ac.uk/%7Eball1714/Variance%20normalisation.pdf. These results were initially motivated by the problem of moral uncertainty, arising out of conversation between us, though we had very little input on the proofs. However, they are interesting results within social choice theory, too. We state the arguments informally here; for the full proofs, see the paper.

IV. Two Arguments for Variance Voting

Distance from the Uniform Theory

Consider a uniform choice-worthiness function—one that assigns the same degree of choice-worthiness to all options. If any theory's choice-worthiness function were normalized to be essentially uniform before applying MEC,[17] then that theory would not affect the final decision. Such a normalization would give that theory no 'say'. We could thus measure how much 'say' a theory has by how 'far away' its normalized choice-worthiness function is from the uniform choice-worthiness function. Remember that by 'say' we are thinking of the degree to which the theory may influence the choice between options, for a fixed degree of credence in that theory.

Imagine starting each theory off with a uniform choice-worthiness function and an equal amount of credit, where this credit can be spent on moving the choice-worthiness function away from the uniform function. Every move away from the uniform choice-worthiness assignment increases the 'say' of that theory, and uses up a proportionate amount of credit. On this account, giving every theory 'equal say' means giving them an equal amount of starting credit. In this section, we will spell out this suggestion, explain the motivation for it, and demonstrate that variance voting is the only normalization method that gives every theory 'equal say', so understood.

Let us begin by considering different theories that *are* intertheoretically comparable. It should be clear that a completely uniform theory, according to which all options are equally choiceworthy, has no 'say' at all: it never affects what it's appropriate to do. We'll say that it gives all options choice-worthiness 0, though we could have just as well said it gives all options 17, or any other number. Next, consider a theory, T_1, which differs from the uniform theory only insofar as its choice-worthiness function gives one option, A, a different choice-worthiness, x. There are two ways in which a theory T_2 might have more 'say' than T_1. First, it could have the same choice-worthiness ordering as T_1, but its choice-worthiness function could give A a higher numerical value (remembering that, because we are talking about theories that are intertheoretically comparable, this is a meaningful

---

[17] If a theory is represented by a choice-worthiness function f, it is also represented by $0.1f$, $0.01f$, $0.001f$, and so on. These limit to a uniform choice-worthiness function, and if we are far enough down the sequence then the representative will be close enough to uniform to make no difference.

difference between these two theories). If it gave A a numerical value of $2x$, so that the choice-worthiness difference between A and any other option is twice as great according to T_2 than according to T_1, then T_2 would have twice as much 'say' as T_1. A second way in which a theory could have more 'say' than T_1 is if it assigned non-zero numerical values to another option in addition to A. Then it would have 'equal say' with respect to A, but would have a greater 'say' with respect to the other options.

But what does 'moving away' from the uniform theory mean? We can take this idea beyond metaphor by thinking of choice-worthiness functions geometrically. To see this, suppose that there are only two possible options, A and B, and three theories, T_1, T_2 and T_3, whose choice-worthiness functions are represented by Table 4.3.

Using the choice-worthiness of A as the x-axis and the choice-worthiness of B as the y-axis, we may represent this geometrically as follows (see Figure 4.4).

Any point on this graph represents some choice-worthiness function and those corresponding to T_1, T_2 and T_3 are marked. The diagonal line represents all the uniform choice-worthiness functions. The dotted lines show the distance from each of T_1, T_2 and T_3 to their nearest uniform choice-worthiness function. These distances allow a way of precisely defining 'equal say'. Giving each theory 'equal say' means choosing a (normalized) choice-worthiness function for each theory such that, for every choice-worthiness function, the distance from that choice-worthiness function to the nearest uniform choice-worthiness function is the same.

It turns out that the distance from a choice-worthiness function to the nearest uniform function is always equal to the standard deviation of the distribution of choice-worthiness values it assigns to the available options.[18] So treating all choice-worthiness functions as having 'equal say' means treating them as lying at the same distance from the uniform function, which means treating them such that they have the same standard deviation and thus the same variance. variance voting is thus the unique

Table 4.3

	T_1	T_2	T_3
A	−4	3	4
B	1	4	1

[18] Proof of this is given in Cotton-Barratt, 'Geometric Reasons for Normalising Variance to Aggregate Preferences'.

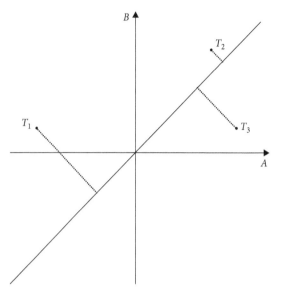

Figure 4.4

normalization method for preserving 'equal say' on this understanding of 'equal say'.

We can now look at the geometric interpretation of normalizing theories by their variance (see Figure 4.5).

The dashed lines in this diagram represent all the choice-worthiness functions that are distance of 1 from the nearest uniform function.[19] This means that they also have a standard deviation of 1 and hence a variance of 1. In order to normalize each theory so that they have the same amount of 'say', we move each theory to the closest point on one of the dashed lines (the arrows show these moves). This corresponds to linearly rescaling all of the theory's choice-worthiness values so that their variance is equal to 1, while keeping their means unchanged. This doesn't change the ordering of the options by that theory's lights, it just compresses it or stretches it so that it has the same variance as the others. One can then apply MEC to these normalized choice-worthiness functions.

This all works in the same way for any finite number of options.[20] A choice-worthiness function gives an assignment of a real number to each

---

[19] We could have chosen any non-zero value here, but 1 is especially convenient.

[20] This argument applies only in the case where there are finitely many options, and makes an assumption of symmetry in the weight we attach to each. This is the simplest case for inter-theoretic value comparisons, and any method should at least behave well in this base case.

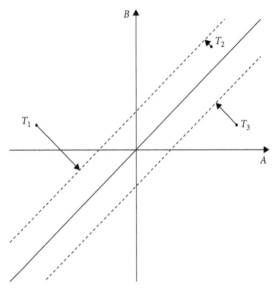

Figure 4.5

option, so if there are n options, a choice-worthiness function can be represented as a collection of n real numbers. Just as pairs of real numbers give us Cartesian coordinates in the plane and triples give us coordinates in three-dimensional space, so we can interpret this collection as the coordinates of a point in n-dimensional Euclidean space. We can then proceed the same way, looking at the distance in this n-dimensional space from a choice-worthiness function to the nearest uniform theory, equating this to 'say', and normalizing to make the distances the same. Just as before, the distance corresponds to the standard deviation, and so normalizing to equalize variance is the unique way to provide 'equal say'.

While there is no need to normalize the means of the choice-worthiness functions (it does not affect the MEC calculation, as we are ultimately interested in comparing between options) it could be convenient to normalize them all to zero, by adding or subtracting a constant from each choice-worthiness function. If so, then the choice-worthiness functions are in the familiar form of 'standard scores' or 'z-scores' where the mean is zero and the unit is one standard-deviation. These z-scores are commonly used in statistics as a way to compare quantities that are not directly comparable, so it is particularly interesting that our approach to intertheoretic choice-worthiness comparisons for non-comparable theories could be summarized as 'compare them via their z-scores'.

The Expected Choice-Worthiness of Voting

The previous argument cashed out the idea of 'equal say' as 'equal distance from a uniform choice-worthiness function'. For our second argument, we shall borrow a concept from voting theory: *voting power*. An individual's voting power is the a priori likelihood of her vote being decisive in an election, given the assumption that all the possible ways for other people to vote are equally likely. It is normally used for elections with just two candidates, but the concept is perfectly general.

We shall extend this concept to flesh out 'equal say'. A first challenge is that while voters all have just one vote, theories come with different credences. We want theories with the same credence to have the same voting power and for voting power to go up on average as the credence increases.[21] We can resolve this by looking at the voting power of a small increase in the credence of a particular theory.

A second challenge is that by a theory's own lights it doesn't just matter that one's credence in it is decisive in determining which option gets chosen, it matters how much better this chosen option is than the option that would have been chosen otherwise. Getting its way in a decision about whether to prick someone with a pin matters a lot less, for utilitarianism, than getting its way in a decision about whether to let a million people die. If we are normalizing to provide 'equal say', we should take that into account as well. Since theories come with a measure of this difference between the options (the choice-worthiness difference), and they use its expectation when considering descriptive uncertainty, it is natural to use this here. This means we should speak not just of the likelihood of being decisive, but of the increase in expected choice-worthiness. We thus achieve 'equal say' when, from a position of complete uncertainty about how our credence will be divided over different choice-worthiness functions, an increase in our credence in a theory by a tiny amount will increase the expected choice-worthiness of the decision by the same degree regardless of which theory it was whose credence was increased.

There is one final challenge. If each theory had one canonical choice-worthiness function, this definition would work. But since each theory is described by infinitely many different choice-worthiness functions (positive

---

[21] The qualification 'on average' is needed as it is possible for a theory to get its way all the time when it is given a credence that is slightly less than 1 and from that point increases in credence will not improve its power. This is analogous to how a voting block might already have all the power with less than 100% of the votes.

affine transformations of each other), we do not yet know which choice-worthiness function to use to represent each theory and so cannot come up with a unique value for the 'expected choice-worthiness'.

However, we can resolve this by considering that the normalization used to choose an option in a decision situation should be the same normalization used to measure 'equal say' in terms of this version of voting power. This doesn't sound like a strong constraint, but it is enough to let us prove that there is a unique normalization method that satisfies it and equalizes voting power.[22]

Given that we have found two independently plausible ways of cashing out the principle of 'equal say' that both lead to the same conclusion, we think it is warranted to think of variance voting as strongly supported by that principle. We'll now turn to discuss two issues regarding how to precisely formulate variance voting.

V. Option-Individuation and Measure

An objection that one can make to both the Borda Rule and to variance voting is that they are both extremely sensitive to how one individuates options.[23] To illustrate this with respect to the Borda Rule, consider the following case.

Trolley Problems

Sophie is watching as an out-of-control train hurtles towards five people working on the train track. If she flips a switch, she will redirect the train, killing one person working on a different track. Alternatively, she could push a large man onto the track, killing him but stopping the train. Or she could do nothing. So she has three options available to her.

A: Do nothing.
B: Flick the switch.
C: Push the large man.

She has credence in three moral theories.

---

[22] See Cotton-Barratt, 'Geometric Reasons for Normalising Variance to Aggregate Preferences'.
[23] This problem is analogous to the problem of 'clone-dependence' in voting theory, which itself is a generalization of the idea of vote-splitting. For discussion of clone-dependence, see Tideman, 'Independence of Clones as a Criterion for Voting Rules'. We thank Graham Oddie for pressing this criticism of the Borda Rule. The example is Oddie's.

40% in utilitarianism, according to which: $B>C>A$
30% in simple Kantianism, according to which: $A>B\sim C$
30% in sophisticated Kantianism, according to which: $A>B>C$

In this case, according to the Borda Rule, B is the most appropriate option, followed by A and then C.[24] But now let us suppose that there are actually two Switching options:

A: Do nothing.
B':   Flick the switch to the left.
B'':   Flick the switch to the right.
C: Push the large man over the railing to stop the track

Sophie has the same credences in moral theories as before. Their recommendations are as follows:

Utilitarianism: $B'\sim B''>C>A$
Simple Kantianism: $A>B'\sim B''\sim C$
Sophisticated Kantianism: $A>B'\sim B''>C$

Given these choice-worthiness rankings, according to the Borda Rule, A is the most appropriate option, then B' and B'' equally, then C.[25] So, according to the Borda Rule, it makes a crucial difference to Sophie whether she has just one way of flicking the switch or whether she has two: and if she has two ways of flicking the switch, it's of crucial importance to her to know whether that only counts as one option or not. But that seems bizarre.

To see how this problem plays out for variance voting, suppose that there are only four possible options, all of which are available to the decision-maker, and suppose that the decision-maker has credence in only two theories (see Table 4.4).

---

[24] Now that some theories posit tied options, we return to using our 'official' definition of a Borda Score in our working. Option A receives a score of $0 + 30 \times 2 + 30 \times 2 - (40 \times 2 + 0 + 0) = 40$. B's score is $40 \times 2 + 0 + 30 \times 1 - (0 + 30 \times 1 + 30 \times 1) = 50$. C's score is $40 \times 1 + 0 + 0 - (40 \times 1 + 30 \times 1 + 30 \times 2) = -90$.

[25] Option A receives a score of $0 + 30 \times 3 + 30 \times 3 - (40 \times 3 + 0 + 0) = 60$. B' and B'' each receive a score of $40 \times 2 + 0 + 30 \times 1 - (0 + 30 \times 1 + 30 \times 1) = 50$. C's score is $40 \times 1 + 0 + 0 - (40 \times 2 + 30 \times 1 + 30 \times 3) = -160$.

Table 4.4

	T_1	T_2
A	18	10
B	16	4
C	6	4
D	0	22

Table 4.5

	T_1	T_2
A	18	10
B	16	4
C	6	4
D'	0	22
D"	0	22

These two theories have been normalized in accordance with their variance. For both T_1 and T_2, the mean choice-worthiness is 10 and the variance is 54. But now suppose that the decision-maker comes to believe that option D can be broken down into two distinct options, D' and $D"$. There is no morally relevant difference between the two options, so the decision situation now looks as in Table 4.5.

Now, the mean of T_1 is 8 and the variance is 59.2, while the mean of T_2 is 12.4 and the variance is 66.2. So the variance in T_2 is now larger than in T_1 and they would need to be renormalized. This would require compressing the distribution of choice-worthiness numbers in T_2, giving it less 'say' relative to T_1 than it had before we divided D. This means that the variance of a theory depends crucially on how we individuate options, which seems problematic.[26] (Note that this was not a problem for PEMT because it normalized by the range of choice-worthiness and, unlike the variance, the range of a distribution is not sensitive to how many times a number occurs in it.)

However, there is a principled and satisfying response to this objection: that we need to have a *measure* over the space of possible options, and that

---

[26] There is a close analogy here to the 'independence of clones' property in voting theory, whereby the outcome of an election should not be sensitive to whether a new candidate that is very similar to an existing one joins the race.

we were neglectful when we didn't initially include a measure in our definition of the Borda Rule or of variance voting[27] A measure will define the
'sizes' of different options, allowing an option to be divided into two smaller
options without affecting the variance. Technically, we will use a 'probability
measure': a function that assigns non-negative numbers to subsets of a set
(in this case the set of all possible options), assigns 0 to the empty set, 1 to
the whole set, and where the number assigned to the union of two disjoint
sets is the sum of the numbers assigned to each of the smaller sets. Note that
this does *not* necessarily mean we're talking about the decision-maker's credences in the likelihood of different options; the term 'probability measure'
simply signifies that the whole set of options is assigned measure 1.

A way to visualize the idea of a measure is to think of the entirety of
the space of possibilities as the area of a two-dimensional shape. When we
talk about an 'option' we are talking about some area within the shape.
What a measure does is give sense to the intuitive idea of the size of
the space of possibilities, and so gives us the resources to say that one option
takes up twice as much of the space as another, or a specified fraction of the
whole space.

With the concept of a measure on board, we can reformulate the definition of an option's Borda Score as follows: that an option's *Borda Score* is
equal to the sum on the measure of the options below it minus the sum of
the measure of the options above it. Once we've defined a Borda Score in
this way, then we can use all the other definitions as stated. Nothing will
change in terms of its recommendations in the cases we've previously discussed. But it resolves the option-individuation problem.

To see how this resolves the option-individuation problem, consider
again the case given above. Let us suppose that the measure of each option,
A, B and C, is 1/3.[28] If so, then, as before, according to the Borda Rule, B is
the most appropriate option, followed by A and then C.[29] Now, however,
when we split the option B into options B' and B", we have to also split the
measure: let us suppose that the measure splits equally, so that B' and B"
each have measure 1/6.[30] If so, then according to the Borda Rule, B is still

---

[27] We thank Owen Cotton-Barratt for this suggestion.

[28] Note that there would be no difference to our argument if the measure were split
unequally among options A, B, and C.

[29] Option A receives a score of $0 + 30 \times (2/3) + 30 \times (2/3) - (40 \times (2/3) + 0 + 0) = 13\ 1/3$. B's
score is $40 \times (2/3) + 0 + 30 \times (1/3) - (0 + 30 \times (1/3) + 30 \times (1/3)) = 16\ 2/3$. C's score is $40 \times (1/3) + 0 + 0$
$(40 \times (1/3) + 30 \times (1/3) + 30 \times (2/3)) = -30$.

[30] Note that there would be no difference to our argument if the measure did not divide
evenly between B' and B".

the most appropriate option, followed by A and then C.[31] In general, the addition of a measure means that we can make sense of a 'size' of an option, and will therefore avoid the option-individuation problem.

Similarly, once we use a measure, the problem of variance voting's dependence on how we individuate options dissolves: we normalize the variance of the distribution of choice-worthiness by taking the choice-worthiness of each option weighted by that option's measure. So, let us suppose that each of the options A–D had measure $1/4$. In this case, as before, in the first decision-situation the mean of T_1 is 10 and the variance is 54. However, this stays the same in the second decision-situation. When we split D into the smaller options D' and D'', the measure is split, too. Let's suppose, then, that each new option gets measure $1/8$ (though the argument would work just as well if the measure was split unequally). If so, then the mean and variance of both T_1 and T_2 is the same in the second decision-situation as it is in the first decision-situation. And that's exactly the result we wanted.[32]

There are additional benefits to the incorporation of a measure. First, it means that the Borda Rule can handle situations in which the decision-maker faces an infinite number of options.[33] Before we had defined a measure over possibility space and incorporated that into an option's Borda Score, one could have objected that the Borda Rule can't handle infinite option sets. For, if the number of options below or above one option A were infinite, then there would be no answer to the question of what that option's Borda Score is.

Having a measure over possibility space resolves this problem, because one can have an infinite number of options with a measure that sums to some finite number. For example, suppose that below option x there are an infinite number of options, with measure $1/4, 1/8, 1/16, 1/32\ldots$ In this case, even though there are an infinite number of options there is a fact about the sum of the measure of options below A: namely, $1/2$. Indeed, because

---

[31]   Option A receives a score of $0 + 30 \times (2/3) + 30 \times (2/3) - (40 \times (2/3) + 0 + 0) = 13\ 1/3$. B' and B'' each receive a score of $40 \times (2/3) + 0 + 30 \times (1/3) - (0 + 30 \times (1/3) + 30 \times (1/3)) = 16\ 2/3$. C's score is $40 \times (1/3) + 0 + 0 - (40 \times (1/3) + 30 \times (1/3) + 30 \times (2/3)) = -30$. That is, the scores are just the same as they were prior to the more fine-grained individuation of option B.

[32]   In Chapter 2, we criticized My Favorite Theory in part because of the problem of theory-individuation. One might wonder: if both our account and MFT have individuation problems, doesn't this undermine our earlier objection? However, the use of measure gives us a principled solution to this problem, whereas we cannot see a way of using a measure to solve the theory-individuation problem. So we think our earlier objection still stands.

[33]   We thank an anonymous reviewer at *Mind* for pressing this objection.

the measure of the set of all possible options is 1, the measure of options above or below any particular action will always be finite. So the Borda Score of an option will always be well-defined, even when there are an infinite number of options available to the decision-maker.

Second, it means that variance voting will avoid a problem that faces other structural accounts. Many moral theories are often unbounded: theories according to which there can be situations where there is no maximally choiceworthy or no minimally choiceworthy option. For example, any theory that accepts the Total View of population ethics is unbounded above and below: one can keep making a world better by adding to it additional happy people; and one can keep making a world worse by adding to it lives that aren't worth living. Sepielli objects that the PEMT has nothing to say concerning how to normalize such unbounded moral theories in situations where there is no best or worst option. A very similar problem afflicts max-mean and mean-min.

We take it as a virtue of variance voting that it is able, once we have incorporated the idea of a measure, to normalize many unbounded theories. Just as unbounded distributions can have a mean (if the chance of getting an extreme value falls off quickly enough compared to the growth of the extreme values), so too can they have a variance.

So we now have the resources to state variance voting precisely. Because of the arguments we have given, we propose that, in conditions of moral uncertainty and intertheoretic incomparability, decision-makers should choose the option with the highest expected choice-worthiness, where the (measure-weighted) variance of choice-worthiness should be treated as the same across all considered theories.

VI. Broad vs Narrow

For both the Borda Rule and variance voting we have a choice about how to define the theory. When we normalize different theories at their variance, should we look at the variance of choice-worthiness over all possible options, or the variance of choice-worthiness merely over all the options available to the decision-maker in a given decision situation? Similarly, when we say that an option's Borda Score, on a given theory, is the sum of the measure of the options ranked lower than it by the theory minus the sum of the measure of the options ranked higher than it, should we sum over all the options in a given decision-situation, or should we sum over all conceivable options? These two approaches will give very different answers concerning what it's appropriate to do in a given situation. Following Sen, we will say that Broad accounts are defined across all conceivable options and that Narrow accounts are defined over only the options in a particular decision-situation.[34] In this section we argue that Narrow is the best approach, though we are not confident.

We have two key reasons for preferring Narrow accounts. First, Narrow accounts are able to provide a principled solution to the infectious incomparability problem, in a way that Broad accounts are not—we discuss this further in Chapter 5. Second, Narrow accounts are more action-guiding. For example, if you use the Broad Borda Rule, then, for any option you face, you'll have simply no idea what Borda Score it should receive—we would need to know the total measure of all options above and below the option in question, and that seems very difficult or impossible. We could do it approximately if we could know in what *percentile* the option ranks among all possible options—but how are we meant to know even that? Similar difficulties plague variance voting. In contrast, you can come to at least a rough approximation of the options facing you in a particular decision-situation. So we are able to actually use Narrow methods, at least approximately.

However, there are arguments against Narrow accounts. In his extensive criticism of Lockhart's PEMT, Sepielli gives four arguments against the PEMT that arise in virtue of the fact that it makes intertheoretic comparisons only within a decision-situation (rather than across all decision situations).[35] One might therefore think that our account will also be susceptible to these arguments.

His first two arguments are as follows. First, he argues that the Narrow PEMT cannot make sense of the idea that some decision-situations are higher-stakes for some theories than for others. Second, he argues that the PEMT generates inconsistent choice-worthiness comparisons: in one decision-situation, the difference in choice-worthiness between A and B, on T_1 is the same as the difference in choice-worthiness between A and B on T_2, but in another decision-situation the difference in choice-worthiness between A and B, on T_1 is larger than the difference in choice-worthiness between A and B on T_2

---

[34] The terminology of 'broad' and 'narrow' for this distinction comes from Amartya Sen, *Choice, Welfare, and Measurement*, Cambridge, MA: MIT Press, 1982, p. 186.
[35] Sepielli, 'Normative Uncertainty for Non-Cognitivists'.

However, in the context of our project, these criticisms lose their force. First, we are using the Borda Rule and variance voting not as accounts of how theories actually compare, but as a way of coming to a principled decision in the face of incomparable theories. So there isn't a fact of the matter about some decision-situations being higher stakes for some of these theories rather than others. And these accounts aren't generating inconsistent assignments of choice-worthiness, because they aren't pretending to make claims about how choice-worthiness actually compares across theories. Rather, they are simply giving an account of what it's appropriate to do given that choice-worthiness doesn't compare across theories.

A separate argument against Narrow Borda and Narrow Variance accounts is that they violate *Contraction Consistency*.

Contraction Consistency: Let $\mathcal{M}$ be the set of maximally appropriate options given an option-set $\mathcal{A}$, and let $\mathcal{A}'$ be a subset of $\mathcal{A}$ that contains all the members of $\mathcal{M}$. The set $\mathcal{M}'$ of the maximally appropriate options given the reduced option-set $\mathcal{A}'$ has all and only the same members as $\mathcal{M}$.

For simplicity, we'll just focus on this criticism as aimed at the Narrow Borda Rule, but just the same considerations would apply to Narrow variance voting.

To see that the Borda Rule violates *Contraction Consistency*, consider again the *Hiring Decision* case.

Hiring Decision

Jason is a manager at a large sales company. He has to make a new hire, and he has three candidates to choose from. They each have very different attributes, and he's not sure what attributes are morally relevant to his decision. In terms of qualifications for the role, applicant B is best, then applicant C, then applicant A. However, he's not certain whether that's the only relevant consideration. Applicant A is a single mother, with no other options for work. Applicant B is a recent university graduate with a strong CV from a privileged background. And applicant C is a young black male from a poor background, but with other work options. Jason has credence in three competing views.

30% credence in a form of virtue theory. On this view, hiring the single mother would be the compassionate thing to do, and hiring simply on the basis of positive discrimination would be disrespectful. So, according to this view, $A>B>C$.

30% credence in a form of non-consequentialism. On this view, Jason should just choose in accordance with qualification for the role. According to this view, $B>C>A$.

40% credence in a form of consequentialism. On this view, Jason should just choose so as to maximize societal benefit. According to this view, $C>A>B$.

As we noted, C is, both intuitively and according to the Borda Rule, the uniquely most appropriate option. Now, however, suppose that it were no longer possible to hire candidate A. In which case, Jason's credence distribution would look as follows.

30% credence in virtue theory, according to which $B>C$.
30% credence in non-consequentialism, according to which $B>C$.
40% credence in consequentialism, according to which $C>B$.

In this new decision-situation, B is now the uniquely most appropriate option. The appropriateness of options is highly sensitive to which other options are within the option-set.

How strong of an objection to Narrow accounts is the violation of *Contraction Consistency*? We're not sure. We think it would be reasonable if one found this violation to be compelling, and therefore wanted to endorse a Broad account, despite Broad accounts' other problems. But, on balance, we think that those other problems are more grave, because we think that the two primary reasons one might have for endorsing *Contraction Consistency* are not compelling in this case.

First, one might worry that violation of *Contraction Consistency* would lead one to be open to money-pumps, choosing B over A, C over B, and A' (a strictly worse option than A) over C. But such arguments are of dubious cogency. Though we don't have space in this book to delve into the extensive literature around money-pumps, we point the reader to some compelling recent work arguing that agents with cyclical preferences across choice-situations are not vulnerable to money-pumps.[36]

Second, a reason why *Contraction Consistency* is thought desirable in the voting context is that violating it leads to susceptibility to tactical voting. Again, consider *Hiring Decision*. If the virtue theory could pretend that its

---

[36] See Arif Ahmed, 'Exploiting Cyclic Preference', *Mind*, vol. 126, no. 504 (October 2017), pp. 975–1022.

preference ordering was $B>A>C$ rather than $A>B>C$, then it could guarantee that its second-favoured option would 'win', rather than its least-favoured option. And, indeed, the Borda Rule is often dismissed for being extremely susceptible to tactical voting. However, as we have noted, while tactical voting is a real problem when it comes to aggregating the stated preferences of people, it is no problem at all in the context of decision-making under moral uncertainty. Theories aren't agents, and so there's no way that they can conceal their choice-worthiness ordering. If a decision-maker pretends that one theory's choice-worthiness ordering is different than it, in fact, is, she deceives only herself.

So we think there are some positive reasons in favour of our account being Narrow, and that the arguments against Narrow accounts are not strong. So we tentatively conclude that the Narrow version of our account is to be preferred.

VII. How to Act in Varying Informational Conditions

In Chapter 2, we discussed how to take moral uncertainty into account in conditions where theories' choice-worthiness is interval-scale measurable and intertheoretically comparable. In Chapter 3, we discussed how to take moral uncertainty into account in conditions where theories give merely ordinal choice-worthiness. And, earlier in this chapter, we discussed how to take moral uncertainty into account in conditions where theories give interval-scale measurable choice-worthiness but are intertheoretically incomparable. But how should we put these different criteria together? In accordance with our *information-sensitive* view, we want our account to take into account all the relevant information that theories provide to us, but not to demand more of theories than they can provide.

One natural approach takes the form of multi-step procedure: doing what you can with the most informationally rich theories, then falling back to more general techniques to fold in theories which provide less and less information.[37] The idea is as follows. At the first step, aggregate each set of interval-scale measurable and mutually intertheoretically comparable theories. For each set, you produce a new choice-worthiness function R_i, where

---

[37] The following is very similar to the account one of us defended in William MacAskill, 'How to Act Appropriately in the Face of Moral Uncertainty', BPhil thesis, University of Oxford, 2010.

R_i assigns numbers to options that represent each option's expected choice-worthiness (given the theories in that set). R_i is given a weight equal to the sum total of the credence of all the theories within the set. At the second step, you use variance voting to aggregate all the new choice-worthiness functions (the R_i) with every interval-scale measurable but non-comparable choice-worthiness function, producing another new choice-worthiness function S. S is weighted by the sum of the decision-maker's credences in all interval-scale theories. Then, at the third and final stage, you aggregate S and all merely ordinal theories using the Borda Rule.

However, that proposal suffers from the following significant problem. Consider a decision-maker with the following credence distribution:[38]

4/9 credence in T_1: $A>B>C$.

2/9 credence in T_2: $CW_2(A) = 20$, $CW_2(B) = 10$, $CW_2(C) = 0$.

3/9 credence in T_3: $CW_3(A) = 0$, $CW_3(B) = 10$, $CW_3(C) = 20$.

T_1 is merely ordinal, while T_2 and T_3 are interval-scale and comparable. If we use the multi-step procedure, then at the first step, we aggregate T_2 and T_3 to get the following output ordering.

5/9 credence in R_1: $C>B>A$

At the second step, we aggregate T_1 and R_1 using the Borda Rule, which gives option C as the winner. However, this seems like the wrong result. In particular, consider the following credence distribution.

4/7 credence in T_1: $A>B>C$.

0 credence in T_2: $CW_2(A) = 20$, $CW_2(B) = 10$, $CW_2(C) = 0$.

3/7 credence in T_3: $CW_3(A) = 0$, $CW_3(B) = 10$, $CW_3(C) = 20$.

In this decision-situation, using the multi-step procedure would give A as the most appropriate option. So having *lower* credence in T_2 makes the appropriateness ordering better by the lights of T_2. This means that the multi-step procedure violates the *Updating* condition given in Chapter 3. The reason this happens is because, in the first decision-situation, though T_2's and T_3's choice-worthiness orderings cancel out to some extent, the multi-step procedure washes this fact out when it pits the aggregated

---

[38] The possibility of such a problem was first suggested to us by Owen Cotton-Barratt.

ordering R_1 against the ordinal theory T_1. We consider this violation of *Updating Consistency* to be a serious problem for the multi-step procedure.

In private communication, Christian Tarsney has argued that even a single-step procedure will violate *Updating Consistency*. Consider the following variant on the previous case. Suppose that the decision-maker has three options available to her, positive credence in two (cardinal and incomparable) normative theories, T_1 and T_2, and positive credence in two descriptive states of the world, S_1 and S_2. T_1 assigns the same degrees of choice-worthiness to each option regardless of the state of the world but, according to T_2, the choice-worthiness of A and C depends on the state of the world. Here's the credence distribution.

4/9 credence in T_1: $CW_1(A) = 20$, $CW_1(B) = 10$, $CW_1(C) = 0$.

2/9 credence in T_2 & S_1: $CW_{2/1}(A) = 20$, $CW_{2/1}(B) = 10$, $CW_{2/1}(C) = 0$.

3/9 credence in T_2 & S_2: $CW_{2/2}(A) = 0$, $CW_{2/2}(B) = 10$, $CW_{2/2}(C) = 20$.

On this credence distribution, if we normalize at each moral theory's ranking of options in terms of their expected choice-worthiness, then we will also violate *Updating Consistency*. The expected choice-worthiness of options on T_2 is $CW_2(A) = 8$, $CW_2(B) = 10$, $CW_2(C) = 12$, so when we normalize T_1 and T_2 at their variance, C comes out as the most appropriate option. However, if the decision-maker then reduces her credence in S_1 to 0, distributing her credence proportionally among T_1 & S_2 and T_2 & S_2 (such that she has 4/7 credence in T_1 and 3/7 credence in T_2 & S_2), then, using the same procedure as before, A will come out as the most appropriate option. But that means that A has become more appropriate in virtue of becoming less confident in a view (namely, T_2 & S_1) on which A is the top option. We've therefore violated updating consistency.

Now, insofar as we have assumed descriptive certainty in this book, strictly speaking this problem does not arise for us. However, it is clearly a problem that needs to be addressed.

We are not confident about what is the best way to do so, but our currently favoured response is to construe our account as taking an expectation over both empirical and normative states of the world jointly, rather than over empirical-belief-relative orderings. That is: we make a hard distinction between moral theories, which order outcomes in terms of choice-worthiness, and a theory of rationality, which tells us what to do in conditions of either empirical or normative uncertainty or both. This has the disadvantage that we cannot accommodate uncertainty over normative theories that do not endorse expected utility theory. Even if a moral theory endorsed maximin or some other procedure for decision-making in the face of uncertainty, we would still aggregate empirical uncertainty, conditional on that theory, in an expectational way. One could argue that this is therefore not being appropriately responsive to the decision-maker's true uncertainty across different moral views.

In response, we note that, as argued in Chapter 1, we have to go external-ist somewhere. We consider norms that govern decision-making in the face of uncertainty to be norms of rationality, and are inclined to endorse strict liability when it comes to norms of rationality. So the way we should really understand a non-expectational moral theory is as the conjunction of a moral theory (which assigns choice-worthiness to outcomes) and a theory of rationality (which, in this case, happens to be non-expectational). Our account is not sensitive to uncertainty about rationality, in which case the fact that our account 'overrides' the decision-maker's credence in a view that endorses some non-expectational decision theory should not be sur-prising to us.

We, therefore, very tentatively endorse a one-step theory. What we suggest is that we should normalize the Borda Scores of the ordinal theories with choice-worthiness functions by treating the variance of the interval-scale theories' choice-worthiness functions and the variance of the ordinal theories' Borda Scores as the same.[39] Of course, we are not claiming that these nor-malized Borda Scores represent choice-worthiness on these theories; to say that would be to pretend that ordinal theories are really cardinal. All we are suggesting is that this might be the correct way of aggregating our moral uncertainty in varying informational conditions.

If we take this approach, we need to be careful when we are normalizing Borda Scores with other theories. We can't normalize all individual compar-able theories with non-comparable theories at their variance. If we were to

---

[39] Doing this does not alter the Borda Rule as presented in Chapter 2 when each theory has a strict choice-worthiness ordering over options. However, it *does* make a difference when some theories rate some options as equally choiceworthy to one another (which is discussed in Chapter 3, footnote 26). The account given in the previous chapter gives the standard way of dealing with ties under the Borda Rule. But when taking the variance of each theory's Borda Scores to be the same, a theory that ranks $A{\sim}B{>}C{\sim}D$ will weigh comparatively more heavily against $D{>}C{>}B{>}A$ than it would under the account we stated in the previous chapter. However, the standard way of giving Borda Scores to tied options is typically defended with recourse to something like the principle of 'equal say', and implicitly invokes average-distance-to-the-mean as the correct account of 'equal say'. Now that we have seen that normalizing at the variance is the best account of 'equal say', we should use the method of dealing with tied options that nor-malizes at the variance, rather than at distance to the mean.

do so, we would soon find our equalization of choice-worthiness-differences to be inconsistent with each other. Rather, for every set of interval-scale theories that are comparable with each other, we should treat the variance of the choice-worthiness values of all options on that set's common scale as the same as the variance of every individual non-comparable theory.

An example helps to illustrate the proposal. Consider four theories, T_1-T_4, in order from left to right (see Figure 4.6).

T_1 is a merely ordinal theory. The diagram illustrates the Borda Scores that T_1 assigns to options. T_2 is interval-scale measurable but is not comparable with any other theory. T_3 and T_4 are interval-scale measurable and comparable with each other. What the single-step procedure does is to treat the variance of T_1's Borda Scores as equal with the variance of T_2's choice-worthiness function and as equal with the variance of the choice-worthiness of options across *both* T_3 and T_4. As should be clear from the diagram, the variance of T_3 is smaller than the variance of T_4. But if T_3 and T_4's variances were each individually normalized with T_2, then the variance of T_3 and T_4 would be the same. So we should not normalize T_3 and T_4 individually with T_2. Rather, it's the variance of the distribution of choice-worthiness on T_3 and T_4's common scale that we treat as equal with other theories.

With their variances treated as equal in the correct way, the theories would look approximately as in Figure 4.7.

Then, once we have done this, we maximize the expectation of the normalized scores given to each option by each theory.

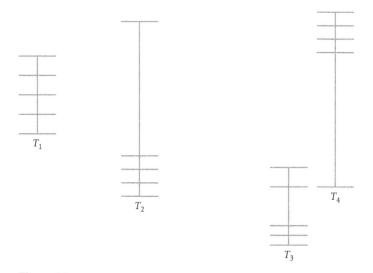

T_1

T_2

T_4

T_3

Figure 4.6

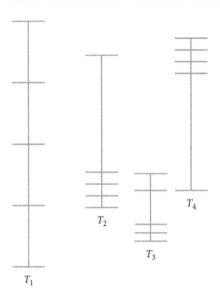

Figure 4.7

This single-step aggregation method wouldn't be possible if we didn't use a scoring function as our voting system in the situation involving merely ordinal theories. If, rather than a scoring function, we had defended a Condorcet extension as the correct way to take into account moral uncertainty over merely ordinal theories, we would be forced to endorse the multi-step procedure. But the objection to the multi-step procedure given above looks fatal. So we take this to provide additional support in favour of the use of a scoring function to aggregate merely ordinal theories, rather than a Condorcet extension.

As a final comment on this, we should note that the above account is effectively taking an expectation over all moral theories. So, even though one of the authors (William MacAskill) initially thought that the problems of merely ordinal theories and intertheoretic incomparability were reasons to reject MEC as a *general* theory, we ultimately end up with a sort of extension of MEC as a general account of decision-making under moral uncertainty, for the informational conditions we consider. Of course, we have only considered a small number of informational conditions, so it remains to be seen whether this will remain true when further work considers a wider range of informational conditions.[40]

---

[40] We thank Christian Tarsney for emphasizing this to us.

Conclusion

In this chapter, we considered how to take moral uncertainty into account in the situation where the decision-maker has non-zero credence in only interval-scale measurable theories that are intertheoretically incomparable. Arguing that the Borda Rule is unsatisfactory in this context, and arguing against Lockhart's PEMT among others, we argued in favour of variance voting, on the basis that it best respects the principle of 'equal say'. We then showed how one should aggregate one's uncertainty in varying informational conditions.

This concludes our account of what we believe to be the best theory for how to make decisions under moral uncertainty. However, we don't yet know much about when theories are comparable and when they are not, nor do we know what makes theories comparable, if and when they are comparable. Chapter 5 tackles these issues.

5

Intertheoretic Comparisons
of Choice-Worthiness

Introduction

So far, we have given an account of how to make decisions in the face of
moral uncertainty that can be applied even when some of the theories in
which one has credence are not comparable with each other. This raises the
question: how often are differences of choice-worthiness comparable across
theories? (In this book, we only consider the issue of intertheoretic comparisons of choice-worthiness differences. There is a separate question of
whether *levels* of choice-worthiness are comparable across theories. However,
as noted in the introduction, we do not discuss level-comparability of
choice-worthiness in this book. When we use the term *comparable* in every
instance we're referring to comparability of differences of choice-worthiness,
not level-comparability.)

Three distinct lines of argument suggest that intertheoretic comparisons
of choice-worthiness differences are impossible or, if possible, are bound to
lead to implausible normative results.

First, the *appeal to cases* argument. In many cases there seems to be
no intuitive way in which to compare two moral theories. As noted in
Chapter 4, even for theories as similar as utilitarianism and prioritarianism,
there appears to be no principled way of determining whether prioritarianism is agreeing with utilitarianism about the value of wellbeing-increases
for the well-off but claiming that those for the badly-off get extra weight, or
whether it is agreeing for the badly-off and claiming that wellbeing-
increases for the well-off matter less (or some third option).

Second, the *swamping* argument. Even in some cases where there does
seem to be a 'natural' way to compare the two theories, this natural comparison quickly leads to implausible results, causing one theory to 'swamp'
the other in the expected choice-worthiness calculation. Brian Hedden
makes this argument with respect to Average and Total Utilitarianism

Moral Uncertainty. William MacAskill, Krister Bykvist and Toby Ord, Oxford University Press (2020).
© William MacAskill, Krister Bykvist and Toby Ord.
DOI: 10.1093/oso/9780198722274.001.0001

(where he considers equating a unit of total wellbeing with a unit of average wellbeing):[1]

> Suppose that the agent has the choice of increasing the world's population from 6 billion to 24 billion people at the cost of halving the average happiness level…maximizing intertheoretic expectation will recommend that the agent implement the population-increasing policy (i.e. doing what Totalism recommends) unless she is over 99.9999999916% confident that Averagism is right. But this seems crazy.

After considering different ways of giving the two theories a common unit (or 'normalizing' those theories), he concludes that the problem is unresolvable: 'No matter what value functions we use to represent Averagism and Totalism, once we fix on proposed decrease in average happiness, Averagism will swamp Totalism for smaller population increases while Totalism will swamp Averagism for larger population increases.'

Again, however, the fact that these are both such similar theories should make us worried. If we can't make plausible choice-worthiness comparisons across two very similar versions of utilitarianism, what hope do we have to make comparisons across very different sorts of theory, such as utilitarianism and virtue ethics?[2]

The third and most general argument is the *arbitrary unit* argument.[3] The natural way of understanding *intra*theoretic comparisons of choiceworthiness differences, so the argument goes, is in terms of how a theory orders prospects under empirical uncertainty: that what it means for the difference in choiceworthiness between A and B (where A is more choiceworthy

---

[1] Brian Hedden, 'Does MITE Make Right? On Decision-Making under Normative Uncertainty', *Oxford Studies in Metaethics*, vol. 11 (2016), p. 108. As he notes, this argument can also be found in William MacAskill, 'Normative Uncertainty', DPhil Thesis, University of Oxford, 2014; the progenitor of the case is Toby Ord. The example of average and total utilitarianism is also given by John Broome, *Climate Matters: Ethics in a Warming World*, New York: W. W. Norton, 2012, p. 185 as part of an assertion that intertheoretic comparisons are almost always impossible, though he doesn't make the *swamping* argument. These cases are considered in depth in Hilary Greaves and Toby Ord, 'Moral Uncertainty about Population Axiology', *Journal of Ethics and Social Philosophy*, vol. 12, no. 2 (November 2017), pp. 135–67. The authors are inclined to accept the *swamping* conclusion as a *modus ponens*.
[2] A different response would be to say that the problem is not with the intertheoretic comparison, but with maximizing expected choice-worthiness (which allows some theories to swamp others). We discuss a related issue in our section on 'fanaticism' in Chapter 6.
[3] This argument is made in Ittay Nissan-Rozen, 'Against Moral Hedging', *Economics and Philosophy*, vol. 31, no. 3 (November 2015), pp. 349–69.

than B) to be equally as large as the difference in choice-worthiness between B and C (where B is more choiceworthy than C) is that a guarantee of B is equally as good as the prospect of a 50/50 chance of either A or B. More precisely, if a theory orders all possible prospects in terms of their choice-worthiness and satisfies the von Neumann–Morgenstern axioms, then it can be represented as maximizing expected choice-worthiness, where choice-worthiness can be represented on an interval scale.[4] However, for each theory, the numerical representation of its choice-worthiness ordering is unique only up to a positive affine transformation: the unit is arbitrary. So if there is nothing more to choice-worthiness than an individual theory's choice-worthiness ordering over prospects (and this is an assumption we will return to later in the chapter), then the choice of unit is arbitrary for the representation of the choice-worthiness ordering of each moral theory, and it's meaningless to say that one unit of choice-worthiness, on one theory, is greater than, smaller than, or equal to one unit of choice-worthiness on another theory.

These worries have given rise to three classes of response. The *sceptics* argue that choice-worthiness differences are either always incomparable across theories[5] or are almost always incomparable across theories.[6]

The *structuralists* claim that intertheoretic comparisons are often possible, and that intertheoretic comparisons should be made only with reference to structural features of the theories' qualitative choice-worthiness relation (such as the choice-worthiness of the best option and worst option) or mathematical features of its numerical representation (such as the mean, sum, or spread of choice-worthiness). One might believe, for example, that variance voting is not merely the best way to act if theories are incomparable, but that it is the correct way to actually make intertheoretic comparisons; this would be a structural account.[7] The non-structuralists deny

---

[4] Von Neumann and Morgenstern, *Theory of Games and Economic Behavior*. Note, though, that their concern is preference-orderings rather than with choice-worthiness orderings. For discussion of von Neumann and Morgenstern's result to moral theories see Broome, *Weighing Goods*.

[5] Hudson, 'Subjectivization in Ethics'; Gracely, 'On the Noncomparability of Judgments Made by Different Ethical Theories'; Gustafsson and Torpman, 'In Defence of My Favourite Theory' and perhaps Hedden, 'Does MITE Make Right?'

[6] John Broome, 'The Most Important Thing about Climate Change', in Jonathan Boston, Andrew Bradstock, and David L. Eng (eds), *Public Policy: Why Ethics Matters*, Acton, ACT: Australia National University E Press, 2010, pp. 101–16; Broome, *Climate Matters*, p. 122.

[7] One interpretation of Lockhart, *Moral Uncertainty and Its Consequences* is that he's a structuralist. Other structural accounts are suggested by Sepielli, 'Normative Uncertainty for Non-Cognitivists'.

structuralism, and take into account something more than just positional features of theories' choice-worthiness functions.[8]

In this chapter we will argue against both scepticism and structuralism. We believe that understanding why both scepticism and structuralism are false helps us to understand the scope of possibilities within non-structural accounts; our arguments will therefore also provide some positive reasons in favour of non-structuralism, and some suggestions of possible non-structural accounts.

I. Against Scepticism

The first two arguments in favour of scepticism appealed to specific cases, where either there were no intuitive comparisons to be made, or where the natural comparison would lead to swamping, which was taken to be an implausible result.

However, one can only draw a limited conclusion by appealing to specific cases. At most, one can show that *sometimes* intertheoretic comparisons do not hold between two theories. One cannot, thereby, show that they (almost) *never* hold between two theories, or that they are impossible. Usually, the *appeal to cases* and *swamping* arguments have been made in the context of arguing against MEC. A presupposition has been that if intertheoretic comparisons of choice-worthiness differences are *sometimes* impossible, then MEC cannot be a perfectly general account of what to do under normative uncertainty. But that presupposition is false; as we have seen in the previous chapters, by using Borda and variance voting we can apply a modified form of MEC even in conditions of intertheoretic comparability and even in conditions of merely ordinal theories.

Moreover, there are also many cases where two different moral views intuitively *do* seem comparable. We describe three classes of cases.

The first class of cases is the most compelling cases of MEC-style reasoning, where the two moral viewpoints differ with respect to only one moral issue. Consider, for example, the following statements.[9]

---

[8] Non-structural accounts are suggested by Ross, 'Rejecting Ethical Deflationism', pp. 763–4 and Sepielli, ' "Along an Imperfectly Lighted Path" '.

[9] In each example statement we give in this section, we will use the natural English locution to make the intertheoretic comparison. However, strictly speaking we should consider the natural English as shorthand. So, when we imagine someone saying, 'If animals have rights in the way that humans do, then killing animals is a much more severe wrongdoing than if they don't

If animals have rights in the way that humans do, then killing animals is a much more severe wrongdoing than if they don't.

If Singer is right about our duties to the poor, then our obligation to give to development charities is much stronger than if he's wrong.

These are cases where we're not really comparing two different complete theories, considered in the abstract. We're comparing two different moral views that differ with respect to just one moral issue. In these cases, the intertheoretic comparison seems obvious: namely, that choice-worthiness differences are the same between the two views with respect to all moral issues other than the one on which they differ.

The second class is *variable-extension* cases: unlike the former, these are cases involving complete theories, considered in the abstract.[10] Consider, for example, two forms of utilitarianism. They both have exactly the same hedonistic conception of welfare, and they both agree on all situations involving only humans: they agree that one should maximize the sum total of human welfare. They only disagree on the extension of bearers of value. One view places moral weight on animals; the other places no moral weight on animals, and they therefore disagree in situations where animals will be affected. Between these two theories, the intertheoretic comparison seems obvious: they both agree on how to treat humans, and therefore it seems clear that the choice-worthiness difference of saving one human life compared to saving no human lives is the same on both theories. Other similar examples can be given. If we consider a form of utilitarianism that claims that only presently existing people have moral weight and we should maximize the sum of their wellbeing, and compare that to total utilitarianism, again there is an intuitively obvious comparison: the choice-worthiness differences are the same in situations that only affect presently existing people.

---

and common-sense morality is correct', we should really understand them as saying, 'If animals have rights in the way that humans do, then the difference in choice-worthiness between killing an animal and not-killing an animal (in some particular situation) is much greater than the difference in choice-worthiness between killing an animal and not-killing an animal (in some particular situation) if animals don't have rights and common-sense morality is correct.' Given how laborious this would be to say, it's not surprising that natural English would use a slightly less precise shorthand.

[10] See Tarsney, 'Rationality and Moral Risk', Appendix B and sect. 6.3.1, and Christian Tarsney, 'Intertheoretic Value Comparison: A Modest Proposal', *Journal of Moral Philosophy*, vol. 15, no. 3 (June 2018), pp. 324–44.

The third class of cases are those where we make comparisons of people's moral viewpoints, whether between different people, or within one person's life and across times. Consider, for example, the following statements.

Laura used to think that stealing from big corporations was only mildly wrong, but now she thinks it's outrageous.

James thinks that extramarital sex is a minor wrong, but Jane thinks it's an abomination.

Both of these seem to be perfectly meaningful statements. But they are claims about intertheoretic comparisons. Reflecting on these statements suggests that sometimes we make intertheoretic comparisons by taking a detour via preferences. For example, if the first statement is true, then, assuming Laura is a morally conscientious agent, her preference to not-steal from big corporations has increased in strength, in proportion with her belief about the wrongness of stealing. It's part of common sense that we can make comparisons of preference-strength across people, or across changes in preference within one person's life.[11] But if we can make comparisons of preference-strength when those preferences are in proportion with the agent's moral views, then we can make comparisons of choice-worthiness differences, too.

Our intuitions about intertheoretic comparisons are therefore mixed: in some cases, they seem possible; in other cases, they don't. But this is enough to undermine the arguments for scepticism that were based on appeal to intuitions about particular cases.

The sceptic could respond by trying to debunk the intuitions we've appealed to above. She could argue that, rather than comparisons of choice-worthiness differences, our intuitions are simply tracking the ordinal rank of an option on different theories' choice-worthiness orderings. When we say, 'James thinks that extramarital sex is a minor wrong, but Jane thinks it's an abomination', we are really saying something like, 'James thinks that extramarital sex is approximately in the 40th percentile of choice-worthiness of options (more severe wrong than jay walking, but not as severe a wrong as lying), whereas Jane thinks it's in approximately the 20th percentile (a more severe wrong than lying, but not as severe a wrong as murder).'

---

[11] Though of course, it has been the subject of considerable debate within economics. For an overview, see, for example, Ken Binmore, *Rational Decisions*, Princeton, NJ: Princeton University Press, 2009. We are unable to enter into that debate here, so what we say should be taken to be on the assumption that the common-sense view about comparisons of preference-strength is correct.

In order to make true statements such as these, we don't need to make intertheoretic comparisons of choice-worthiness differences.

However, this debunking argument seems to misrepresent our judgements in these cases. In many instances of moral uncertainty, MEC-style reasoning seems plausible. As we argued in Chapter 2, if Sophie is a morally conscientious person and is fairly uncertain about whether animals have rights, then it seems plausible that, by her own lights, she shouldn't order factory-farmed chicken, even if she thinks it's more likely than not that ordering the chicken is slightly more choiceworthy than not ordering the chicken. If we were just talking about ordinal rank when we made what seem like intertheoretic comparisons, however, then MEC would be inapplicable. So the best explanation of the fact that we find MEC-style reasoning plausible is that we can make intertheoretic comparisons.

The reasonable view, then, on the basis of the intuitive evidence, is that sometimes intertheoretic comparisons are obvious; sometimes they are unobvious or perhaps impossible. The *appeal to cases* argument and the *swamping* argument therefore give us no argument for intertheoretic incomparability in general. It may be that, ultimately, we want to reject our intuitions about intertheoretic comparisons as confused. But this is a conclusion that we should only draw at the end of enquiry, after we have tried our best to come up with a general account of intertheoretic comparisons and failed.

Things are different for the *arbitrary unit* argument, which is a perfectly general argument against the possibility of intertheoretic comparisons. In light of the examples given above, however, the *arbitrary unit* argument seems to prove too much. If it were correct, it would show that *no* intertheoretic comparisons are possible. Yet we have seen many cases where they do seem to be possible. So we are left with a puzzle. On the one hand we have an argument that the choice of unit in a theory's choice-worthiness function is arbitrary; on the other hand we have specific cases where the choice of unit seems *not* to be arbitrary. The rest of the chapter will discuss accounts of intertheoretic comparisons that might resolve this puzzle. To this end, let's first consider structural accounts of intertheoretic comparisons.

II. Structural Accounts

Let us define a structural account of intertheoretic comparisons as follows.

A *structural account* is a way of giving different moral theories a common unit that only invokes structural features of the theories' qualitative choice-worthiness relation (such as the choice-worthiness of the best option and worst option) or mathematical features of its numerical representation (such as the mean, sum, or spread of choice-worthiness). The identities of particular options have no relevance; only positional properties matter.

If we were to interpret Lockhart's PEMT as an account of how theories actually compare (rather than an account of what to do in conditions when they are incomparable), then it would be a structural account. Similarly, one could go further than we claimed in Chapter 4 and suggest that variance voting is the correct account of how two theories compare, when they are comparable. This would also be a structural account.

Structural accounts are appealing for at least two reasons. First, they confront the 'arbitrary unit' argument for intertheoretic incomparability head on. If some structural account is correct, then we do not require anything more from moral theories other than that they provide an interval-scale measurable choice-worthiness function. In order to normalize two theories, all they need is that those two theories both provide a choice-worthiness ordering over prospects that satisfies the von Neumann–Morgenstern axioms.

Second, they alleviate the swamping worry, too. In virtue of *only* looking at each theory's choice-worthiness function, they attempt to ensure that no theory gets more 'say' than another. Lockhart, for example, explicitly defends the PEMT on these lines:

> The PEMT might be thought of as a principle of fair competition among moral theories, analogous to democratic principles that support the equal counting of the votes of all qualified voters in an election regardless of any actual differences in preference intensity among the voters.[12]

We have found that structural accounts have regularly been endorsed in conversation for these reasons. However, though structural accounts have some theoretical appeal, we believe that all such accounts are flawed. To show this, we provide five arguments against structural accounts; moreover, seeing why structural accounts fail will help us to see how non-structural accounts could succeed.

These five objections share a common theme. According to structural accounts, there is only *one* possible way to make intertheoretic comparisons between any two theories. In order to reject structuralism we therefore don't

---

[12] Ted Lockhart, *Moral Uncertainty and Its Consequences*, p. 86.

need to argue that two theories definitely do compare in a certain way that is inconsistent with any structuralist view. All we need to argue is that an agent is not making a mistake if she has a belief that two theories compare in a way that structural accounts cannot countenance. Each of the five objections that follow show a different way in which this is the case.

III. Five Arguments against Structural Accounts

Varied-Extension Cases

In cases where two theories agree in every respect except on the extension of the class of things that are fundamental bearers of value, there seems to be an intuitive way in which these two theories compare. For example, consider humans-only utilitarianism (HO-U) and all-sentient-creatures utilitarianism (ASC-U). The natural and obvious way to compare these two theories is to suppose that the value of humans is the same according to both theories; certainly it seems epistemically permissible for a decision-maker to have a credence distribution such that this is so. But structural accounts have to deny this. Because structural accounts are only sensitive to features of a theory's choice-worthiness function, they can't 'peer inside' the theories to see that they have parts in common, and they can't allow one theory to be higher-stakes in general than another.

To see this, let's suppose that ASC-U regards (non-human) animal lives as half as valuable as human lives (due to some aspect of their reduced cognitive capacities). And let's suppose, for simplicity, that there are only three possible options: one in which there are no sentient creatures, one in which there are 100 humans, and 0 other animals, and one in which there are 100 humans and 800 other animals. In Table 5.1 those two theories are represented in the most intuitive way.

This fits our intuition that, since they have the same account of human value, the second option is considered just as valuable by each theory. It also fits our intuition that if you lived in the world with many animals and came to change your beliefs from a theory that neglected animals to one that recognized them, you would find the world to be much more valuable than before and to think that there was more at stake.

This, however, is not how structural accounts would normalize them. For example, the broad PEMT would normalize them as in Table 5.2.

Table 5.1

	HO-U	ASC-U
0 humans, 0 animals	0	0
100 humans, 0 animals	100	100
100 humans, 800 animals	100	500

Table 5.2

	HO-U	ASC-U
0 humans, 0 animals	0	0
100 humans, 0 animals	100	20
100 humans, 800 animals	100	100

The broad PEMT therefore has to deny that the two theories agree on the value of human lives. The same would be true if we normalized the two theories at the difference between the maximum and mean choice-worthiness, at their variance, or at any other features of their choice-worthiness function. Structural accounts have to say that, according to ASC-U, humans are of less value than they are according to HO-U, and that a decision-maker is making a mistake if she believes them to be otherwise. But this seems wrong. They therefore fail to capture our intuitions about intertheoretic comparisons in varied-extension cases.

The structuralist might be inclined to reject the starting intuition we appealed to. But it was intuitions like those concerning varied-extension cases that made us think that intertheoretic comparisons were possible at all. Insofar as structural accounts reject those intuitions, they, therefore, undermine part of the motivation for denying scepticism in the first place.

Discontinuity with Universal Indifference

A second problem for structural accounts is that it seems, intuitively, that some theories can be higher stakes than others. This means that structural accounts must create a discontinuity between *universal indifference*—the view on which all options are equally choiceworthy—and discerning moral theories.

For example, suppose that Meursault originally adheres to common-sense ethics, but then reads more and more nihilist literature. He becomes progressively convinced that universal indifference is true. However, the way he becomes convinced is not that he increases his credence in universal indifference and decreases his credence in common-sense ethics. Rather, he progressively realizes that certain things he used to think were of positive value are neutral in value. First, he realizes that art and literature and non-personal goods have no intrinsic positive or negative value. Then he realizes that there are no other-regarding reasons, and retreats to egoism. At each step, Meursault becomes more despondent. Finally, he realizes that even his own happiness is also merely neutral in value, and he comes to accept full-blown universal indifference.

A natural and intuitive way to understand this is that the ethical viewpoints that Meursault adheres to become progressively closer and closer to universal indifference. Meursault progressively thinks that there is less and less positive value in the world, until eventually he thinks there is no positive value at all in the world. Again, it seems at least epistemically permissible for Mersault to think about his changes in moral beliefs in this way. However, structuralist accounts cannot understand Meursault's progression in beliefs in this way. According to structuralist accounts, when Meursault rejects the value of art, his other beliefs compensate and he comes to believe that personal moral reasons were much more important than he had previously thought; when Meursault rejects moral reasons, he must also come to believe that his own happiness is much more important than he had previously thought. The amount of value Meursault thinks exists in general is the same right up until the point when he embraces universal indifference. At that point, there is a stark discontinuity. Insofar as structural accounts cannot countenance the possibility that Mersault comes to have progressively lower-stakes beliefs, we have another reason against accepting structural accounts.

Incoherent Beliefs—Weighing Values

Our third argument against structural accounts rests on the fact that how we think we should compare two theories can be affected by our beliefs in theories other than the two in question.[13]

---

[13] The idea that pluralistic theories can serve as 'bridges' to establish intertheoretic comparability between other theories, based on cases like the one described below, is defended in Tarsney, 'Rationality and Moral Risk', pp. 202–4 and 323–7.

Let us suppose that Abel has the following beliefs. He is a consequentialist, but isn't sure if pleasurable experiences are of value, or if artistic and scientific accomplishments are of value, or if both are of value, and, therefore, he isn't sure about the relative choice-worthiness of options that promote happiness and those that promote accomplishments. However, he has no doubts at all about how to weigh the value of increased pleasurable experiences against the value of artistic and scientific accomplishments, if they are both of value.

That is, he has credence in three different theories: T_1, according to which only pleasurable experiences are of value; T_2, according to which only artistic and scientific accomplishments are of value, and T_3, according to which both are of value.

Abel believes that the intratheoretic comparison between pleasure and accomplishments on T_3 provides a basis for the intertheoretic comparison between T_1 and T_2. He believes that one unit of pleasurable experience is worth the same on T_1 and T_3 and he believes that one unit of accomplishment is worth the same on T_2 and T_3. Does this set of beliefs seem irrational? We believe not. But structural accounts would have to say that these beliefs are irrational.

To illustrate, suppose for simplicity that there are only three possible options, A, B, and C. On T_3, the pleasure produced by option A is of value 100, the achievement produced by option B is of value 200, the pleasure produced by option C is of value 50, and the achievement produced by option C is of value 100. Given our description of Able's beliefs, we would therefore represent these theories as in Table 5.3.

However, structural accounts will not be able to represent theories in this way. The broad PEMT, for example, will represent them as in Table 5.4.

For any comparison between two theories, structural accounts are blind to the decision-maker's beliefs about other theories. But this seems like a mistake. In the case given above, Abel is sure about how pleasure and accomplishment should be weighed against each other if they are both of

Table 5.3

	T_1	T_2	T_3
A: Lots of pleasure, little achievement	100	0	100
B: Lots of achievement, little pleasure	0	200	200
C: Moderate amounts of both pleasure and achievement	50	100	150

Table 5.4

	T_1	T_2	T_3
A: Lots of pleasure, little achievement	100	0	0
B: Lots of achievement, little pleasure	0	100	100
C: Moderate amounts of both pleasure and achievement	50	50	50

value. But even though he is certain that if both pleasure and accomplishment are of value they weigh against each other in such-and-such a way, according to structural accounts he must believe that, when it comes to the intertheoretic comparison between pleasure and accomplishment, they *must* weigh against one another in a different way. That seems wrong.

Incoherent Beliefs—Too Much Comparability

Our fourth argument is that structural accounts generate too much intertheoretic comparability. Structural accounts must claim that *all* moral theories that can be represented by an interval-scale measurable choice-worthiness function are intertheoretically comparable. But that seems much too strong.

Consider Beth, who, like Abel is unsure about whether pleasure or accomplishment or both are of value. However, unlike Abel, she is absolutely certain that if both pleasure and accomplishment are of value, then, because of the nature of those two values, they are absolutely incomparable in value. Like with Abel, we can represent her as having credence in three theories: T_1, according to which only pleasurable experiences are of value; T_2, according to which only artistic and scientific accomplishments are of value; and T_3, according to which both are of value, but the value of each is (intratheoretically) incomparable.

Further, let us suppose that Beth believes that T_1 and T_2 are absolutely incomparable. Given that she believes that, if pleasure and accomplishment are both of value, then they are absolutely incomparable, this seems like a natural and reasonable set of beliefs. But structural accounts cannot make sense of this. For structural accounts, T_1 and T_2 are no different from any other theories that provide choice-worthiness functions, and can be normalized in the same way. But this seems to force Beth to have strange beliefs:

believing that, though pleasure and accomplishment would be absolutely incomparable if they were both of value, nonetheless they are perfectly comparable when considered intertheoretically.

The advocate of structural accounts could respond by supposing that her account is only an account of how values compare across theories when those two theories are intertheoretically comparable; and that the account remains silent on *when* theories are intertheoretically comparable. But this drastically reduces the attractiveness of the structural accounts. One of the virtues of the account was its generality, and the fact that it served as a response to the worry that intertheoretic value comparisons are not possible at all. With this modification, we are left with no way of knowing when, if ever, two theories are intertheoretically comparable. If the structuralist wishes to assuage this worry by developing an additional account of when two theories are intertheoretically incomparable, then they will run into other problems. For that account would have to appeal to information other than information concerning the structure of the theory's choice-worthiness function. Such an additional account would therefore go against the very spirit of structural accounts, and should make us wonder why we were attracted to them in the first place.

Amplified Theories

Our final argument is that structural accounts can't account for a possible way in which a decision-maker might believe two theories to be related. Introducing some new terminology, let us say that two theories T_i and T_j have the same *interval-scale structure* iff there exists a constant c and a constant $k > 0$, such that for all options A: $CW_i(A) = k\, CW_j(A) + c$, where $CW_i(A)$ represents the choice-worthiness of A on moral theory T_i. And let us say that T_i is an *amplified* version of T_j iff they have the same interval-scale structure and the difference in choice-worthiness between any two options A and B on T_i is greater than the difference in choice-worthiness between those same two options A and B on T_j. Figure 5.1 (which is to scale) represents this idea.

Suppose that A–E are the only possible options. If so, then T_2 is an amplified version of T_1. T_1 and T_2 agree that the difference between B and C is four times the difference between A and B. But the difference between A and B, according to T_2, is twice the difference between A and B, according to T_1. So T_2 is an amplification of T_1.

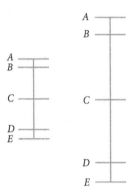

Figure 5.1

With this on board, we can state our final argument against structuralism.

(P1)   It's epistemically permissible to believe in two distinct theories, one of which is an amplified version of the other.

(P2)   If (P1), then all structural account are false.

(C3)   Therefore, all structural accounts are false.

(P2) is uncontroversial. If structural accounts are correct, we can only appeal to information concerning the theory's choice-worthiness function, which is unique only up to a positive affine transformation. So, on structural accounts, all theories with the same interval-scale structure must be normalized in exactly the same way. Providing an example where it seems epistemically permissible to believe that one theory is an amplified version of another theory would thereby show that structural accounts are not correct. Here we suggest an example of such a pair of theories.

Sophie's Change of View

Sophie initially believes in a partialist form of utilitarianism, which posits both impartial and agent-relative value. Though she thinks that human welfare is of value in and of itself, she also thinks that the presence of certain relationships between her and others confers additional value on those with whom she has the relationship. For that reason, she believes that the welfare of her family and friends is more valuable than that of distant strangers, though she thinks that both have value.

Sophie then revizes her belief, and comes to believe that the welfare of all humans is of equal value. However, she realizes that there are two ways in which she could come to hold this view. First, she could come to believe that there's no such thing as agent-relative value; no relationships confer additional value on the welfare of others. In which case the value of the welfare of distant strangers would be the same as she had previously thought, but the value of the welfare of close family and friends would be less than she had previously thought. Second, she could come to believe that, morally, she should 'be a brother to all', and she should regard her relationship with all other humans as being morally valuable in just the same way that she had thought that blood relationships and friendships were morally valuable. In which case, the welfare of her family and friends would be just as valuable as she had always thought; it's just that the value of the welfare of distant strangers is greater than she had thought. She is unsure which she should believe.

Let's call the first view that Sophie considers *Benthamite utilitarianism* and the second view *kinship utilitarianism*. Intuitively, it seems perfectly meaningful to think that Sophie could be uncertain between these two views. And it also seems meaningful for her to think that her relationships would have been downgraded in value, if Benthamite utilitarianism were true, but that the value of distant strangers would have increased in value, if kinship utilitarianism were true.

One might think that there is no *meaning* to the idea of one theory being an amplified version of another theory. But we can point to five distinctions between the two theories in order to further explain the meaningfulness of amplified theories.

First, Benthamite utilitarianism and kinship utilitarianism differ on the grounding of choice-worthiness: they disagree on facts concerning in virtue of what are certain actions wrong. Benthamite utilitarianism would claim that saving a human life is good because saving that life would increase the sum total of human welfare. On Benthamite utilitarianism, there is just one fact in virtue of which saving a human life is a good thing. In contrast, kinship utilitarianism would claim that saving a human life is good both because saving that life would increase the sum total of human welfare, and also because one has a certain sort of relationship to that person. On kinship utilitarianism, there are two facts in virtue of which saving a human life is a good thing. That is, Benthamite utilitarianism and kinship utilitarianism disagree on what the *right-makers* are.

In general, there is often more to a moral theory than a choice-worthiness function: there is also a metaphysical account of why that choice-worthiness function is correct. This provides some grounds for thinking that the *arbitrary unit* argument, which appealed to the idea that there is nothing more to a moral theory than its choice-worthiness function, is mistaken. Theories differ in their metaphysics, and, intuitively, that metaphysical account can make a difference to the amplification of a theory. On Benthamite utilitarianism, one does *one* wrong thing by killing another person (namely, reducing the amount of welfare in the world), whereas, on kinship utilitarianism, one does *two* wrong things (reducing the amount of welfare in the world, and violating a an obligation that arises out of a special relationship that one has). Committing both wrong X and wrong Y is worse than committing just wrong X. So it's a more severe wrong to kill, according to kinship utilitarianism, than it is according to Benthamite utilitarianism.

A second way in which we can make sense of amplified theories is with reference to the relationships in which they stand to other theories. Benthamite utilitarianism and kinship utilitarianism differ in their relationship to partialist utilitarianism. Benthamite utilitarianism has a part in common with partialist utilitarianism—the part that concerns strangers. Kinship utilitarianism also has a part in common with partialist utilitarianism, but it is a different part: the part that concerns family and friends. Because of these different relationships, we can make sense of kinship utilitarianism being an amplified version of Benthamite utilitarianism.

Third, it seems that which attitudes it is fitting for Sophie to have, given revision of her initial belief, depends on which amplification of utilitarianism she comes to believe. If she comes to believe Benthamite utilitarianism, it seems fitting for her to be disappointed: she has lost something of value, as her family and friends are merely as valuable as distant strangers. In contrast, the same is not true if she comes to believe kinship utilitarianism. Perhaps, instead, it would be fitting for her to feel a sense of wonder and new connectedness with those whom she doesn't know.[14]

Fourth, it seems plausible to us that the epistemological facts can differ depending on which theory we are discussing, and that they can differ in virtue of the amplification of the theory. Perhaps the idea of downgrading

---

[14] Note that we use the term 'fitting' rather than 'ought'. That an attitude is fitting does not entail, necessarily, that one ought to have that attitude. Analogously, one might reject the idea that the requirements of etiquette affect what you ought to do while still acknowledging that it's against the requirements of etiquette to eat with one's elbows on the table.

the value of her family and friends seems abhorrent to her; or perhaps she finds the idea that certain relationships should confer additional value on welfare metaphysically spooky. Either of those views seem reasonable, and either one would mean that she'd find one of the two theories more plausible than the other.

Fifth, facts about what it's appropriate to do under moral uncertainty can differ depending on which amplification of utilitarianism Sophie has credence in. If she has 20% credence in kinship utilitarianism and 80% credence in non-consequentialism, then, if she follows MEC, she will more often act in accordance with utilitarianism than if she has 20% credence in Benthamite utilitarianism and 80% credence in non-consequentialism. This is because things are higher-stakes in general for kinship utilitarianism than for Benthamite utilitarianism.

One might complain that we have only given one example, and that we shouldn't trust our intuitions if they pertain to merely one case. But we could give more examples. Consider Thomas, who initially believes that human welfare is ten times as valuable as animal welfare, because humans have rationality and sentience, whereas animals merely have sentience. He revizes this view, and comes to believe that human welfare is as valuable as animal welfare. He might now think that human welfare is less valuable than he previously thought because he has rejected the idea that rationality confers additional value on welfare. Or he might now think that animal welfare is more valuable than he previously thought, because he has extended his concept of rationality, and thinks that animals are rational in the morally relevant sense.

Or consider Ursula, who initially believes that wrong acts are ten times as wrong as wrong omissions, but then comes to believe that acts and omissions are on a par. Does she come to believe that wrong omissions are worse than she had thought, or does she come to believe that wrong acts aren't as wrong as she had thought? If the former, then it might be fitting for her to feel horror at the idea that, insofar as she had let others die, she had been doing things as bad as murder all her life. If the latter, then it might be fitting for her to feel less blame towards those who had killed others.

In exactly the same way as with Sophie, we can explain the distinction between these pairs of amplified theories by looking at differences in rightmakers, differences in fitting attitudes, differences in epistemological reasons, and differences in facts about what it is appropriate to do under moral uncertainty.

For these reasons, we believe that we should reject structural accounts of intertheoretic comparisons.

IV. Non-structural Accounts

In the course of our arguments in favour of amplified theories, we saw that two theories with the same interval-scale structure can differ in a number of ways—their metaphysical underpinnings, their relationship to other theories, their relationship to epistemic reasons, the reactive attitudes that are fitting, and the actions that are rational given credence in them—and that these differences have some relationship to intertheoretic comparisons. Each of these has the potential to enter into an explanation of the possibility of intertheoretic comparisons. We could say, for example, that such-and-such an intertheoretic comparison is true *because* of certain facts about what attitudes it is fitting to have;[15] or we could say that it's true *because* of facts about what it's rational to do under moral uncertainty.[16] And in the course of some of our other arguments, we saw that sometimes we can make intertheoretic comparisons via comparisons of preference-strength. If we want to compare T_1 and T_2, perhaps we can do so by comparing the preference-strengths of morally conscientious person A, who fully believes T_1, and morally conscientious person B, who fully believes T_2. And we sometimes saw that we can appeal to relationships between theories— if we can explicate the notion of some aspect of a theory being 'shared' across two theories, then again we would have a way of making intertheoretic comparisons.[17]

Our problem, therefore, is not that we have no way of making the comparison, but that we have too many. There are many ways in which theories differ that seem to relate to intertheoretic comparisons. But we don't yet know which of these aspects are the grounds of intertheoretic comparisons, and which are consequences of intertheoretic comparisons.

Even without having a specific account in hand, however, we may have the basis for optimism about the extent of the applicability of MEC. If we allow the possibility of amplified theories, then we should reconsider what

---

[15] This account is suggested by Sepielli, '"Along an Imperfectly Lighted Path"'.
[16] This account is suggested by Ross, 'Rejecting Ethical Deflationism'.
[17] This idea is suggested Ross, 'Rejecting Ethical Deflationism' and then explicated by Sepielli, 'What to Do When You Don't Know What to Do' (who recants the view in '"Along an Imperfectly Lighted Path"').

we call moral theories. Rather than thinking of 'utilitarianism' as designating one particular theory, really it designates an entire class of theories, each of different levels of amplification. We can therefore return to the 'hard cases' for intertheoretic comparisons with a new perspective. For example, rather than thinking that there is simply no way to make the comparison between utilitarianism and prioritarianism, we might instead think that we are just unsure about which, of all the prioritarian theories within the class of theories with the same interval-scale structure, is most plausible. Some forms of prioritarianism clearly seem implausible, such as the form of prioritarianism according to which the value of one extra year of healthy life given to a typical member of an affluent country is one million times as large as the value of one extra year of healthy life given to a typical member of an affluent country according to utilitarianism. When we were initially thinking about the comparison between utilitarianism and prioritarianism, the argument was that, because there was no privileged way to make the comparison, we should conclude that there is no comparison. But in light of the discussion of amplified theories, the lack of a privileged normalization shouldn't be so worrying to us. Instead, we should distribute our credences over many different prioritarianisms with the same interval-scale structure. And we have intuitions about that: it's clear we should have much higher credence in the prioritarianism that values one year of healthy life given to a typical member of an affluent country approximately the same as utilitarianism does than we should to the prioritarianism that values that year of life as one million times as much as utilitarianism does. But if we even have a probability distribution over different prioritarianisms of different levels of amplification, that's sufficient to use MEC.

However, the arguments that we've given might make us even more worried than we were by swamping. Consider, for example, someone who is unsure between prior-existence utilitarianism and total utilitarianism. If our arguments are correct, the natural way to normalize these two theories is via the part on which they agree, namely the value of presently existing people. However, if so, then it seems that total utilitarianism will swamp prior-existence utilitarianism: whereas the number of people who presently exist is 7 billion, it seems that the expected number of people who exist in the future is at least in the tens of trillions.[18] For almost any decision that

---

[18] For context, *Homo sapiens* have already been around for 200,000 years and the average mammalian species lasts for 1 to 2 million years. If we had even a one in ten chance of surviving for as long as a typical mammalian species, that would be an expected 10 to 20 trillion

has some effect on the long-term future of the human species, the action with the highest expected choice-worthiness will accord with total utilitarianism rather than present-existence utilitarianism, even if one has a very small credence in total utilitarianism.

However, we think that the correct response is to deny that the *swamping* argument is a good argument against certain intertheoretic comparison claims. If we take seriously the idea that there are norms governing decision-making under moral uncertainty, then presumably we do so because of the analogies between decision-making under moral uncertainty and decision-making under empirical uncertainty. But a *swamping* argument against an empirical hypothesis would be absurd. For example, prior to the first atomic test, physicist Edward Teller raised the possibility that a nuclear blast might 'ignite' the atmosphere by causing a self-propagating fusion reaction between nitrogen nuclei, thereby destroying the planet.[19] Prior to extensive physical calculations, this hypothesis would have swamped the expected utility calculation of undertaking a first atomic test. But that wasn't a reason for supposing that the destruction of the planet wouldn't be as bad, if Teller's hypothesis is true, than if Teller's hypothesis is false. If one empirical hypothesis regards a decision-situation as higher-stakes than another, we should represent it as such; the same is true for moral theories. A theory on which there is more to gain or lose in a situation (or in general) should have greater weight in the calculation concerning what to do: that's precisely the point of taking into account both the probability that the theory is true *and* the strength of the choice-worthiness differences according to the theory.

Partly, we think that our concerns about swamping are influenced by concerns about whether maximizing an expectation is the right way to make decisions in the face of tiny-probability but extremely-high-value outcomes; this is the 'fanaticism' problem that we discuss in Chapter 6. We agree that it is a worrying problem that maximizing an expectation might require one to pursue actions that have almost no chance of producing a good outcome. But this is a problem for decision theory in general, whether under moral or

more individuals. Given any real chance of spreading beyond Earth, the expected number would be much higher.

[19] See Richard Rhodes, *The Making of the Atomic Bomb*, London: Simon & Schuster, 1986, pp. 418–19.

empirical uncertainty.[20] It has nothing to do with intertheoretic comparisons in particular.

Given this, it seems that the class of non-structural accounts of intertheoretic comparisons is promising to explore. We can divide non-structural accounts into two categories. According to what we call *common ground* accounts, intertheoretic comparisons are true in virtue of different theories' having parts that are shared between them. Ross, Sepielli, and Tarsney have proposed common ground accounts.[21]

According to *universal scale* accounts, intertheoretic comparisons are true in virtue of the fact that there is some independent choice-worthiness scale that is the same across different theories. Ross and Sepielli have both proposed universal scale accounts, in addition to the common ground accounts that they have proposed. We defend a different universal scale account later in this chapter.

We can represent these different accounts diagrammatically. Let us consider two theories, T_1 and T_2 (see Figure 5.2).

Structural accounts normalize with respect to some features of each theory's choice-worthiness function. In the diagram below, we have normalized them with respect to the range of the choice-worthiness function. The key question for structural accounts is at which features of each theory's

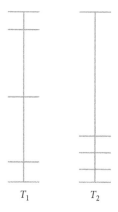

$$T_1 \qquad T_2$$

Figure 5.2

[20] See, for example, Alan Hájek, 'Waging War on Pascal's Wager', *The Philosophical Review*, vol. 112, no. 1 (January 2003), pp. 27–56 and Nick Bostrom, 'Pascal's Mugging', *Analysis*, vol. 69, no. 3 (July 2009), pp. 443–5.

[21] Ross, 'Rejecting Ethical Deflationism', pp. 764–5; Sepielli, 'What to Do When You Don't Know What to Do'.

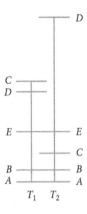

Figure 5.3

choice-worthiness function to normalize (such as the range, or the variance, or the maximum choice-worthiness minus the mean choice-worthiness).

Common ground accounts attempt to find some choice-worthiness-differences between specific options that are agreed on by both theories. As opposed to structural accounts, common ground accounts require us to be able to identify options across theories (rather than merely identifying them by their position in the choice-worthiness function). The key questions for common ground accounts are: (i) to elucidate what it means for a theory to 'share parts'; and (ii) to identify the options A and B whose choice-worthiness difference the two theories under consideration agree upon. In Figure 5.3, we have supposed that the two theories agree on the choice-worthiness difference between A and B.

According to universal scale accounts, the two theories are already plotted on some shared scale, represented in black in Figure 5.4.

The key question for universal scale accounts is to explain the nature of this shared scale, and give reasons for thinking that this shared scale exists.

V. Against Two Common Ground Accounts

On a common ground account that is suggested by both Ross and Sepielli,[22] the idea, in Ross's words, is to look at 'cases in which, for some pair of

---

[22] Ross, 'Rejecting Ethical Deflationism', pp. 764–5; Sepielli, 'What to Do When You Don't Know What to Do'.

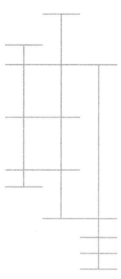

Figure 5.4

options, we know that the difference between their values is the same according to both ethical theories.'[23] We then can use that difference to define one unit of choice-worthiness that is comparable across both theories.

The trouble with this account is that neither Ross nor Sepielli give an explanation of what it is for some choice-worthiness difference to be 'shared' between two options. Sepielli is clearest: he takes agreement between theories to consist in the fact that two theories agree where some part of their choice-worthiness functions have the same interval-scale structure. More precisely, Sepielli's view is as follows. For some three particular options A, B, and C:

$$\text{If } \frac{CW_i(A)-CW_i(B)}{CW_i(B)-CW_i(C)} = \frac{CW_j(A)-CW_j(B)}{CW_j(B)-CW_j(C)}$$
$$\text{then } CW_i(A)-CW_i(B) = CW_j(A)-CW_j(B).$$

But this account is internally inconsistent, and therefore the claim above is false.[24] We saw this in Chapter 4, section I, with respect to utilitarianism

---

[23] Ross, 'Rejecting Ethical Deflationism', p. 764.
[24] Sepielli recants this view, because of this objection, in Sepielli, ' "Along an Imperfectly Lighted Path" '.

and prioritiarianism (where we assumed the prioritarian's concave function is the square root function). To recap: suppose that Annie and Betty have lived for sixteen years so far, and if you save their lives they'll each live a further nine years. Both utilitarianism and prioritarianism agree that the difference in choice-worthiness between saving both Annie and Betty and saving Annie only is the same as the difference in choice-worthiness between saving Annie only and saving neither. According to the prioritarian, the choice-worthiness difference between saving Annie only and saving neither is $\sqrt{25} - \sqrt{16}$, which equals 1. According to the utilitarian, the difference is $25 - 16$, which equals 9. So, according to Ross's and Sepielli's view, 1 unit of choice-worthiness on prioritiarianism equals 9 units of choice-worthiness on utilitarianism.

But now suppose that Annie and Betty had lived for sixty-four years, and would live a further nine years. Again, both utilitarianism and prioritarianism agree that the difference in choice-worthiness between saving both Annie and Betty and saving Annie only is the same as the difference in choice-worthiness between saving Annie only and saving neither. But, according to the prioritarian, the choice-worthiness difference between saving Annie only and saving neither is $\sqrt{73} - \sqrt{64}$, which is approximately 0.5. According to the utilitarian, the difference is 9, as before. So, according to Ross's and Sepielli's view, 1 unit of choice-worthiness on prioritiarianism equals 18 units of choice-worthiness on utilitarianism. But this is different from what we concluded in the previous paragraph, when Annie and Betty had lived shorter lives. So Ross's and Sepielli's account generates inconsistent pronouncements about how choice-worthiness compares across two theories. So their account should be rejected.

Christian Tarsney suggests a variant of Ross and Sepielli's account.[25] On Tarsney's view, the common ground between different theories is not some specific ratio of choice-worthiness differences, but instead is a shared *category of reasons*. So, for example, if we consider one theory that values both pleasure and beauty, and another theory that values both beauty and knowledge, then ceteris paribus, we should think that these two theories agree on how strong the reasons to promote beauty are.

One might think that this suffers from internal inconsistency in much the same way that Ross and Sepielli's accounts do. Consider a decision-maker who has 1/3 credence in each of the following three theories: T_1 values pleasure and knowledge; T_2 values knowledge and beauty; T_3 values

---

[25]   Tarsney, 'Rationality and Moral Risk', Appendix B.

beauty and pleasure. Let's call the relevant choice-worthiness units hedons, epistemons, and aesthetons. And let's suppose that, on T_1, increasing the value of the world by 1 hedon (and leaving everything else as it is) is as choiceworthy as increasing the value of the world by 1 epistemon (and leaving everything else as it is). Similarly, the exchange rate on T_2 between epistemon and aesthetons is 1:1, but on T_3 the exchange rate is 1 aestheton to 2 hedons.

There seems to be nothing irrational with having such a credence distribution. But if a decision-maker did have such a credence distribution, then it would seem that Tarsney's 'categories of reasons' would give inconsistent conclusions on how T_1, T_2 and T_3 compare with each other.

However, the precise account that Tarsney defends does not suffer from this problem, because he claims that (i) a decision-maker should only *ceteris paribus* believe that the value of a hedon is independent of what other bearers of value there are, but that (ii) if there is a difference in how hedons and other bearers of value trade off against each other, the decision-maker needs to have some belief that explains why hedons have more or less value on one theory than another. So, on Tarsney's account, insofar as the above decision-maker lacks such a belief, she is indeed irrational.

However, it seems to us that this is now just begging the question. In order to make his account consistent, Tarsney has required the decision-maker to have beliefs about how theories intertheoretically compare (namely, that, *ceteris paribus*, one hedon is worth the same across all theories). Whereas the very claim of the intertheoretic comparability sceptic is that a decision-maker needn't have any such belief.

Indeed, we believe that Tarsney misrepresents the dialectic on the problem of intertheoretic comparisons. Tarsney argues that, 'Opponents of any kind of intertheoretic comparability … must hold that Alice should accept [that the value of a hedon if aesthetons have non-derivative value is incomparable with the value of a hedon if aesthetons don't have non-derivative value].' But in our view, the aim of an account of intertheoretic comparability is not to merely show that the positive position that 'theories are intertheoretically incomparable' is as justified or unjustified as any other position. The aim is to provide an account of *why* intertheoretic comparisons hold, if they do. (In the same way that the aim of responding to the external-world sceptic is to help us understand how we know we have hands, not to simply show that believing we're a brain in a vat is also an unjustified position.) Claiming that decision-makers do (or ought to) have certain beliefs in intertheoretic comparisons does not help us in that end. So we ultimately find this account, at least as Tarsney has currently developed it, unsatisfactory.

Another common ground account that Sepielli briefly suggests[26] is that there might be 'paradigms' of morally acceptable actions, and paradigms of morally heinous actions, which are definitive of choice-worthiness. So just as one might think that the International Prototype Kilogram defines what it means to have 1 kg of mass, so one might think that the difference in choice-worthiness between some two particular, extremely well-specified options (listening to music, and killing for fun, for example), defines one unit of choice-worthiness.

The problem with this account, as a fundamental explanation of how intertheoretic comparisons are possible, is just that there is far too much disagreement among moral theories for this to be a plausible general view. According to ethical egoism, the difference in choice-worthiness between listening to music and killing for fun will be very different compared to the difference in choice-worthiness between listening to music and killing for fun, according to utilitarianism.

The same will be true for any pair of options. One might think that the difference in choice-worthiness between options that only affect the agent—such as, for me, the option to drink a cup of tea right now and the option to keep writing—should be considered the same across all possible moral theories. But this account will result in a clash between separable and non-separable moral views: for example, on average utilitarianism the difference in value between my drinking an enjoyable cup of tea and continuing writing is smaller the larger the number of people there are (because that action affects the average wellbeing by a smaller amount the more people there are); but on total utilitarianism, the value remains constant. So we would have to pick one particular population size in order to put average and total utilitarianism on the same scale, and it's hard to see how this could be done in a non-arbitrary way.

VI. Against Two Universal Scale Accounts

The discussion of amplified theories made some suggestions about ways in which we can tell the difference between two theories with the same

---

[26] Sepielli, '"Along an Imperfectly Lighted Path"', p. 186.

interval-scale structure. This idea motivates some different accounts of intertheoretic comparisons.

We mentioned that the amplification of a theory can make a difference to facts concerning what it's appropriate to do under moral uncertainty. So perhaps it's those facts that make it the case that a certain intertheoretic comparison holds. This is a view suggested by Ross.[27]

As we understand this suggestion, the claim is that facts about how choice-worthiness differences compare across theories are determined by facts about what it is appropriate to do in light of uncertainty between those theories. If an agent faces options A and B, and has 10% credence in T_1, according to which $CW_1(A) > CW_1(B)$, and 90% credence in T_2, according to which $CW_2(B) > CW_2(A)$, and it is appropriate for her to do A, then, *because* it is appropriate for her to do A in this situation, $(CW_1(A)-CW_1(B))$ is at least 9 times greater than $(CW_2(B)-CW_2(A))$.

The obvious objection to this account is that it puts the cart before the horse. Consider Kate, who has 80% credence in common-sense views about how she should spend her money, and 20% credence in Singer's view that she has strong obligations to donate much of her money to alleviate extreme poverty. In this case, intuitively it's appropriate for her to donate the money. But we have that intuition because it seems clear how the choice-worthiness differences compare across the two moral views in which she has credence. It's not that we have the intuition that it's appropriate for Kate to donate part of her income, and thereby infer what the respective choice-worthiness differences between the common-sense view and Singer's view are. Ross's proposal therefore seems to get the order of explanation the wrong way around.

A different sort of meta-scale account is suggested by Sepielli.[28] He wishes to use degrees of blameworthiness as the scale by which choice-worthiness difference may be compared. The exact nature of his proposal is unclear. But it seems to us that his principal initial proposal is that a decision-maker believes that $(CW_i(A)-CW_i(B)) = (CW_j(C)-CW_j(D))$ iff the strength of the decision-maker's disposition to blame for doing A rather than B, conditional on T_i, is the same as the strength of the decision-maker's disposition to blame for doing C rather than D, conditional on T_j. It should be fairly clear that this isn't the right account. The decision-maker might just have the sort

[27] Ross, 'Rejecting Ethical Deflationism', p. 763. It is also endorsed by Stefan Riedener ('Maximising Expected Value under Axiological Uncertainty') and by John Broome (private communication, June 2013).
[28] Sepielli, '"Along an Imperfectly Lighted Path"', p. 183.

of personality where she wouldn't be terribly disposed to blame, if some very demanding moral theories were true. Or it might be that she would be deeply depressed if one particular theory were true, and therefore her dispositions to do anything would be weaker than they ordinarily are. But these factors don't seem to affect how choice-worthiness differences compare across the different theories in which she has credence.

One might try to tweak Sepielli's account by claiming that choice-worthiness differences are measured by how disposed to blame one *ought* to be. But that account would suffer from problems as well. On utilitarianism, how disposed to blame one *ought* to be is not perfectly correlated (indeed, is sometimes highly uncorrelated) with the degree of wrongness of a particular action. So this account would misrepresent choice-worthiness differences according to utilitarianism.

Instead, the best account in this area, we think, is that choice-worthiness differences are measured by the degree to which is it *fitting* to blame for a certain action (or, as we will use the term, the degree to which an action is *blameworthy*). More precisely: $(CW_i(A) - CW_i(B)) = (CW_j(C) - CW_j(D))$ iff the blameworthiness of the decision-maker for doing B rather than A, conditional on T_i, is the same as the blameworthiness of the decision-maker for doing D rather than C, conditional on T_j. Note that, on this view, fittingness is a *metaethical* fact: on the assumption of a certain metaethics being true, the relationship between fittingness-to-blame and strengths of reasons is not something that different moral views can disagree about.

We think that this account has at least something going for it: in our discussion of amplified theories, we suggested that there is a link between the amplification of a theory and which attitudes it is fitting to have. The principal question, again, however, is whether choice-worthiness differences should be explained in terms of fitting attitudes, or the other way around. And this fitting-attitude account suffers from the following problem, which is that it cannot explain where interval-scale measurable degrees of blameworthiness come from.[29] It cannot, for example, use probabilities to provide the interval-scale measure. To do so would require making claims such as:

S is equally blameworthy for choosing (i) A and the guarantee that T_1 is true, as she is for choosing (ii) a 50% probability of B and T_2 being true, and a 50% probability of C and T_2 being true

[29] We owe this point to Riedener, 'Maximizing Expected Value under Axiological Uncertainty'.

(which would show that the difference in choice-worthiness between $T_2(B)$ and $T_1(A)$ is the same as the difference between $T_1(A)$ and $T_2(C)$). But if 'probability' in that sentence means objective chance, then it doesn't make any sense, because there can't be objective chances about which theories are true (except 1 and 0). If 'probability' means either 'subjective credence' or 'rational credence', then the account becomes extremely similar to Ross's 'facts about appropriateness' account, which, as we saw, got the order of explanation the wrong way around. So we don't think that this account is satisfactory, either.

VII. A Universal Scale Account

We believe that we can make progress on understanding intertheoretic comparisons by learning from work that has been done in the literature on the metaphysics of quantity. Indeed, we seem to be able ask very similar questions about intertheoretical comparisons of quantities and intertheoretical comparisons of choice-worthiness.

P1. Does physical theory P_1 assign greater mass to object x than P_2 does?

P2. Does physical theory P_1 assign twice as much mass to object x than P_2 does?

P3. Does P_1 assign a greater difference in mass to x and y than P_2 does?

T1. Does moral theory T_1 assign greater choice-worthiness to option A than T_2 does?

T2. Does moral theory T_1 assign twice as much choice-worthiness to option A as T_2 does?

T3. Does moral theory T_1 assign a greater difference in choice-worthiness to A and B than T_2 does?

If the questions about intertheoretical comparisons of mass (P1–P3) are meaningful, which they surely seem to be, why should we not say the same thing about the questions about the intertheoretical comparison of choice-worthiness (T1–T3)?

The debate around the metaphysics of quantity addresses questions such as: 'In virtue of what is this object more massive than this other object?' or 'In virtue of what is it true that this object is 2 kg and that object is 4 kg?' There are two classes of answers. Comparativists answer that it is the mass-relations ('x is more massive than y') that are fundamental, and claims about intrinsic mass properties ('x is 4 kg') are grounded in mass-relations. Absolutists answer that it is the intrinsic mass properties of objects that ground mass-relations. For absolutists, the fact that x is heavier than y is true in virtue of facts about the intrinsic properties of the objects themselves; for comparativists, it is the other way around.

Though work on the metaphysics of quantity has, so far, entirely focused on scientific quantities ('mass', 'size', 'temperature', etc), we can ask just the same questions about the metaphysics of quantities of value, or of choice-worthiness. We can ask: If it is true that the difference in choice-worthiness between A and B is twice as great as the difference in choice-worthiness between B and C, is that true in virtue of the fact that A, B and C each have an intrinsic property of a certain degree of choice-worthiness? Or is the metaphysical explanation the other way around? Moreover, in the same way as the possibility of amplified theories is a crucial issue in the debate concerning intertheoretic comparisons, the possibility of a world in which everything is identical except insofar as everything is twice as massive is a crucial issue in the debate between absolutists and comparativists.[30]

Within the metaphysics of quantities literature, it is generally recognized that absolutism is the more intuitive position.[31] Yet it seems to us that all the discussion of intertheoretic comparisons so far has assumed comparativism about quantities of value or choice-worthiness. If we reject that assumption, then we can provide a compelling metaphysical account of intertheoretic comparisons. In what follows, we'll first present the comparativist account of mass, then quickly sketch Mundy's elegant absolutist account of mass, then explain how something like this account could be applied to value and choice-worthiness.

The standard comparativist account of mass is to analyze mass in terms of the relation 'x is more massive than y', and the concatenation operator 'x and y are together equally as massive as z'. Three things are important to note about standard comparativist accounts. First, the account is first-order: the variables, x, y, and z are variables over *objects* (rather than over properties, which would make the account second-order). Second, for this reason, the account is nominalist: it gives an account of mass without any reference to the properties of objects. And, third, the account is empiricist: attempting

---

[30] Shamik Dasgupta, 'Absolutism vs Comparativism about Quantity', *Oxford Studies in Metaphysics*, vol. 8 (2013), pp. 105–48.
[31] See, for example, Shamik Dasgupta, 'Absolutism vs Comparativism about Quantity'.

to give an analysis of mass solely in terms of observable mass-relations. (So, for example, both '*x* is more massive than *y*' and '*x* and *y* are equally as massive as *z*' can be defined operationally, identifying them with the behavior of those objects on scales: *x* is more massive than *y* iff, when *x* and *y* are placed on opposite sides of the scale, the scale will tip in *x*'s direction; *x* and *y* are together equally as massive as *z* iff, when *x* and *y* are placed on one side of the scale, and *z* on the other side, then the scale will not tip in ether direction.) Using those two relations, and several axioms,[32] it can be shown that the '*x* is more massive than *y*' relation can be represented using numbers, where $M(x) > M(y)$ iff *x* is more massive than *y*, where the numerical representation is unique up to a similarity transformation ($f(x) = kx$).[33]

In contrast, Mundy's[34] account is second-order, defined over properties as well as objects. Letting *X* refer to the mass of *x* and *Y* refer to the mass of *y* (etc.), the fundamental mass relations, on Mundy's account, are '*X* is greater than *Y*' and '*X* and *Y* are equal to *Z*'. That is, the fundamental massrelations are defined over the mass-properties of objects, rather than over those objects themselves. It is therefore clearly realist rather than nominalist: it posits the existence of properties (which are abstract entities), over and above the existence of objects. And it is Platonist rather than empiricist, because properties are abstract entities that can exist without being instantiated. Using this framework, Mundy is able to give a full formal account of quantities of mass; he then argues that there are significant *empirical* reasons for preferring it to the traditional, first-order, comparativist accounts. In

---

[32] We will use the axiomatization given in Patrick Suppes and Joseph Zinnes, 'Basic Measurement Theory', in R. Duncan Luce, Robert R. Bush, and Eugene Galanter (eds), *Handbook of Mathematical Psychology*, New York: John Wiley & Sons, 1963, vol. 1, pp. 3–76. Let *A* be the set of all objects, and let '*Rxy*' mean '*x* is either less massive or equally as massive as y'. Let *x*°*y* refer to a binary operation from *A* x *A* to *A*: the 'concatenation' of *x* and *y* (where 'concatenation' of *x* and *y* may be defined as, for example, placing *x* and *y* on the same side of a scale). The axioms are as follows.

1. Transitivity: If *Rxy* and *Ryz*, then *Rxz*.
2. Associativity: $(x°y)°cRx°(y°c)$.
3. Monotonicity: If *Rxy* then $R(x°z)(z°y)$.
4. Restricted Solvability: If not *Rxy*, then there is a *z* such that $Rx(y°z)$ and $R(y°z)x$.
5. Positivity: Not *x*°*yRx*.
6. Archimedean: If *Rxy*, then there is a number *n* such that $Ry(nx)$ where the notation (nx) is defined recursively as follows: $1x = x$ and $nx = (n-1)x°x$.

As Suppes and Zines note, axiom 5 in conjunction with the order properties of *R* and the definition of ° imply that the set *A* is infinite.

[33] See David H. Krantz et al., *Foundations of Measurement*, New York: Academic Press, 1971, vol. 1.

[34] For Mundy's full account, see Brent Mundy, 'The Metaphysics of Quantity', *Philosophical Studies*, vol. 51, no. 1 (1987), pp. 29–54.

particular: in order to prove the representation theorem that mass is representable on a ratio-scale, the traditional comparativist account of mass needs to assume that, for any two objects, there is an actual third object that is equal in mass to those two objects. But the universe may well be finite, and if so then this assumption would be false. But it seems very plausible that objects have mass-quantities *whether or not* the universe is finite.

There is considerable debate between absolutists and comparativists. The key issue, however, when it comes to quantities of value or of choice-worthiness, is that absolutism about quantities of choice-worthiness can neatly solve the problem of intertheoretic choice-worthiness comparisons. And, going further, we can develop an analogue of Mundy's account and solve the intertheoretic comparisons problem by appeal to a *second order* universal scale, which measures primitive abstract degrees of choice-worthiness.

Consider the issue of whether there could be a world w_1, where all the relations between objects are the same as in world w_2, but where all objects are twice as massive in w_1 as they are in w_2. It is generally regarded as a problem for comparativism that it cannot make sense of the idea that w_1 and w_2 could be distinct worlds: the mass-relations between all objects in w_1 are the same as the mass-relations in w_2, so, according to comparativism, there is no difference between those two worlds. In contrast, absolutism is able to explain how those two worlds are distinct. Properties necessarily exist; so the two worlds differ in the intrinsic properties that objects in those two worlds instantiate. Note, also, that, if w_1 and w_2 are distinct worlds, then we have conclusive evidence for the existence of inter-world mass relations: we can say that object x in w_1 is twice as massive as it is in w_2.

Similarly, now, consider the issue of whether there could be two theories T_1 and T_2, where T_1 has the same interval-scale structure as T_2, but where the choice-worthiness differences between all options are twice as great on T_1 as they are on T_2. In our argument against structural accounts of inter-theoretic comparisons, we argued that this is a genuine possibility. But, if so, then we have a good argument against comparativism about choice-worthiness, according to which the only fundamental facts about choice-worthiness are facts about choice-worthiness relations between options. (One could try to explicate this idea in comparativist terms using Ross's universal scale account; but we saw that that account was unsatisfactory, getting the order of explanation the wrong way around.) In contrast, if we endorse absolutism about choice-worthiness, then we have an explanation for how T_1 and T_2 could be distinct theories. The same choice-worthiness quantities exist in many different epistemically possible worlds, so we can use them as the measuring rod to compare the choice-worthiness of A in the world in which T_1 is true and the choice-worthiness of A in the world in which T_2 is true. Moreover, we have an answer to the question of grounds: the choice-worthiness difference between A and B on T_1 is different from the difference in choice-worthiness between A and B on T_2 in virtue of the fact that A and B instantiate different intrinsic choice-worthiness quantities in the world in which T_1 is true than in the world in which T_2 is true.

In general, on the account we suggest, if it is true that $CW_i(A) - CW_i(B) = CW_j(C) - CW_j(D)$, then it is true in virtue of the fact that the difference in the magnitude of the property of choice-worthiness that A instantiates and the magnitude of the property of choice-worthiness that B instantiates, in the epistemically possible world in which T_i is true, is the same as the difference in the magnitude of the property of choice-worthiness that C instantiates and the magnitude of the property of choice-worthiness that D instantiates, in the epistemically possible world in which T_j is true. In fact, as long as we know to take the following second-order claim at face-value, rather than analyze it in comparativist terms, we can state this claim in very natural language, namely: if $CW_i(A) - CW_i(B) = CW_j(C) - CW_j(D)$ is true, then it is true in virtue of the fact that the difference between the choice-worthiness of A and the choice-worthiness of B, in the epistemically possible world in which T_i is true, is the same as the difference between the choice-worthiness of C and the choice-worthiness of D, in the epistemically possible world in which T_j is true.

Absolutism about choice-worthiness takes statements about choice-worthiness at face value: as ascribing an intrinsic property to an option. And once we allow the existence of necessarily existent choice-worthiness properties, then we have the resources to explain how intertheoretic comparisons are possible.[35] The absolutist about choice-worthiness mimics the

---

[35] One objection, raised to us by Christian Tarsney, is that there is a difficulty in moving from the fact that in the actual world, theories instantiate irreducibly monadic choice-worthiness properties to the conclusion that all moral theories in which the decision-maker has credence must be understood as committed to such properties. The former is a metaphysical claim; the latter a conceptual one. In other words: for our account to work, we need it to be the case that *all* the views in which the decision-maker has some credence must involve imputing irreducibly monadic choice-worthiness properties.

We believe that there are two ways in which one can respond to this worry. First, one could argue that the meaning of concepts like 'choice-worthiness' is determined by reference magnetism, and that theories that do not refer to such properties are simply changing the subject. However, though we find plausible the general idea that reference magnetism helps to determine the meaning of concepts, the claim that those with different metaethical views aren't even making coherent moral claims seems implausibly strong to us. So we prefer a second approach,

absolutist about mass in this respect: the absolutist about mass takes statements about the mass of objects at face value (as ascribing an intrinsic property of mass to an object), and then uses this to explain how inter-world mass relations are possible (as in the mass-doubled world case).

Before concluding this chapter, we note that it is not ad hoc to side with absolutism about choice-worthiness, rather than comparativism. This is for three reasons.

First, there are strong independent reasons that motivate absolutism. Not only can it explain intertheoretic comparisons of choice-worthiness, it can also explain other sorts of value-comparisons. For example, it can explain how we can make comparisons across *worlds*: we can understand 'x could have been better than x is' as saying that the value x has in the actual world is less than the value x has in some different possible world. Also, it can explain how we make comparisons of value across *time*: we understand 'x is better now than it used to be' as saying that the value x has now is greater than the value x used to have. Finally, it can explain comparisons of value between *mental attitudes* and the *world*: we understand 'x is better than I thought it was' as 'the value x has is greater than the value I thought x had'. These explanations are all intuitively simple. In contrast, it is unclear how the comparativist could offer equally intuitive and simple explanations of value-comparisons.

Second, we argued above that amplified theories are possible and that intertheoretic comparisons are clearly possible sometimes. Insofar as absolutism can give a natural and plausible explanation of that, whereas comparativism seemingly cannot, we have reason to prefer absolutism about choice-worthiness.

Third, the principal reason for rejecting absolutism about quantities of mass (and other scientific quantities) is a worry about needing to posit abstract entities such as properties in one's ontology. Whether or not this argument is successful in general, it is considerably weaker in the case at hand. In Chapter 7, we argue that moral uncertainty is inconsistent with non-cognitivism and, for the purpose of the project in this book, we must assume that error theory is false (otherwise there would be no subject matter for us

which is to distinguish metaethical uncertainty and normative uncertainty. Our account of how to make intertheoretic comparisons makes sense conditional on a particular metaethical view. We do not take ourselves to give an account of how to make intertheoretic comparisons across all metaethical views. In particular, insofar as the decision-maker should retain some credence in comparativism about choice-worthiness, any moral theories that are conditional on the comparativist view may be incomparable with moral theories that are conditional on absolutist views.

to investigate). That leaves us with some form of moral realism. And if we believe moral realism, then, though not an inconsistent combination of views, it certainly seems like an *odd* combination of views to be happy with the existence of moral facts, but to be sceptical of the existence of moral properties.[36]

VIII. The Metaphysical and Epistemic Questions

Once we have accepted that the correct account of intertheoretic comparisons is non-structural, the problem of intertheoretic comparisons divides into two problems. The *metaphysical* problem is about what *grounds* intertheoretic comparisons.[37] That is: in virtue of what are intertheoretic comparisons true, when they are true? As we have argued, we think that the relations between abstract quantitative choice-worthiness properties ground intertheoretic comparisons.

But there is a further problem to be resolved. This is the *epistemic* problem: how can we tell which intertheoretic comparisons are true, and which are false?

Answering the first problem tells us about the nature of intertheoretic comparisons—what makes intertheoretic comparisons true. Answering the second problem would enable us, at least to some extent, to more confidently make intertheoretic comparisons: to more confidently know how two theories compare, when they do compare; and to more confidently know whether two theories are comparable at all.

In response to the epistemic problem, our view is rather deflationary. Because we endorse a universal scale account, we believe that, for any theory T_1 and for any real number k, we can make sense of another theory T_2 whose

---

[36] An additional objection, given to us by Christian Tarsney, is whether, on our view, it is possible to have an amplified credence distribution: that is, whether it is possible for there to be two decision-makers, D_1 and D_2, that have all the same credences in all the same moral theories and intertheoretic comparison claims, except that all theories in which D_1 has credence are amplified versions of the theories in which D_2 has credence. If this is possible, it seems we then get into trouble—we now have to choose between an infinite number of credence distributions, and whichever one we pick we are basically guaranteed to be wrong.

We accept that amplified credence distributions are indeed a possibility on our account. Our response, here, is to appeal to a very weak form of reference magnetism: of all the possible amplifications of her credence distribution that she could have, the credence distribution she actually has is determined by what choice-worthiness properties are instantiated in the actual world. This is also what guarantees that at least some of her beliefs are (at least approximately) true.

[37] For discussion of the idea of grounding, see Kit Fine, 'Guide to Ground', in Fabrice Correia and Benjamin Schnieder (eds), *Metaphysical Grounding: Understanding the Structure of Reality*, Cambridge: Cambridge University Press, 2012, pp. 37–80.

choice-worthiness function is k times that of theory T_1. That is: every possible amplification of T_1 is itself a distinct theory. So when we ask: 'How, if at all, do utilitarianism and this rights-based non-consequentialist theory compare?' we're really asking: 'Which, of the infinitely many different theories that have the same interval-scale structure as utilitarianism, and which, of the infinitely many different rights-based non-consequentialist theories, should we have most credence in?'

This means that the 'epistemic question' of which intertheoretic comparisons are true is really a question about how we ought to apportion our credences across different amplifications of a given class of equivalent interval-scale theories. And we believe that the methodology for answering that should be approximately the same as the methodology for first-order normative ethics in general: relying on intuitions about particular cases and appealing to more theoretical arguments.

To take an earlier example, consider Sophie, who initially believed partialist utilitarianism, but then became unsure between that view and the view according to which all persons have equal moral weight. The question about how to make intertheoretic comparisons between those two views reduced to the question of which, of all infinitely many theories within the class of classical utilitarian theories (including what we called kinship utilitarianism and Benthamite utilitarianism) she should come to have credence in. If she was moved to classical utilitarianism because it is a simpler theory, then it seems plausible that she should come to have most credence in Benthamite utilitarianism. If she was moved to classical utilitarianism by reflecting on the fact that there is a deep arbitrariness in whom she happens to have special relationships with, then it seems plausible that she should come to have most credence in kinship utilitarianism. Either way, we can explain why, as is intuitive, she should come to have most credence in one of those theories, rather than a different theory (according to which, perhaps, the value of distant strangers' welfare is 1 million times as great as it is on the partialist theory). Basic epistemic conservatism suggests that she should alter her beliefs as little as possible in order to accommodate new evidence (in this case, new arguments). Having partial belief in partialist utilitarianism, and partial belief in anything other than kinship or Benthamite utilitarianism, would be oddly incoherent.

If the account we have given is correct, this is an exciting development for first-order normative ethics. Moral theories, when they have been given, have really been *classes* of moral theories. And different views within this class can me more or less plausible than other views within this class. So there may be scope to revisit old ethical theories, and assess which specific versions of those theories are most plausible.[38]

Conclusion

In this chapter, we have argued against both sceptics and structuralists. Sceptics cannot account for the fact that we have intuitions about intertheoretic comparisons in many cases, and they have not provided a compelling general argument for their view. Structuralists cannot account for the ways in which aspects of theories other than their choice-worthiness functions seem to make a difference to how those theories should be normalized. We should therefore look for a theory of intertheoretic comparisons within the class of non-structural accounts. We defended an account analogous to Mundy's account of the metaphysics of natural quantities, arguing that intertheoretic comparisons are meaningful because of the relations between quantitative choice-worthiness properties.

Having completed our discussion of informational issues arising for MEC, let us next turn to two potential problems for our account.

---

[38] For example, Frances Kamm and Thomas Nagel claim that utilitarianism is implausible because it does not posit the existence of rights, and therefore that humans do not possess the value of dignity that can only be conferred by the possession of rights (Frances Kamm, 'Non-Consequentialism, the Person as an End-in-Itself, and the Significance of Status', *Philosophy & Public Affairs*, vol. 21, no. 4 (Autumn 1992), pp. 354–89; Thomas Nagel, 'The Value of Inviolability', in Paul Bloomfield (ed.), *Morality and Self-Interest*, New York: Oxford University Press, 2008, pp. 102–16). But neither Kamm nor Nagel distinguish between two different versions of utilitarianism. According to the first, no one has any rights, and so humans are indeed of less value. According to the second, people do have rights not to be killed (for example), but they also have equally strong rights to be saved. Both have the same interval-scale structure. But, according to the latter form of utilitarianism, humans *do* have the value of dignity that can only be conferred by having rights. So Kamm's and Nagel's argument would not go through. See Shelly Kagan, *The Limits of Morality*, Oxford: Oxford University Press, 1989, ch. 3.

6

Fanaticism and Incomparability

Introduction

In this chapter, we discuss two further problems that face accounts of decision-making under moral uncertainty, and are particularly pressing for theories that involve maximizing expected choice-worthiness.

In section I, we address the 'fanaticism' problem—that the expected choice-worthiness of options might be primarily determined by tiny credences in theories that posit huge amounts of value. In section II, we consider the 'infectious incomparability' problem—that any credence in theories with radical incomparability might render the expected choice-worthiness of almost every option undefined.

I. Fanaticism

One might worry that our account will result in *fanaticism*: that is, the expected choice-worthiness will be dominated by theories according to which most moral situations are incredibly high stakes.[1] Consider the following case.

Doug's Lie

Doug is uncertain between two moral theories: utilitarianism, and an absolutist form of non-consequentialism. Doug has the option to tell a lie, and, in doing so, to mildly harm another person, in order to save the lives of ten people. For utilitarianism, the difference in choice-worthiness between saving ten people and saving none, all other things being equal, is 10. The difference in choice-worthiness between doing nothing and telling a lie, all other things being equal is 0.01. Absolutism agrees that it is choiceworthy to

[1] This problem was first raised by Ross, 'Rejecting Ethical Deflationism', p. 765.

Moral Uncertainty. William MacAskill, Krister Bykvist and Toby Ord, Oxford University Press (2020).
© William MacAskill, Krister Bykvist and Toby Ord.
DOI: 10.1093/oso/9780198722274.001.0001

save lives, and that it's more choiceworthy to save more lives. However, according to the absolutist, telling a lie is absolutely wrong, such that it is never permissible to tell a lie, no matter how grave the consequences. Doug is almost certain that utilitarianism is correct, but has a very small credence that the absolutist view is true.

In the above case, it seems obvious, intuitively, that it's appropriate for Doug to lie: he's almost certain both that it's the right thing to do, and that it's extremely important that he tells the lie. But, so the objection goes, this is not what MEC would recommend.

According to this objection, the most natural way to represent the absolutist theory decision-theoretically is to say that the wrong of telling a lie has infinite severity according to absolutism. If so, then, no matter how small Doug's credence is in absolutism, then the expected choice-worthiness of telling a lie is less than that of refraining from telling a lie. That is, the decision-situation looks as in Table 6.1.

If so, then, no matter how small Doug's credence is in absolutism, the expected choice-worthiness of telling a lie is less than that of refraining from telling a lie, and so refraining from lying is the appropriate option. But this seems like an absurd conclusion.

We'll consider two responses that Jacob Ross makes to this problem but then reject them and give our own response. Ross's first response is to bite the bullet, that is: 'to endorse the Pascalian conclusion, however counterintuitive it may seem at first.'[2] His second response is to suggest that one should not have a non-infinitesimal credence in fanatical theories:

If, therefore, one is subject to rational criticism in this case, it is not in choosing to accept [a fanatical theory] but rather in having a positive, non-infinitesimal degree of credence in a theory that is so fanatical that its

Table 6.1

	Utilitarianism—99%	Absolutism—1%
Lie	+9.99	$-\infty$
Don't lie	0	0

[2] Ross, 'Rejecting Ethical Deflationism', p. 766.

contribution to the expected values of one's options swamps that of all other theories.[3]

We cannot endorse either of these responses. Regarding the second, it is deeply implausible to claim that one should have zero credence or infinitesimal credence in any fanatical theories. We believe that absolutist theories are incorrect, but they are not so implausible as to warrant credence 0. On the standard understanding of credences,[4] to have credence 0 in a proposition is to be certain that one could never gain any evidence that would change one's view away from credence 0. But we can clearly imagine such evidence. For example, if all our intellectual peers came to believe in absolutism after lengthy philosophical reflection, we would have reason to have positive credence in absolutism. Or if we discovered that there is a God, and His booming voice told us that absolutism is true, that would also provide evidence for absolutism. Nor, we think, does the idea of merely infinitesimal credence fare much better. First, doing so requires departing from standard Bayesianism, according to which a credence function maps onto real numbers (which does not include infinitesimals).[5] But, second, even if we allow the possibility of rational infinitesimal credences, it seems overconfident to have such a low credence in absolutist views, despite the testimony of, for example, Kant and Anscombe, on at least some interpretations of their views. And if it's true that even some decision-makers should rationally have very small but non-infinitesimal credences in absolutist theories, then the fanaticism problem still looms large.

Regarding Ross's first response, the fanaticism problem does not merely generate grossly counterintuitive results in cases like *Doug's Lie*. Rather, it simply *breaks* MEC. In any real-life variant of *Doug's Lie*, Doug should have some non-zero credence in a view according to which it's absolutely wrong not to save those lives. In which case, the expected choice-worthiness of not lying is also negative infinity. And this will be true for any decision a real-life decision-maker faces. For any option, the decision-maker will always have some non-zero credence in a theory according to which that

[3] Ross, 'Rejecting Ethical Deflationism', p. 767.

[4] Though see Alan Hájek, 'What Conditional Probability Could Not Be', *Synthese*, vol. 137, no. 3 (December 2003), pp. 273–323 for arguments against the standard view.

[5] For arguments against using hyperreals in our models of credences, see Kenny Easwaran, 'Regularity and Hyperreal Credences', *The Philosophical Review*, vol. 123, no. 1 (January 2014), pp. 1–41. For discussion of how invoking infinitesimals fails to help with the 'fanaticism' problem within decision theory under empirical uncertainty, see Hájek, 'Waging War on Pascal's Wager'.

option is infinitely wrong, and some non-zero credence in a theory according to which that option is infinitely right. If an option has some probability of an infinitely bad outcome, and some probability of an infinitely good outcome, then the overall expected choice-worthiness of that option will be undefined.[6] Insofar as this is true for all options that we ever face, it means that MEC is never able to recommend one option as more appropriate than another.

A better response is simply to note that this problem arises under empirical uncertainty as well as under moral uncertainty. One should not give 0 credence to the idea that an infinitely good heaven exists, which one can enter only if one goes to church; or that it will be possible in the future through science to produce infinitely or astronomically good outcomes. This is a tricky issue within decision theory and, in our view, no wholly satisfactory solution has been provided.[7] But it is not a problem that is unique to moral uncertainty. And we believe whatever is the best solution to the fanaticism problem under empirical uncertainty is likely to be the best solution to the fanaticism problem under moral uncertainty. This means that this issue is not a distinctive problem for moral uncertainty.

This is our primary response to the objection. However, there are, we think, two more moral uncertainty-specific things that one can say on this issue, so we briefly mention them before moving on. They both pertain to how to make comparisons of magnitudes of choice-worthiness across theories.

First, one could argue that, really, we should not understand absolutist theories as giving a quantitative measure of choice-worthiness. Instead, we should understand them as merely ordinal theories: they provide a ranking of options in terms of choice-worthiness but there is no meaning to the idea of *how much* more choiceworthy one option is than another. Absolutist theories would always rank any option that involves lying as less choiceworthy than any option that involves violating no side-constraints, but there would be no meaning to the idea that lying is 'much' more wrong than failing to save lives; there is no ratio of the difference in choice-worthiness between

[6] For further discussion of the problems that infinite amounts of value pose for decision-theory, see Hájek, 'Waging War on Pascal's Wager'.
[7] The standard response is to endorse prudential and moral theories whose choice-worthiness functions are bounded above and below. But this idea has severe problems of its own: making the choice-worthiness of decisions oddly dependent on facts about the past, and making bizarre recommendations when the decision-maker is close to the bound. For discussion, see Nick Beckstead, 'Recklessness, Timidity and Fanaticism', unpublished MS.

telling a lie and doing nothing and the difference in choice-worthiness between doing nothing and saving ten lives.

If so, then in accordance with the account we have defended in previous chapters, we would use the Borda Rule to aggregate our uncertainty over these theories. And if we do this, then absolutist theories would not swamp our decision-making. Our second response is that, even if one does suppose that absolutism is best represented as assigning an infinite severity of wrongness to lying, we think that the fanaticism problem is not as bad as it seems. Instead of holding that the theories agree on the choice-worthiness of saving a life, we could hold that they agree on the choice-worthiness of lying. This is still compatible with absolutism's claim that not lying is infinitely more important than saving a life, since it could treat saving a life as having a relatively infinitesimal effect on choice-worthiness—merely breaking ties in cases where the number of lies the agent told is equal. If so, then on MEC the appropriate option for Doug is to lie.[8]

Admittedly, the first way of making the intertheoretic comparison seems intuitively more plausible to us. But we're not certain that that's true. So a decision-maker like Doug should split his credence between the two different ways of making the intertheoretic comparison, giving higher credence to the one that seems more intuitively plausible. This can be spelled out more precisely, representing a theory with two kinds of choice-worthiness as a pair (c_1, c_2) in which the first element is given lexical priority, and representing the credence in the two types of normalization as credence in two types of utilitarianism: one where the choice-worthiness of promoting pleasure is treated as c_1 and one where it is treated as c_2. If so, then Doug would have uncertainty over absolutism and two different normalizations of utilitarianism, as in Table 6.2.

Utilitarianism-1 is the normalization of utilitarianism that agrees with absolutism about the magnitude of the choice-worthiness of saving a life. Utilitarianism-2 is the normalization of utilitarianism that agrees with absolutism about the magnitude of the choice-worthiness of refraining from telling a lie. If Doug is uncertain over these two different normalizations of utilitarianism, then as long as Doug has at least one-99th as much credence in Utilitarianism-2 as he has in absolutism, MEC would recommend lying.

---

[8] Christian Tarsney points out that there is a question of how this discussion interacts with the universal scale account that we defend in the previous chapter. Insofar as the idea that choice-worthiness is multidimensional is incompatible with the particular account of choice-worthiness properties that we defend in our universal scale account, we have to note that this discussion makes sense only conditional on some other metaethical view (such as that there are absolute choice-worthiness properties, but that they are multidimensional).

Table 6.2

	Utilitarianism–1	Utilitarianism–2	Absolutism—1%
Lie	(0, 9.9)	(99, 0)	(−1, 10)
Don't lie	(0, 0)	(0, 0)	(0, 0)

Taking into account uncertainty about how to normalize across theories therefore seems to get reasonably intuitive conclusions concerning what it is appropriate for one to do in real-life cases even when one has credence in what is seems initially to be a 'fanatical' moral theory.

II. Infectious Incomparability

In this book, we are largely putting aside the issue of theories that have incomplete choice-worthiness orderings. However, one might worry that in doing so we have dodged a potentially devastating problem by mere stipulation. So in this section we consider the question of whether allowing theories that posit incomparability between values, and which therefore have incomplete choice-worthiness orderings, poses an insurmountable problem for theories of decision-making under moral uncertainty.

In particular, we recast and develop further an argument taken from MacAskill, as follows.[9] We can divide cases of incomparability into *mild* incomparability and *radical* incomparability. In cases of mild incomparability, one can sometimes (but only sometimes) make trade-offs between two different types of values. For example, perhaps you have two career paths open to you: you could be a clarinetist, or a philosopher.[10] On the mild incomparability views, sometimes you can make trade-offs: if you have the option to become an outstanding clarinetist or a mediocre philosopher, then it's more choiceworthy to become the clarinetist. But, other times, such as if you have the option to become an excellent clarinetist or an excellent philosopher, there is simply no choice-worthiness relation between your

---

[9] William MacAskill, 'The Infectiousness of Nihilism', *Ethics*, vol. 123, no. 3 (April 2013), pp. 508–20.
[10] We take this example from Joseph Raz, *The Morality of Freedom*, Oxford: Clarendon Press, 1986, p. 332.

options: it's neither equally as choiceworthy to become the clarinetist or the philosopher, nor is one option more choiceworthy than the other.[11]

Views that posit mild incomparability are reasonably plausible. However, we think they are unlikely to pose a grave problem for theories of decision-making under moral uncertainty. They require that we develop an account in cases of decision-making in conditions of uncertainty and incomparability; but it seems likely that one can do this in a fairly natural way. Work has already been done on this problem by Caspar Hare, for example.[12] One way of extending MEC to account for incomparability would be to claim that:

> (i) A is more appropriate than B iff A has greater expected choice-worthiness than B on all coherent completions of every moral theory in which the decision-maker has credence. (Where a choice-worthiness function CW'_i is a *coherent completion* of a moral theory T_i iff for all A, B, if A is at least as choiceworthy as B according to T_i, then $CW'_i(A) \geq CW'_i(B)$, and where the resulting choice-worthiness function has ordinal significance if the theory that is completed is ordinal, and cardinal significance if the theory that is completed is cardinal, and so on.)
>
> (ii) A is equally as appropriate as B iff A and B have equal expected choice-worthiness on all coherent completions of every moral theory in which the decision-maker has credence.

Let us call this the *coherent completion* account. If we took this approach, the effect will be that, given some credence in theories that posit mild incomparability, some pairs of options will be neither equally appropriate nor will one be more appropriate than the other, but most of the time (given a reasonable credence distribution) one option will be more appropriate than the other. That's a result that we can live with.

Theories that posit radical incomparability, however, are different. On these views, for some pairs of values (such as esthetic and prudential value) there are *no* trade-offs that can be made between those two types of values: any time that one option A increases one value by more than B does and B increases the other value by more than A does, then there is no positive

[11] Ruth Chang (ed.), *Incommensurability, Incomparability, and Practical Reason*, Cambridge, MA: Harvard University Press, 1997.

[12] See Caspar Hare, 'Take the Sugar', *Analysis*, vol. 70, no. 2 (April 2010), pp. 237–47; Riedener, 'Maximising Expected Value under Axiological Uncertainty'.

choice-worthiness relation between these two options. On many such views, there are very few positive choice-worthiness relations between options because almost all important moral decisions involve trade-offs between different types of value. This is what MacAskill calls the *infectious incomparability* problem.[13]

Views that posit radical incomparability aren't plausible, in our view. However, they are certainly epistemic possibilities, so we should assign some positive credence to them. But now suppose we try to use the coherent completion account. Because there are so few positive choice-worthiness relations, the range of possible coherent completions of a theory that posits radical incomparability is vast. This means that on our account, there will be almost no pairs of options where all the completions agree, which would be necessary for a positive appropriateness relation.

To see this, consider an example. Suppose that the decision-maker has credence in two moral views. First, she is 99.99% certain of utilitarianism. Second, she has 0.01% credence in a radical incomparabilist view on which there is no fact of the matter about how wellbeing compares between any two people; the only instances where option A is at least as choiceworthy than option B is where A is better for some people than B and worse for no one. And suppose, further, that the decision-maker is certain that there is no intertheoretic comparability between those two views. The decision-maker has the option to save one hundred lives, or to prevent the headache of a different person. On utilitarianism, let us suppose the ratio of choice-worthiness differences between A and B and B and C is 1,000,000:1. On the radical incomparabilist view A and B are incomparable in value. We can represent this as in Table 6.3.

Table 6.3

	Utilitarianism —99.99%	Radical Incomparabilism —0.01%
A: Save one hundred lives	1,000,000	Maximally choiceworthy
B: Prevent one (different person's) headache	1	Maximally choiceworthy
C: Do nothing	0	0

---

[13] William MacAskill, 'The Infectiousness of Nihilism,' *Ethics*, vol. 123, no. 3 (April, 2013), pp. 508–20.

Clearly, the intuitively appropriate option is A. However, if we use the coherent completion approach, we must conclude that A and B stand in no positive appropriateness relation with each other. Any numbers can represent a coherent completion of the choice-worthiness relationship between A and B. On one coherent completion of the radical incomparabilist view, B is given choice-worthiness 1 trillion and A is given choice-worthiness 1 (which would make the expected choice-worthiness of B greater than that of A).

Our response to this problem is to point out that the argument above relies on the assumption that we can make an intertheoretic comparison between the coherent completions of the incomparabilist moral views and the other views in which the decision-maker has credence. In the example just given, we implicitly considered all possible completions of interpersonal incomparabilism *and all possible intertheoretic comparisons*. But this is not the natural way of doing things. There's no reason that we should treat the coherent completions of interpersonal incomparabilism as comparable with utilitarianism. After all, if there is rampant incomparability *within* the theory, why should we act as if there were comparability *between* it and other theories?

If, instead, we treat the coherent completions of the interpersonal incomparabilist view as incomparable with the utilitarian view, then we do not get the same infectious incomparability problem. For the purposes of working out the expected choice-worthiness of different options, we would normalize the coherent completions of infectious incomparabilism with utilitarianism at the variance of the two theories' choice-worthiness functions (which is, we argued in the last chapter, how we should in general handle theories that are incomparable with each other). If this is how we do things, then the incomparability that the theory posits is not perniciously infectious. In the above case, if we normalize the two choice-worthiness functions at their variance, there is no coherent completion of interpersonal incomparabilism such that B has a greater expected value than A.[14]

---

[14] To see this, consider the coherent completion of radical incomparabilism that disagrees most strongly with utilitarianism. On this coherent completion, the choice-worthiness of A is epsilon greater than 0, whereas the choice-worthiness of B is 1. In which case, the mean of radical incomparabilism's choice-worthiness function is ~1/3 and the variance is ~2/9. Next, consider utilitarianism. Because the unit is arbitrary, we can divide the choice-worthiness values given in table 6.3 by 1,000,000 for convenience. After doing this, the mean of utilitarianism's choice-worthiness function is ~1/3 and the variance is ~2/9.

Given variance normalization, the difference in choice-worthiness between A and B on utilitarianism is therefore approximately the same as the difference in choice-worthiness between B

So our account would get the correct answer: that *A* is the most appropriate option.[15]

Conclusion

In this chapter, we discussed the fanaticism and infectious incomparability objections to accounts of decision-making under moral uncertainty. While we do not claim to have completely resolved them, we think we have showed that neither of them look like insuperable problems for our account. So let us now turn to some implications of our account of moral uncertainty.

and *A* on radical incomparabilism, on the coherent completion we're considering. Because utilitarianism has a much higher credence assigned to it, *A* will be the option with the highest expected value. Because we considered the coherent completion of radical incomparabilism that disagreed most strongly with utilitarianism, we can therefore see that under variance normalization, *A* will be the option with the highest expected choice-worthiness under all coherent completions of radical incomparabilism.

[15] Christian Tarsney gave us the following objection to our account. Consider two theories: T_1, which is classical hedonistic utilitarianism, and T_2, which is a theory that posits both hedonic and esthetic value but holds that these two kinds of value are absolutely incomparable. Intuitively, it seems that these two views should agree on the hedonic value. So our view that we should treat these views as entirely incomparable cannot be correct.

In response, we're not wholly convinced that it is wrong to treat these views as incomparable. But, if one does find this unintuitive, there is another response one can give. In Chapter 4 we argued that the right way to make rational decisions in the face of incomparability between theories is by treating the theories as agreeing on their variance. We could broaden this account, and use it as a way of making decisions in the face of radical in comparability in general. On this view, if a theory has two value-bearers *X* and *Y* that are absolutely incomparable, then our account would, for the purposes of rational decision-making, normalize those two value-functions at their variance. If so done, then we could make the intuitive intertheoretic comparison between T_1 and T_2 above, without getting into problems with radical incomparability.

7

Metaethical Implications

Cognitivism versus Non-Cognitivism

Introduction

So far, our discussion has almost entirely been focused on normative issues, about what is morally choiceworthy and what is appropriate to do in the face of moral uncertainty; apart from our discussion of metaethical nihilism in the previous chapter, we have not discussed issues of metaethics. In this chapter, however, we will show that moral uncertainty creates a challenge for another metaethical view, namely, non-cognitivism, according to which moral judgements are desires, or some other desire-like states, rather than beliefs. We will show that it is surprisingly difficult, though perhaps not impossible, for non-cognitivists to accommodate moral uncertainty.

Now, one could of course turn this argument on its head and say the fact that non-cognitivism cannot accommodate moral uncertainty (if it is a fact) shows that there is no such thing as moral uncertainty. This would be an incredible thing to say, however, since it seems so obvious that we can be uncertain about fundamental moral matters—just recall the intuitive examples we gave in Chapter 1. Furthermore, the leading non-cognitivists of today agree that it is important to accommodate fundamental moral uncertainty in a way that does not force them to give up on mundane facts such as that we can be more or less certain that an action is right (including the possibility that one can be fully certain that an action is right), and that we can be less certain that an action is right than that some non-moral proposition is true.[1] Indeed, they think it is important to 'earn the right' to other realist-sounding notions as well, such as 'truth', 'fact', and 'evidence',

---

[1] See, for instance, James Lenman, 'Non-Cognitivism and the Dimensions of Evaluative Judgement', Brown Electronic Article Review Service, 15 March 2003. http://www.brown.edu/Departments/Philosophy/bears/homepage.html; Michael Ridge, 'Ecumenical Expressivism: The Best of Both Worlds?', *Oxford Studies in Metaethics*, vol. 2 (2007), pp. 51–77; Simon Blackburn, 'Dilemmas: Dithering, Plumping, and Grief', in H. E. Mason (ed.), *Moral Dilemmas and Moral Theory*, Oxford: Oxford University Press, 1996, pp. 127–39.

Moral Uncertainty. William MacAskill, Krister Bykvist and Toby Ord, Oxford University Press (2020).
© William MacAskill, Krister Bykvist and Toby Ord.
DOI: 10.1093/oso/9780198722274.001.0001

THE CHALLENGE FOR NON-COGNITIVISM

since these notions permeate ordinary moral talk. So we do not think we are stacking the cards against non-cognitivism by assuming that fundamental moral uncertainty is a fact that needs to be accommodated by any plausible metaethical theory.

I. The Challenge for Non-cognitivism

According to a simple form of non-cognitivism, to make a moral judgement is to express a desire (a non-cognitive attitude) rather than a belief (a cognitive attitude). As we pointed out above, there is general agreement even among non-cognitivists that a metaethical theory needs to explain (and not explain away) fundamental moral uncertainty. Since moral uncertainty involves having some degree of certainty, less than full, in a moral judgement, one cannot accommodate moral uncertainty without accommodating degrees of certainty (call this *certitude*). So, non-cognitivists need to be able to give an account of degrees of moral certainty.

Another feature in need of explanation is the uncontroversial fact that we can ascribe degrees of value or normative importance to states of affairs or actions (call this *importance*). The challenge for non-cognitivism is that desires seem to have too little structure to account for both certitude and importance, where certitude is assumed to obey at least some of the axioms of probability theory. If certitude is identified with degrees of desire strength (so that the stronger the expressed desire is, the more certain you are about the moral judgement), then there is nothing left to explain importance. On the other hand, if importance is identified with degrees of desire strength (so that the stronger the expressed desire is, the more value or importance is ascribed to the act or state of affairs), then there is nothing left to explain certitude. Of course, this would not be a problem if certitude and importance always co-varied, but that is not true. One might, for example, invest *low* certitude in the belief that leading an autonomous life is of *great* intrinsic value and a *great* degree of certitude in the belief that experiencing bodily pleasure is of *moderate* intrinsic value. Similarly, one might have *low* certitude in the belief that one has a *strong* reason to save a stranger's two children at the cost of the life of one's own child and *high* certitude in the belief that one has a *weak* reason to satisfy one's whims.[2]

---

[2] This way of stating the problem for non-cognitivists is found in Michael Smith, 'Evaluation, Uncertainty, and Motivation', *Ethical Theory and Moral Practice*, vol. 5 no. 3

Obviously, the cognitivist, who identifies moral judgements with beliefs, has no problem capturing these cases. Degrees of moral judgements are simply degrees of beliefs and the degree of belief in a moral proposition can vary independently from the degree of moral importance ascribed to an action or a state of affairs. But for the non-cognitivist it is a real challenge.

The non-cognitivist could try to break out of this dilemma by identifying degrees of certitude with the degree to which one is insensitive to new information and reflection, so the less one is prone to change one's expressed desires in light of new information and reflection, the more certain one is about one's moral judgements. But this would be to conflate certitude with *robustness*. One can have high certitude in a moral judgement that is not robust. Just think of someone who vacillates between strong moral opinions depending on which newspaper she reads and which TV programme she watches. Or think about someone who starts off with very low credence in a moral judgement she has not seen much evidence for, e.g. that insects have moral rights. When more information comes in, she may retain the same low level of certainty in this judgement, i.e. the same high level of certainty in the judgement that insects do not have rights, even though the robustness of her judgement that they do not have rights increases.

The challenge to account for moral uncertainty also spells trouble for non-cognitivists who think that moral judgements express intention-like states, such as plans. Since it is doubtful that intentions or plans come in degrees, it seems *prima facie* difficult to account for certitude and importance.[3] The challenge is thus relevant to Gibbard's recent account, according to which judging that one ought, all things considered, to do something is to plan to do it.[4] The challenge is thus relevant to a wide family of non-cognitivist views.

A possible non-cognitivist rejoinder is to represent importance in terms of first-order attitudes and certitude in terms of *second-order* attitudes. This version of non-cognitivism says that a moral judgement that some action type, φ, is right expresses a second order desire—a desire to desire to φ. For instance, when Mary judges that she has a reason to keep her promises, she

---

(September 2002), pp. 305–20. In fact, the argument was broached a decade earlier in a textbook by Lars Bergström (*Grundbok i värdeteori*, Stockholm: Thales, 1990, pp. 35f).

[3] At least this seems so for *all-out* intentions that constitute decisions to act, which is the relevant notion of intention for an account of all things considered judgements of moral rightness. For the notion of partial intentions that function as inputs for decisions, see Richard Holton, 'Partial Belief, Partial Intention', *Mind*, vol. 117 (2008), pp. 27–58.

[4] Allan Gibbard, *Thinking How to Live*, Cambridge, MA: Harvard University Press, 2003.

expresses a desire to desire that she keeps her promises. The strength of the first-order desire could be taken to represent importance. So the more strongly Mary desires to keep her promises, the more important she considers it to keep her promises. The strength of the second-order desire, on the other hand, represents her degree of certitude in the claim that that keeping her promises is right. So the more strongly she desires to desire to keep her promises, the more certain she is that it would be right for her to keep her promises. This proposal, which we might call the *attitudinal ladder proposal*, faces several objections.

First, the attitudinal ladder proposal is plagued by arbitrariness: what is the rationale for representing importance in terms of the strength of the relevant first-order desire and certitude in terms of the strength of the relevant second-order desire rather than the other way around?[5]

Second, unlike degree of belief, desire-strength does not come in a neat interval with a clearly defined minimum and maximum. Certitude can vary from complete uncertainty (credence 0) to complete certainty (credence 1), but there is no obvious analogy for desire strength. Complete indifference might be seen as the weakest possible desire, but what is it to *completely* desire (to desire) something? As we shall see, this problem recurs for other forms of non-cognitivism to be considered below.

A final problem for the attitudinal ladder proposal is that strengths of second-order attitudes and moral certitude may come apart. According to the attitudinal ladder proposal, the stronger Mary desires to desire to φ, the more certain she is that she has reason to φ. But it seems possible that there are cases in which Mary desires to desire to φ without being at all certain that she has reason to φ. Think of a case where an evil demon threatens to harm your family if you do not desire always to keep your promises. The demon does not care about whether you actually keep all your promises; he cares only about whether you desire to do so. In this case, you may well strongly desire to have the desire that you keep all your promises while you lack certainty that you actually have reason to keep all your promises.

II. Ecumenical Non-cognitivism

It has recently become popular to argue that *ecumenical* non-cognitivism is the version of non-cognitivism that is best equipped to meet the challenge

---

[5] Smith, 'Evaluation, Uncertainty, and Motivation', p. 318.

of moral uncertainty and thus to accommodate both certitude and importance. As the label suggests, ecumenical non-cognitivism is a hybrid view
that incorporates both cognitivist and non-cognitivist components. It inherits
from traditional non-cognitivism the idea that moral judgements express
desires and it inherits from cognitivism the view that moral judgements
express beliefs.[6] What makes it an ecumenical version of non-cognitivism
rather than an ecumenical version of cognitivism is that the contents of the
beliefs expressed in moral judgements do not provide truth conditions of
moral judgements and sentences.[7]

More specifically, the idea is that a moral judgement concerning, e.g. the
rightness of an action expresses (1) a general desire for actions insofar as
they have a certain natural property; and (2) a belief that the particular
action in question has that property. The belief component thus makes
direct reference back to the property mentioned in the desire component.[8]

According to the simplest version of ecumenical non-cognitivism, what
the property in question is depends on the first-order moral view endorsed
by the speaker. To give a simple example, a utilitarian who endorses the
judgement that sticking to a vegetarian diet is morally right expresses
approval of actions insofar as they tend to maximize overall happiness and
a belief that sticking to a vegetarian diet has *that property*, i.e. the property
of tending to maximize overall happiness. The sentence 'Sticking to a vegetarian diet is morally right' lacks truth-value, since the expressed belief is
not assumed to provide the truth-conditions for this sentence.

Since ecumenical non-cognitivists claim that moral judgements express
both desires and beliefs, they seem to be in a better position to accommodate both importance and certitude. One obvious solution is to say that
certitude is represented by the strength of the *belief* expressed by a moral
judgement. So, one's certitude that sticking to a vegetarian diet is morally
right is identified with the degree of one's belief that sticking to a vegetarian diet tends to maximize overall happiness. Importance could then be

---

[6] As James Lenman reminded us, the idea that moral judgements have both non-cognitive
and cognitive meaning is not new. R. M. Hare famously argued that the primary meaning of
moral judgements is prescriptive, while their secondary meaning is descriptive. See *The
Language of Morals*, Oxford: Clarendon Press, 1952, ch. 7. The similarities between Ridge's ecumenical expressivism and Hare's prescriptivism are discussed in John Eriksson, 'Moved by
Morality: An Essay on the Practicality of Moral Thought and Talk', dissertation, Uppsala
University, 2006, pp. 199–204.

[7] Ridge, 'Ecumenical Expressivism', p. 54; Lenman, 'Non-cognitivism and the Dimensions
of Evaluative Judgement', sect. 2.

[8] Ridge, 'Ecumenical Expressivism', p. 55.

represented by the strength of the expressed desire. Given that one believes that sticking to a vegetarian diet tends to maximize overall happiness, the more strongly one approves of actions insofar as they tend to maximize overall happiness, the more moral reason one thinks one has to stick to a vegetarian diet.

One advantage of this account is that it does not have to translate degrees of certainty into degrees of desire, since certainty is here represented by degrees of belief. Another advantage is that it can allow for some cases of motivational maladies. One can judge that one ought to do something and yet still lack a desire to do it. It is true that one's judgement will always express a desire, but it is a *general* desire to do actions insofar as they have a certain property, not a desire to do a particular action. Arguably, a general desire to do an action of a certain type can exist in the absence of a desire to do a particular action of this type. One might, for instance, have a general desire to do some work today, but, in a state of listlessness, fail to have any desire to do some particular kind of work.

The most serious drawback of the account is that it seems unable to capture distinctively *moral* certitude. One's certainty that sticking to a vegetarian diet is morally right depends on one's empirical certainty that doing this tends to maximize overall happiness, but it also depends on one's *moral* certainty that maximizing overall happiness is a morally relevant feature. If one comes to doubt that sticking to a vegetarian diet tends to maximize overall happiness, one will also come to doubt that doing this is morally right. But it is also true that if one comes to doubt that maximizing overall happiness is a morally relevant feature, one will come to doubt that vegetarianism is the morally right option. The ecumenical non-cognitivist seems able to capture only one's *empirical* certainty, not one's distinctively *moral* certainty.

Lenman and Ridge, who both are sensitive to this objection, have advocated a slightly more complex version of ecumenical non-cognitivism. Following Ridge, we will call it the Ideal Advisor version. According to this version, a moral judgement concerning the rightness of an action expresses (1) a desire for actions insofar as they would be approved of by a certain sort of *ideal advisor* and (2) a belief that makes direct reference back to the property of being approved of by that advisor.[9] To judge that sticking to a vegetarian diet is morally right is on this view to express (1) a desire for actions insofar as they would be approved of by one's ideal advisor and (2) a

---

[9] Lenman, 'Non-Cognitivism and the Dimensions of Evaluative Judgement', sects 2, 4; Ridge, 'Ecumenical Expressivism', p. 57.

belief that sticking to a vegetarian diet would be approved of by one's ideal advisor. Different people might have different ideal advisors. Utilitarians, for instance, would think of the ideal advisor as someone who only approves of actions that would maximize overall wellbeing, whereas Kantians would think of the ideal advisor as someone who only approves of actions that are based on universalizable maxims. It is crucial, of course that the belief about one's ideal advisor can be spelled out in purely non-moral terms. Otherwise, this belief would not be a proper belief according to the non-cognitivist.

Common to both Lenman's and Ridge's Ideal Advisor theories is the idea that importance is represented by the motivational strength of the ideal advisor's desires. So, how much reason one takes there to be for one to keep one's promises is represented by how much one thinks one's ideal advisor would want one to keep one's promises. This differs from the simpler view sketched above, according to which importance was identified with the motivational strength of the actual agent's general desires for actions. While Lenman's and Ridge's treatments of importance are closely related, they differ in their treatments of certitude, as we will see.

III. Lenman's Version of Ecumenical Expressivism

Lenman's response to the challenge starts with the proposal that the non-cognitivist can give the following story about moral uncertainty: when a subject, S, wonders whether φ-ing is wrong, S wonders whether an *improved* version of S would disapprove of φ-ing. Certitude is then given by S's degree of belief in what an Improved S recommends, while importance is given by the strength of the Improved S's (dis)approval. This story is consistent with non-cognitivism as long as the improved version of S is described in purely descriptive terms and as long as the judgement that this version of S is improved expresses primarily a pro-attitude to this version of S (that is, as long as the truth condition of the judgement that some version of S is ideal is not provided by the content of a belief). Clearly, Actual S can be more or less certain that Improved S would disapprove of φ-ing.

On Lenman's view, then, S's judgement that she ought not to lie expresses a positive attitude to conforming with the desires of Ideal S (where 'Ideal' is a descriptive specification of a hypothetical version of S that Actual S endorses as improved in the sense that Actual S takes the desires of Ideal S to be action-guiding), together with a belief that Ideal S would desire that S does not lie.[10] For illustrative purposes, let us follow Lenman and say that Ideal S is simply a fully informed and clever version of S, where 'fully informed' and 'clever' are understood descriptively.

Now, S's certitude that she ought not to lie is represented by the strength of her belief that Ideal S would desire that Actual S does not lie. The strength of S's desire not to lie represents how much S cares (*de re*) about acting in accordance with her moral judgements, and the strength of S's general desire to act in accordance with what Ideal S would desire that S does, represents how much S cares (*de dicto*) about acting in accordance with her moral judgements.

Even though Lenman's account can explain certitude in particular moral judgements, such as the judgement that one ought not to lie, it leaves out an important dimension of moral uncertainty: it has no resources to represent uncertainty regarding whether being (dis)approved of by a certain descriptively specified improved agent is indicative of rightness (or wrongness). This means that Lenman's account is unable to account for *fundamental* substantive moral uncertainty.

As Lenman recognizes and as we have hinted more than once, the non-cognitivist must, on pain of circularity, offer a purely descriptive specification of improved agents. But for any descriptive specification of improved agents, there is room for uncertainty as to whether anything of which the improved agent would approve really is right. Lenman's proposal can only account for uncertainty as to whether a descriptively specified ideal agent would (dis)approve of certain actions. But this is uncertainty about purely *empirical* matters of fact, it is not *moral* uncertainty. Lenman's Ideal Advisor version of ecumenical non-cognitivism thus faces a problem similar to the one faced by the simpler version discussed in the previous section. As we shall see in the next section, Ridge is aware of this problem and proposes a way to deal with it.

IV. Ridge's Version of Ecumenical Expressivism

Ridge's favoured version of ecumenical expressivism has several affinities with the account suggested by Lenman. One important difference, though, concerns the representation of certitude. According to Ridge,

---

[10] Lenman notes that Simon Blackburn has suggested a similar account. See Blackburn, *Ruling Passions*, Oxford: Clarendon Press, 2001, pp. 261–9.

An agent's certainty that he should φ is represented by two factors: (a) his certainty (in the ordinary sense) that φ-ing would be approved of by the relevant sort of advisor; and (b) the relative strength of his pro-attitude in favour of actions insofar as they would be approved of by the relevant sort of advisor.[11]

The discussion in the previous section explains why something like clause (b) is called for. We saw that certitude cannot be represented simply in terms of (a) since for any (non-moral) property F (e.g. the property of tending to maximize overall happiness or the property of being favoured by a descriptively specified ideal advisor), a subject can be perfectly certain that an object is F and less than certain that F is a right-making property, or in some other way indicative of rightness.[12] In other words, the addition of (b) is supposed to make Ridge's account succeed where Lenman's account failed, *viz.* in accounting for fundamental substantive moral uncertainty. However, to say that an addition like clause (b) is called for and that it is supposed to fill the gap in Lenman's account is by no means to say that it makes the ecumenical expressivist's account of certitude plausible. In fact, we shall argue in the following section that it makes the account indefensible.

But first, we should take notice of yet another clarification that Ridge makes and that will be relevant to the dilemma we will pose for ecumenical expressivism below. This is the assumption that the motivational strength in (b) is not *absolute* but *relative* to the strengths of the agent's other desires. The point of this assumption is to block the implausible implication that 'perfectly general motivational maladies (depression and listlessness, say) would count as undermining an agent's certainty in all of her moral judgements.'[13] That is to say that even if the absolute strengths of each of an agent's desires are weakened by depression, listlessness, or the like, the relative strength of her desire in (b) might stay the same. (In what follows, we use the terms 'desire' and 'pro-attitude' interchangeably.)

V. Initial Problems and Cross-Attitudinal Comparisons

We know that according to Ridge's ideal advisor version of ecumenical expressivism, a subject S's certitude that some action is morally right is a

---

[11] Ridge, 'Ecumenical Expressivism', p. 71.

[12] Cf. Ridge, 'Ecumenical Expressivism', pp. 71f.

[13] Ridge, 'Ecumenical Expressivism', p. 72.

function of (a) the degree of S's belief that that action would be approved of by the relevant sort of advisor, and (b) the relative strength of S's desire for actions insofar as they would be approved of by the relevant sort of advisor.

Here we shall briefly raise some initial worries about how to interpret this function. We need a procedure that will aggregate degrees of beliefs and (relative) strength of pro-attitudes, so that degree of certitude can only vary from 0 ('complete uncertainty') to 1 ('complete certainty'). Such a procedure is feasible only on the assumption that there are minimum and maximum degrees of desire-strength. As we noted above, complete indifference might be seen as the natural minimum degree of desire-strength but there is no natural maximum degree of desire-strength.

This point is relevant to the possibility of what we might call *cross-attitudinal comparisons*. Intuitively, we should be able to make sense of comparisons of certitude between moral and non-moral beliefs. For instance, a subject S can be more certain that $2 + 2 = 4$ than that utilitarianism is true. But if S's certitude that utilitarianism is true is a function of the degree of S's belief that an ideal advisor would favour actions insofar as they maximize utility and the relative strength of S's pro-attitude to actions insofar as they would be favoured by an ideal advisor, we need to be able to make comparisons in strength between beliefs (such as $2 + 2 = 4$) on the one hand, and combinations of beliefs and desires on the other hand. But what does it mean to say that a belief is stronger than the combination of a belief and a desire? Making sense of such comparisons seems to require a joint scale for beliefs and desires. But, as we have already seen, it is far from clear how to construct such a scale.

VI. A Dilemma

Moral certitude is supposed to be a function of a belief and a desire. But exactly what function? Ridge does not tell us, but one can show that it faces a serious dilemma. To uncover the first horn, recall once again that Ridge defines moral certitude partly in terms of relative desire-strength. The relative strength of S's desire D is most naturally defined—in analogy with relative price—in terms of the ratio between the strength of D and a weighted average of the strengths of all of S's other desires. This means that if the absolute strength of D remains the same while the absolute strengths of some other desires of S's increase, then the relative strength of D decreases. Correspondingly, if the absolute strengths of S's other desires decrease while D's absolute strength remains the same, the relative strength of D increases.

This feature of relative desire-strength generates absurd results. Suppose that you fall in love with a person you have known for many years and, as a result, the strengths of your desires concerning this person shoot up. If the strength of your desire for actions insofar as your ideal advisor would approve of them remains the same, which it is likely to do in most cases since a romantic endeavour need not affect moral commitments, then the relative strength of this desire decreases. But on Ridge's theory this implies that your moral certitude has decreased. Perhaps love can sometimes make you doubt morality, since 'in love everything is permissible', but it is surely not a necessary consequence of falling in love and feeling a strong desire for someone that your moral certitude thereby diminishes. Moral certitude cannot depend on the strength of non-moral desires in this way. Of course, the same point can be made using any non-moral desire, not just love. For instance, if one's desire for eating ice-cream becomes stronger and the strengths of one's other desires stay the same, one's moral certitude has decreased.

It is equally obvious that examples can be given that work in the opposite direction. For instance, if one falls out of love with a person and the strengths of one's desires concerning this person consequently diminish, or if the strength of one's desire for ice-cream diminishes, the relative strength of one's desire for actions, insofar as one's ideal advisor would approve of them, increases. On Ridge's view, this means that one's moral certitude increases. But it is implausible that one's moral certitude is determined in this direct manner on one's falling out of love or on one's desires for ice-cream.

Ridge could reply by defining moral certitude partly in terms of *absolute* rather than *relative* desire-strength, but then he is caught on the second horn of the dilemma. As he himself points out, defining moral certitude in terms of absolute desire-strength would have the unwelcome result that wide-ranging motivational maladies, such as depression and listlessness, will always wipe out one's moral certitude. Recall that for Ridge moral certitude depends in part on the strength of one's general desire to perform actions insofar they would be approved by the ideal advisor. But depression and listlessness can sap one's general desires to perform actions with certain properties without one's moral certitude being greatly affected.

VII. Sepielli's Account

Instead of going for an ecumenical version, Sepielli has recently defended a non-cognitivist account of moral certitude that draws heavily on Schroeder's recent treatment of expressivism.[14] Whereas non-cognitivism is a theory about the nature of the mental state we are in when we make a moral judgement, expressivism is semantic theory, according to which the meaning of a moral statement is identified with (or determined by) the mental state it is conventionally used to express. Most non-cognitivists accept expressivism and are thus committed to the idea that the meaning of a moral statement is the *non-cognitive* mental state (e.g. a desire) it expresses. A notorious problem for expressivism is to account for the meaning of moral terms when they are embedded in complex sentences. This problem goes by various labels, such as the Frege–Geach problem, the problem of embedding, or the negation problem. On Sepielli's view, non-cognitivism can account for moral certitude only if expressivism has enough structure to solve the Frege–Geach problem. Sepielli's basic maneuvre is to apply Schroeder's recent treatment of the Frege–Geach problem to the problem of moral certitude.

Let us follow Schroeder and focus on negation. Consider the sentence:

(1) Jon thinks that murdering is wrong.

There are various places where we can insert a negation in this sentence, e.g. the following:

(2) Jon thinks that murdering is not wrong.

Now, expressivists face at least two challenges. The first is to explain what kind of non-cognitive attitude (2) attributes to Jon. The second is to explain why this attitude is inconsistent with the attitude attributed to Jon in (1). Advocates of traditional expressivism might want to say that (1) attributes to Jon a negative attitude to murdering while (2) attributes to Jon an attitude of toleration to murdering. But then it remains to be explained why a negative attitude to murdering and toleration of murdering are inconsistent attitudes. Since the two attitudes have the same content (murdering), the alleged inconsistency between them cannot be explained in terms of their

---

[14] Sepielli, 'Normative Uncertainty for Non-Cognitivists'.

content. According to Schroeder's diagnosis, traditional expressivism has too little structure to meet the second challenge, so his fix is to add more structure. He does so by introducing the attitude of *being for*. The idea is that to think that an action is wrong, right, etc., is to take the attitude of being for some other attitude to the action in question. To illustrate, sentence (1) should be understood as

(1')   Jon is for blaming for murder

and (2) as

(2')   Jon is for not blaming for murder.

It is easy to see that the content of the attitude attributed to Jon in (1') is inconsistent with the content of the attitude attributed to Jon in (2').[15]

Sepielli's response to this challenge is to claim that degrees of being for are for the non-cognitivist what degrees of belief are for the cognitivist. According to this 'being for' account of normative certitude, being highly certain that murder is wrong is to be strongly *for* blaming for murder. Sepielli identifies degrees of normative importance with degrees of blaming, so having some degree of certitude that there is strong reason not to murder comes out as being, to some degree, for strongly blaming for murdering. As can be readily seen, the degree of being for and the degree of blaming can vary independently. For example, one can be strongly for weakly blaming for not paying taxes, which would capture the case when one is very certain that not paying taxes is a minor wrong. Similarly, one can be weakly for strongly blaming for eating factory-farmed chicken, which would capture the case where one is not so confident that eating factory-farmed chicken is a major wrong.

Another challenge for the non-cognitivist, which we introduced above in our discussion of the ecumenical account, is to solve the 'normalization problem'. This is the problem of finding natural minimum and maximum levels of normative certitude. To elaborate, certitude varies from 0 to 1. To be *fully certain* that P is to believe, to degree 1, that P, and to have 0 degree of belief that not-P. To be *minimally certain* that P is to believe, to degree 0, that P, and to have 1 degree of belief that not-P. Finding minimum and

---

[15] It is perhaps not obvious that this makes the attitudes in (1') and (2') inconsistent. However, for an argument that expressivists can legitimately assume that being for is an 'inconsistency-transmitting' attitude, see Mark Schroeder, *Being For*, Oxford: Oxford University Press, 2008, pp. 42–3, 59–60.

maximum levels of normative certitude is not a problem for cognitivists, since they understand normative certitude straightforwardly in terms of degree of belief, which is taken to vary between 0 and 1.[16] But there is no obvious analogue for non-cognitive, desire-like, attitudes. As suggested above, complete indifference might be seen as the weakest possible desire, but what is it to completely desire something or to desire something to degree 1? In what sense can non-cognitive attitudes be said to vary between 0 and 1? Before we come to Sepielli's solution of the normalization problem, we shall see that the being for account is vulnerable to several problems that can also be pressed against other forms of non-cognitivism.

VIII. Problems for the *Being For* Account of Normative Certitude

Sepielli says that he accepts many of our objections to Lenman and Ridge,[17] but he overlooks the fact that several of these objections have force against the *being for* account of normative certitude too.

Gradability

Sepielli does not say much about the nature of the attitude of being for, but in order not to betray non-cognitivism he must at least maintain that it is a non-cognitive attitude. To accommodate degrees of normative certitude he must maintain that it is a gradable attitude. But this needs to be argued for since it is not obvious that all non-cognitive attitudes come in degrees. Many do, of course, such as desires or wishes, but, as pointed out above, more problematic cases are those of *intentions* or *plans*. It is debatable, of course, whether these are non-cognitive attitudes, but let us assume with expressivists such as Allan Gibbard that they are.[18] It is far from obvious that it makes sense to talk about degrees of intentions or plans, or stronger or weaker

---

[16] To be clear, it is, of course, not an uncontroversial matter how to understand degrees of belief. It is not even uncontroversial that belief does vary in degrees. All we mean to say here is that accounting for degrees of normative certitude is not a special problem for normative cognitivists, whereas it is for normative non-cognitivists. For a recent defense of degrees of belief, see John Eriksson and Alan Hájek, 'What are Degrees of Belief?', *Studia Logica*, vol. 86, no. 2 (July 2007), pp. 185–215.

[17] Sepielli, 'Normative Uncertainty for Non-Cognitivists', p. 194.

[18] Gibbard, *Thinking How to Live*.

intentions or plans. Even if the idea of degrees of being for does make sense, this needs to be argued for. But Sepielli offers no such arguments.

Cross-Attitudinal Comparisons

A plausible account of normative certitude should allow comparisons between normative and non-normative certitude. For instance, one can be more certain that $2 + 2 = 4$ than that it is right to maximize overall happiness. We think that the root of this problem is the lack of a natural maximum level for desire-like attitudes. But even on the assumption that Sepielli has solved the normalization problem for being for and shown that being for varies between 0 and 1, just like belief does, it is not clear that his account can make sense of comparisons between normative and non-normative certitude. Remember that on pain of betraying non-cognitivism, Sepielli must hold that being for is a non-cognitive attitude, i.e. a kind of attitude different from belief. What, then, does it mean to say that one's belief that $2 + 2 = 4$ is stronger than one's attitude of being for blaming actions that do not maximize overall happiness? That does not seem to be a meaningful statement. Even if both degrees of desires and degrees of beliefs are bounded (so that each attitude has a natural minimum degree 0 and a maximum degree 1), they seem too different to be meaningfully calibrated. But intuitively, we *can* make sense of comparisons between normative and non-normative certitude, and for cognitivists this is no problem at all.[19]

Motivational Maladies

Since being for is a non-cognitive attitude, it is sensitive to general changes in a subject's psychology. Falling into a state of depression or listlessness generally has a negative impact on motivational attitudes. It is likely, then, that becoming depressed or listless makes one less for blaming and praising for various actions. Suppose that as a result of falling into a state of general listlessness, a person becomes less for praising for charity work

---

[19] There is a proposal that avoids this problem in Schroeder, *Being For*. Schroeder suggests a non-cognitivist view of belief, according to which belief, too, reduces to the attitude of being for. Roughly, believing that *P* is being for proceeding as if *P*. But as Schroeder notes, this moves has many costs and it is likely that many expressivists will be reluctant to make it.

than she used to be. On Sepielli's view, this means that the listless person's certitude that charity work is right has decreased. But this is an implausible implication. Falling into states of depression or listlessness does not entail that one is less certain about non-normative matters, such motivational maladies do not affect the certitude that $2 + 2 = 4$ or that the CIA planned the murder of JFK. So why should falling into states of depression or listlessness entail that one is less certain about normative matters? Of course, one's interest in being moral may wane when one falls into a depression, but moral interest and moral confidence are different things. It is noteworthy that Lenman's and Ridge's expressivist accounts do take this on board and thus are not vulnerable to the problem of motivational maladies. So this is an aspect in which Sepielli's account is in worse shape than previous accounts.

The Wrong Kind of Reasons

Another serious problem is that the attitude of being for and the degrees to which one is for bearing some relation, such as blaming, to some action can vary independently of moral certitude. For example, a utilitarian might be certain that murder is wrong but not be for blaming for murder since he thinks the attitude of blaming for murder is suboptimal in terms of overall happiness. Or to take another example, one might be very much for blaming omissions to keep one's promises not because one has a high degree of certitude that keeping promises is right but because an evil demon has threatened to torture one's family unless one is for blaming these omissions. That is, the being for account is vulnerable to a version of the notorious wrong kind of reason problem, which has been much discussed recently in other areas of normative theory. In this context, the problem is that one can be for bearing some relation to an action without this having any bearing on one's normative certitude; the reasons for being for bearing some relation (such as blaming) to an action are, in some cases, of the wrong kind to capture normative certitude. There is as yet no general solution to the wrong kind of reason problem that has won general acceptance and it is not easy to see what the solution would be in this particular context.[20]

---

[20] For samples of the recent debate on the wrong kind of reason problem, see e.g. Włodek Rabinowicz and Toni Rønnow-Rasmussen, 'The Strike of the Demon: On Fitting Pro-Attitudes

IX. Normalization of *Being For*

In trying to solve the normalization problem for Being For, Sepielli begins by noting that the normalization axiom is often formulated as prob$(\Omega) = 1$, where 'prob' signifies subjective probability and 'Ω' signifies 'a "universal set" whose members are all possible events'.[21] Informally, this means that the subjective probability that some event or other will occur is 1. Whatever degree of belief one has that some particular event will occur, this degree cannot be greater than the degree to which one believes that some event or other will occur. Sepielli suggests an analogous normalization axiom for the attitude of being for. For example, our certainty that A is wrong or A is not wrong should be understood as the degree of being for (blaming for A or not blaming for A) = 1.

But this normalization procedure has some awkward consequences. Being for is supposed to be a practical, action-guiding attitude:

> [N]ormative thought is tied to action, in the broadest possible sense. When you are for something [...], then other things being equal, this is what you do. So understood [being for] is a motivating state and hence naturally understood as akin to desire, rather than belief.[22]

What are you motivated to do when you are for (blaming for A or not blaming for A)? Sepielli might respond that you are motivated to do precisely that, i.e. to blame for A or not to blame for A. This might seem a curious motivating state, but he can insist that it is simply what it is to be certain that A is wrong or that A is not wrong.

But there is a more worrying implication. Whenever one is less than fully for blaming for A, one must be more for (blaming for A or not blaming for A) than for blaming for A, and thus, in some sense, prefer (blaming for A or not blaming for A) to blaming for A.

To revert to our earlier example, suppose that you have a high degree of certitude that keeping promises is right, but you are less than fully certain.

---

and Value', *Ethics*, vol. 114, no. 3 (April 2004), pp. 391–423; Sven Danielsson and Jonas Olson, 'Brentano and the Buck-Passers', *Mind*, vol. 116, no. 463 (July 2007), pp. 511–22; Gerard Lang, 'The Right Kind of Solution to the Wrong Kind of Reason Problem', *Utilitas*, vol. 20, no. 4 (December 2008), pp. 472–89; Mark Schroeder, 'Value and the Right Kind of Reason', *Oxford Studies in Metaethics*, vol. 5 (2010), pp. 25–55.

[21] Sepielli, 'Normative Uncertainty for Non-Cognitivists', p. 202.
[22] Schroeder, *Being For*, p. 84.

On the being for account, this means that you are strongly—but less than fully—for blaming for breaking promises. Since it seems pretty obvious that if one is more for *A* than for *B*, then one prefers *A* to *B*, Sepielli would then have to say that you must prefer (blaming for breaking promises or not blaming for breaking promises) to blaming for breaking promises, since you must be fully for (blaming for breaking promises or not blaming for breaking promises) and you are less than fully for blaming for breaking promises. But this seems very implausible. First, it is very difficult to even understand what it means to have this kind of preference, at least if preferences are supposed to be action-guiding. How can this preference ever guide one's actions? Second, even if we can somehow make sense of what it means to have this preference, it still seems absurd to have it. As an analogy, consider your attitude towards being happy. You are for being happy, which, plausibly, implies that you prefer being happy to not being happy. But you are not fully for being happy; perhaps you prefer freedom to happiness. Wouldn't it be absurd for you to prefer (being happy or not being happy) to being happy?[23]

We conclude that the being for account of normative certitude is not promising. First, it is vulnerable to several objections we have leveled at previous accounts. Second, its solution to the normalization problem has implausible consequences.

Conclusion

The general conclusion of this discussion is that while cognitivism has an easy time making sense of moral uncertainty, non-cognitivism is still struggling to find a plausible account of moral certitude, which does not conflate certitude with importance or robustness. Lenman's ecumenical account cannot accommodate fundamental moral uncertainty, only moral uncertainty that depends on empirical uncertainty. Ridge's version avoids this problem but has instead the absurd implication that moral credence depends on the strength of non-moral desires. Sepielli's

---

[23] Another way to express the worry about this preference is to say that it violates a famous principle of preference logic, often called *disjunction interpolation*, which is very compelling, at least when it is applied to contradictory pairs of alternatives. If *X* is weakly preferred to not-*X*, then *X* is weakly preferred to (*X* or not-*X*) and (*X* or not-*X*) is weakly preferred to not-*X*. In order words, if *X* is weakly preferred to not-*X*, then (*X* or not-*X*) cannot be ranked above *X* or below not-*X*. For more on this principle, see Sven Ove Hansson, *The Structure of Values and Norms*, Cambridge: Cambridge University Press, 2001, sects 6.6, 7.7.

non-ecumenical account invokes a notion of being for a tautology, which has many problematic implications. Both Ridge and Sepielli have problems with cross-attitudinal comparisons. It is not at all clear that it makes sense to compare strengths of beliefs with strengths of desires (or combinations of desires and beliefs).

Of course, we do not pretend to have shown that there cannot be a plausible non-cognitivist account of fundamental moral uncertainty, but it is at least clear that there are considerable obstacles to overcome.

8

Practical Ethics Given Moral Uncertainty

Introduction

Many of those who have written on moral uncertainty have taken it to have stark implications for at some debates in practical ethics.[1] This literature has principally focused on the topics of abortion and vegetarianism. The argument runs approximately as follows. Consider, first, the following case of decision-making under empirical uncertainty.

Speeding
Julia is considering whether to speed round a blind corner. She thinks it's pretty unlikely that there's anyone crossing the road immediately around the corner, but she's not sure. If she speeds and hits someone, she will certainly severely injure them. If she goes slowly, she certainly will not injure anyone, but will get to work slightly later than she would have done had she sped (see Table 8.1).

In this situation, both expected value reasoning and common-sense recommend that Julia should not speed.

But if we agree with this in a case of purely empirical uncertainty, and we think that we should treat moral and empirical uncertainty analogously, then we should in general think that it's impermissible to eat meat.[2] Consider the following case.

---

[1] Alexander A. Guerrero, 'Don't Know, Don't Kill: Moral Ignorance, Culpability, and Caution'; Lockhart, *Moral Uncertainty and Its Consequences*; Graham Oddie, 'Moral Uncertainty and Human Embryo Experimentation', in K. W. M. Fulford, Grant Gillett, and Janet Martin Soskice (eds), *Medicine and Moral Reasoning*, Cambridge: Cambridge University Press, 1994, pp. 144–61; Dan Moller, 'Abortion and Moral Risk', *Philosophy*, vol. 86, no. 3 (July 2011), pp. 425–43.

[2] See Guerrero, 'Don't Know, Don't Kill' and Moller, 'Abortion and Moral Risk'. Sometimes this and the case against abortion are presented as a *dominance* argument, where vegetarianism, or having a child, is suggested to be certainly permissible (Lockhart, *Moral Uncertainty*

Moral Uncertainty. William MacAskill, Krister Bykvist and Toby Ord, Oxford University Press (2020).
© William MacAskill, Krister Bykvist and Toby Ord.
DOI: 10.1093/oso/9780198722274.001.0001

Table 8.1

	Someone crossing	No-one crossing
Speed	Significant harm to another person	No harm
Go slow	Mild personal cost	Mild personal cost

Table 8.2

	Animals matter	Animals don't matter
Eat meat	Significant wrong	Permissible
Eat vegetarian	Permissible	Mild personal cost

Vegetarianism

Harry is considering whether to eat meat or a vegetarian option for dinner. He thinks it's pretty unlikely animals matter morally, but he's not sure. If he eats meat and animals do matter morally, then he commits a grave wrong. If he eats the vegetarian option, he will certainly not commit a grave wrong, though he will enjoy the meal less than he would have done had he eaten meat. (See Table 8.2.)

Here, the decision situation is analogous to the decision situation in *Speeding*. Even if Harry is highly confident in the view that animals don't matter, his credence in the view that they do matter generates a significant risk of doing something gravely wrong, outweighing the greater likelihood of missing out on a mild prudential benefit. If we thought that Julia shouldn't speed in *Speeding*, then we should think that in *Vegetarianism* the vegetarian meal is the appropriate option for Harry.

A similar argument can be made for abortion.[3] Consider the following case.

and Its Consequences, ch. 2; Weatherson, 'Review of Ted Lockhart, *Moral Uncertainty and Its Consequences*'). However, we think that we should be considering how to make decisions in light of all the possible reasons for action that one has. And if one believes that there is no moral reason against eating meat, whereas there is a prudential reason in favour of eating meat, then eating meat is the most all-things-considered choiceworthy option. So the 'dominance' form of the argument will almost never apply.

[3] See, for example, Oddie, 'Moral Uncertainty and Human Embryo Experimentation'.

Abortion

Isobel is twenty weeks pregnant and is considering whether to have an abortion. She thinks it's pretty unlikely that twenty-week-old fetuses have a right to life, but she's not sure. If she has an abortion and twenty-week-old fetuses do have a right to life, then she commits a grave wrong. If she has the child and gives it up for adoption, she will certainly not commit a grave wrong, though she will bear considerable costs as a result of pregnancy, childbirth, and separation from her child. (See Table 8.3.)

In this case, the prudential cost to the decision-maker is higher than it is in *Speeding* or *Vegetarianism*. But the potential moral wrong, if the view that fetuses have a right to life is correct, is also much greater. So, again, it seems that even if Isobel is fairly confident in the view that fetuses have no right to life, as long as she isn't extremely confident, the risk that fetuses do have a right to life is sufficient to outweigh the significant prudential reason in favour of having the abortion. In which case, the appropriate option for Isobel is to give the child up for adoption.

If this argument works, then it is like the philosopher's stone for practical ethicists: it would mean that we could draw robust lessons for practical ethics even despite extensive disagreement among moral philosophers. As Ted Lockhart comments: 'The significance of this argument is that, if sound, it shows that much of philosophers' discussion of the morality of abortion is for practical (i.e., decision-making) purposes unnecessary.'[4] Some philosophers endorse the implications of moral uncertainty for vegetarianism and abortion;[5]

Table 8.3

	Fetuses have a right to life	Fetuses have no right to life
Have abortion	Very gravely wrong	Permissible
Give up for adoption	Permissible	Significant personal cost

---

[4] Lockhart, *Moral Uncertainty and Its Consequences*, p. 52.
[5] Moller: '[the moral uncertainty argument] does seem to suggest, however, that there is a moral reason—probably not a weak one—for most agents to avoid abortion' ('Abortion and Moral Risk', p. 443). Lockhart: 'In the vast majority of situations in which decision-makers decide whether to have abortions, not having an abortion is the *reasonable* choice of action' (*Moral Uncertainty and Its Consequences*, p. 52)]. Pope John Paul II: 'the mere probability that a human person is involved [in the practice of abortion] would suffice to justify an absolute clear prohibition of any intervention aimed at killing a human embryo' ('Encyclical Letter *Evangelium Vitae*', *Acta Apostolicae Sedis* 87, 1995, pp. 401–522).

others take them to be a *modus tollens*.[6] But all authors so far seem to agree that taking moral uncertainty into account in one's decisions really does have these implications, does so in a rather straightforward way, and does so largely independently of the credences that one has in different moral views, as long as those credences are broadly reasonable.

In this chapter, we're going to make things more complicated, in two ways. First, we show that the *prima facie* implications of moral uncertainty for issues in practical ethics are far more wide-ranging than has been noted in the literature so far.

Second, we show how one can't straightforwardly argue from moral uncertainty to particular conclusions in practical ethics, using abortion and vegetarianism as particular examples. We argue for this on two grounds: first, because of interaction effects between moral issues; and, second, because of the variety of different possible intertheoretic comparisons that one can reasonably endorse. The conclusion we reach is that, before drawing out conclusions from moral uncertainty-based arguments, one first has to do the difficult job of figuring out what one's credences in different moral viewpoints are or ought to be. Taking moral uncertainty seriously undoubtedly has important implications for practical ethics; but coming to conclusions about what those implications are requires much more nuanced argument than has been made so far.

Let us make a caveat before we begin. For the purpose of keeping this chapter focused, we will have to put aside some of the issues that we've discussed so far. In particular, we will assume that all theories in which the decision-maker has credence are complete, interval-scale measurable and intertheoretically comparable and that the decision-maker doesn't have credences that are sufficiently small in theories that are sufficiently high stakes that 'fanaticism' becomes an issue. In a full analysis of the practical implications of moral uncertainty, all these factors would be taken into account. However, philosophers have yet to understand the practical implications of moral uncertainty even with these simplifying assumptions; the task of understanding moral uncertainty's implications for practical ethics without these simplifying assumptions will therefore have to await further work.

---

[6] Weatherson: '[Implications] so striking we might fear for its refutation by a quick modus tollens' ('Review of Ted Lockhart, *Moral Uncertainty and Its Consequences*', p. 694). Guerrero: '[Maximizing expected moral value] is not the reading that we prefer, in part because of cases like [abortion]' ('Don't Know, Don't Kill', p. 91).

I. Implications for Normative Ethics

Though the moral uncertainty literature so far has focused on vegetarian-ism and abortion, there are many issues in normative ethics where there appear to be clear *prima facie* implications of taking moral uncertainty into account in our decision-making, most of which have not yet been noticed.[7] This section provides a brief overview of them.

Beneficence

Consider Peter Singer's argument in 'Famine, Affluence and Morality' that failing to donate to the developing world is as wrong, morally, as letting a child drown in front of you. If one has even a moderate credence in that view, then it seems that under moral uncertainty it's appropriate to donate a substantial proportion of one's resources to save the lives of strangers. Not-donating involves a risk of doing something as wrong as letting a child drown in front of you; whereas donating involves only the risk of needlessly incurring a moderate prudential cost. The situation therefore seems analo-gous to *Speeding*: for someone who is unsure about whether Singer's argu-ments work, it would be inappropriate not to donate.[8]

A distinct argument for the same conclusion can be gained by consid-ering the acts/omissions distinction. Even if you are fairly confident in the moral relevance of the distinction between acts and omissions, you shouldn't be completely certain in that view. You should give some credence to the idea that it's just as wrong to let someone die as it is to intentionally kill them. In which case, you should have some credence that letting dis-tant strangers die because of failing to donate to effective non-profits is

---

[7] The implications of moral uncertainty have been discussed for abortion (Greenwell, 'Abortion and Moral Safety'; Pfeiffer, 'Abortion Policy and the Argument from Uncertainty'; Lockhart, *Moral Uncertainty and Its Consequences*, ch. 3; Moller, 'Abortion and Moral Risk'), embryo destruction (Oddie, 'Moral Uncertainty and Human Embryo Experimentation'), vege-tarianism (Moller, 'Abortion and Moral Risk', pp. 426, 441–3; Guerrero, 'Don't Know, Don't Kill', pp. 76–82), the ethics of killing more generally (Guerrero, 'Don't Know, Don't Kill') and duties of beneficence (Lockhart, *Moral Uncertainty and Its Consequences*, ch. 5; Weatherson, 'Review of Ted Lockhart, *Moral Uncertainty and Its Consequences*'). We don't know of other examples of the practical issues being discussed, so we believe that the suggested implications for partiality, egalitarianism, the suffering/happiness trade-off, theories of wellbeing, welfarism, egoism, and population ethics are novel.

[8] A related argument is made in Tarsney, 'Rejecting Supererogationism'.

184 PRACTICAL ETHICS GIVEN MORAL UNCERTAINTY

roughly as wrong as actively killing them. This gives a second argument for why considerations of moral uncertainty provide an argument for donating a substantial proportion of your resources to save the lives of strangers.

Partiality

Under moral uncertainty, one should give some extra weight to one's family's and friends' interests, even if your preferred moral view is impartial. For even if you are confident that the wellbeing of your family and friends are equally as important as the wellbeing of distant strangers, you should not be certain in that view: you should have some credence that the wellbeing of your family and friends is more important than the wellbeing of distant strangers. However, you should have almost no credence that the wellbeing of distant strangers is *more* important than the wellbeing of your family and friends. So you should therefore give the interests of your family and friends some extra weight, though not as much weight as if you were completely convinced of the partialist moral view. If you could benefit your friend or a stranger by the same amount, it's therefore more appropriate to benefit your friend over the stranger.

Prioritarianism, Equality, Utilitarianism

Under moral uncertainty, you should treat benefits to the badly-off as being more important than providing the same benefits to the well-off, even if you are fairly confident that they should be treated in the same way. The argument for this is analogous to the argument we just made about partiality. You should have some credence in the view that it's more important to give a benefit of a given size to someone who is worse-off rather than to someone who is better-off; this view is entailed by both prioritarianism and egalitarianism. In contrast, you should have almost no credence in the view that one ought to give a benefit of a given size to someone who is better-off rather than worse-off: this is not entailed by any reasonable moral position. So, under moral uncertainty, it will be appropriate to give a benefit of a given size to someone who is worse-off rather than someone who is better-off.

Alleviation of Suffering

Under moral uncertainty you should treat alleviating suffering as more morally important than increasing happiness. Again, the reasoning is analogous to our last two arguments. According to some plausible moral views, the alleviation of suffering is more important, morally, than the promotion of happiness. According to other plausible moral views (such as classical utilitarianism), the alleviation of suffering is equally as important, morally, as the promotion of happiness. But there is no reasonable moral view on which the alleviation of suffering is less important than the promotion of happiness. So, under moral uncertainty, it's appropriate to prefer to alleviate suffering rather than to promote happiness more often than the utilitarian would.

Theories of Wellbeing

Some theories of wellbeing claim that having 'objective' goods, like knowledge or appreciation of beauty, intrinsically make a person's life go better, whereas other theories, such as hedonism and preference-satisfactionism, do not place value on those goods beyond how they contribute to positive mental states or to preference-satisfaction. But no theories of wellbeing claim that possessing objective goods intrinsically makes a person's life go worse.

This means that, given uncertainty about theories of wellbeing but certainty about reason to promote wellbeing, it will be appropriate to promote people's achievement of objective goods.

Welfarism

Similarly, some views, such as utilitarianism, place value only on people's welfare. On other views, there are non-welfarist goods that have intrinsic value, such as great works of art or a well-preserved natural environment. But on no reasonable moral view are the supposed non-welfarist goods of negative intrinsic value. So, if you are unsure between welfarism and non-welfarist views, then under moral uncertainty it will be appropriate to promote non-welfarist goods.

Egoism and Altruism

On egoism, you only have reasons to improve your own welfare. On other moral views, you also have intrinsic reasons to improve the lives of others or respect their rights. But on no plausible moral views is it the case that you have intrinsic reasons to harm others, or violate their rights. So, if you are uncertain between egoism and other moral views, then it will be appropriate to promote the wellbeing of others in addition to your own wellbeing, though not to give promoting the wellbeing of others quite as much weight as you would if you were certain that you had altruistic reasons.

Population Ethics

Extending moral uncertainty to issues of population ethics has three main implications, concerning total versus critical-level views, separable versus non-separable views, and person-affecting versus non-person-affecting views.[9]

First, let us consider only separable non-person-affecting views: that is, views on which the value of adding an additional person to the population is independent of how many other people already exist, who they are, and what their wellbeing levels are. Among such views, there are two plausible theories: the *total* view, according to which the goodness of bringing a new person into existence is given by how much better or worse that person's life is than a 'neutral life', and *critical-level* views, according to which it's good to bring into existence a person if their life is above a certain level of wellbeing c, neutral if their life is at level c, and bad if their life is below c.[10]

Under uncertainty between the total view and critical-level views, bringing a new person into existence would have positive expected choice-worthiness if their lifetime welfare is above an 'expected' critical-level c^*, where c^* is lower than the critical-level claimed by the views in which one has credence, but greater than 0. This is because no plausible critical-level view endorses a

---

[9] For a more comprehensive discussion of these different views, see Hilary Greaves and Toby Ord, 'Moral Uncertainty about Population Axiology', *Journal of Ethics and Social Philosophy*, vol. 12, no. 2 (2017), pp. 135–67.

[10] See, e.g., Charles Blackorby, Walter Bossert and David Donaldson, *Population Issues in Social-Choice Theory, Welfare Economics and Ethics*, New York: Cambridge University Press, 2005. The authors endorse a (positive) critical-level in order to escape the Repugnant Conclusion: that, for any (finite) population of any size and any quality of life, there is some other population of a sufficiently large number of people with lives barely worth living that is better.

negative critical-level, since such a view would imply that bringing into existence lives with negative welfare has positive value. Given that the total view is equivalent to a critical-level view with the critical-level set to zero, the critical-levels over which we are uncertain go from 0 to a positive number, and the 'expected' critical-level must fall within this range.[11]

Second, let us consider uncertainty over separable and non-separable views. Non-separable views include the average view, according to which the goodness of a population is given by the average wellbeing of that population, and views according to which the goodness of a population is determined by both the average wellbeing of the population and the total wellbeing of the population.[12] Under uncertainty between separable views and non-separable views, one will place weight on both the average wellbeing of the population (or other 'quality' measures) and on the sum total of wellbeing that is above c^* minus the total wellbeing that is below c^*.

Finally, we turn to uncertainty between person-affecting and non-person-affecting views. According to person-affecting views, bringing a new person into existence is of neutral moral value; according to non-person-affecting views this is not the case.[13] Note that, given our preceding discussion, if one is uncertain only over non-person-affecting views there will be just one 'neutral' wellbeing level, at which it is neither good nor bad to add some new person to the population; where this neutral level lies will depend on both the expected critical level c^* and the average wellbeing of those who already exist. Under uncertainty between person-affecting and non-person-affecting views, it is therefore almost always the case that adding some new person to the population is of either positive or negative expected choice-worthiness. If they are above the neutral level on the non-person-affecting views in which the decision-maker has credence, then there is some reason to bring them into existence, and no offsetting reason on the person-affecting views. Similarly, if they are below the neutral level on the non-person-affecting views in which the decision-maker has credence, then there is some reason to not bring them into existence, and no offsetting reason against on the person-affecting views.

---

[11] This idea is developed in Hilary Greaves and Toby Ord, 'Moral Uncertainty about Population Axiology'.
[12] See Thomas Hurka, 'Value and Population Size', *Ethics*, vol. 93, no. 3 (April 1983), pp. 496–507; Yew-Kwang Ng, 'What Should We Do about Future Generations?: Impossibility of Parfit's Theory X', *Economics & Philosophy*, vol. 5, no. 2 (October 1989), pp. 235–53.
[13] See Jan Narveson, 'Moral Problems of Population', *The Monist*, vol. 57, no. 1 (January 1973).

II. Interaction Effects

As we noted at the outset, some philosophers have suggested that the implications of maximizing expected choice-worthiness are so clear on some issues in practical ethics that we can cease further work on the first-order philosophical question of which view on the issue is the correct one.[14]

We believe that to be a mistake. So far, commentators haven't noticed just how broad the range of different implications of moral uncertainty-based arguments are. That is obviously an oversight insofar as it means they've underestimated the importance of moral uncertainty-based reasoning. But it's also an oversight insofar as it impacts how moral uncertainty-based arguments should be applied, including in the central examples of vegetarianism and abortion. We cannot simply look at how moral uncertainty impacts on one debate in practical ethics in isolation; moral uncertainty arguments have very many implications for practical ethics, and many of those interact with one another in subtle ways.

Consider vegetarianism. Moller states that, 'avoiding meat doesn't seem to be forbidden by any view. Vegetarianism thus seems to present a genuine asymmetry in moral risk: all of the risks fall on the one side.'[15] Similarly, Weatherson comments that, 'the actions that Singer recommends...are certainly morally permissible...One rarely feels a twang of moral doubt when eating tofu curry.'[16]

That is, the moral uncertainty argument for vegetarianism got its grip because there was supposedly no or almost no possible moral reason in favour of eating meat. Once we consider *all* the implications of moral uncertainty, however, this is no longer true.

We saw that, given moral uncertainty, it's good (in expectation) to bring into existence beings with lives that are sufficiently good (above the critical level c^*). And some types of animals raised for consumption appear to have moderately happy lives, including cows, sheep, humanely raised chickens, and pigs.[17] Depending on exactly how one distributes one's credences across total views and critical-level views, one might reasonably judge that these lives are above the critical level c^*.

---

[14] For example, Lockhart, *Moral Uncertainty and Its Consequences*, p. 52.

[15] Moller, 'Abortion and Moral Risk', p. 441.

[16] Weatherson, 'Review of Ted Lockhart, *Moral Uncertainty and Its Consequences*', p. 693.

[17] An assessment of the welfare levels of various farm animals is given in F. Bailey Norwood and Jayson L. Lusk, *Compassion, by the Pound: The Economics of Farm Animal Welfare*, New York: Oxford University, 2011, p. 223.

Table 8.4

	Animals matter		Animals don't matter
	Non-consequentialist view	Consequentialist view	
Eat meat	Significant wrong	Permissible	Permissible
Eat vegetarian	Permissible	Significant wrong	Mild personal cost

Importantly, when you choose to buy meat, you aren't killing animals. Instead, you are increasing demand for meat, which incentivizes farmers to raise (and then kill) additional animals. By buying and eating cows, sheep, free-range chicken, and pork, you cause fairly happy animals to come into existence that would not otherwise have lived. On some mainstream consequentialist views (such as total utilitarianism), it may therefore be wrong *not* to purchase the meat of such animals.

Our decision situation is therefore more complicated than commentators have suggested. We could represent our decision situation as in Table 8.4.

Importantly, this means we can't state that, given moral uncertainty and any reasonable set of moral credences, one ought to be vegetarian. It might be that you find the total view of population ethics very plausible, in which case eating beef and lamb might have higher expected choice-worthiness than eating vegetarian. Alternatively, you might find the total view of populations ethics very implausible, but find the idea that you shouldn't be complicit in immoral actions very plausible; in which case under moral uncertainty vegetarianism might indeed be the more appropriate course of action. It all depends on controversial conclusions about how confident you should be in different first-order moral theories.

One might respond by restricting the scope of the argument. Rather than claiming that moral uncertainty considerations lead to vegetarianism, one might instead argue that they entail simply not eating those animals (for example, factory-farmed chickens) whose lives have been so bad so as not to be worth living. In this case, the argument that eating meat is good because it brings into existence animals with happy lives would not go through; eating this meat brings into existence animals which appear to have net unhappy lives which, almost everyone would agree, is a bad thing to do. This, one might argue, is still an example where, as Lockhart suggests, philosophers' discussion is unnecessary for practical purposes.

We do think that, for almost any reasonable moral view, the implications of moral uncertainty for the ethics of eating factory-farmed chicken (and other animals with similarly bad lives) will be basically right. But it would still be an oversimplification to say, as Lockhart seems to, that we can make this argument entirely free from at least somewhat controversial assumptions about what credences one ought to have in different moral views. First, it's a question for moral philosophy (in part) what animals have lives that are and aren't worth living; it's not a wholly unreasonable view that even factory-farmed chickens have lives that are worth living. If that were true, then there would be at least one moral view according to which one ought to eat factory-farmed chicken. In order to make moral uncertainty-based arguments entail not-eating factory-farmed chicken, one must argue (at least slightly controversially) that those moral views according to which factory-farmed chickens do not have lives worth living are significantly more plausible than those moral views according to which they have lives that are worth living.

Moreover, remember that consideration of moral uncertainty seemed to show that we have strong duties of beneficence to help the global poor. Restricting your diet costs time and money, which could be used fighting poverty, saving lives in the developing world. Over the course of your life, you could probably save enough time and money to save a life in the developing world.[18] This means that a more accurate representation of the decision situation looks as in Table 8.5.

Table 8.5

	Animals matter		Animals don't matter	
	Obligation to donate	No obligation to donate	Obligation to donate	No obligation to donate
Eat meat	Significant wrong	Significant wrong	Significant wrong	Permissible
Eat vegetarian	Mild wrong	Permissible	Significant wrong	Mild personal cost
Eat cheapest & donate	Permissible	Moderate wrong	Permissible	Mild personal cost

[18] According to the latest estimates from GiveWell, it costs about \$3,200 to do the equivalent amount of good to saving a life in poor countries ('GiveWell Cost-Effectiveness Analysis', November 2016, https://docs.google.com/spreadsheets/d/1KiWfiAGX_QZhRbC9xkzf3I8IqsXC5 kkr-nwY_feVlcM). In order for the costs of a strict vegetarian diet to be greater than the cost to

Again, therefore, we can no longer argue that maximizing expected choice-worthiness would recommend eating vegetarian no matter what reasonable credences one has across moral views. Rather, what conclusion we reach depends on substantive views about (i) how plausible different moral views are, and (ii) the strengths of your obligations, if those views are correct.

Similar considerations apply to abortion. First, even though on Ordinary Morality, the decision whether to have a child is of neutral value, on some other theories this is not the case. In particular, on some moral views, it is wrong to bring into existence even a relatively happy child. On person-affecting views there is no reason in virtue of the welfare of the child to have a child; and if you believe that the world is currently overpopulated, then you would also believe that there are moral reasons against having an additional child. On critical-level views of population ethics, it's bad to bring into existence lives that aren't sufficiently happy; if the critical level is high enough, such that you thought that your future child would probably be below that level, then according to a critical-level consequentialist view you ought not to have the child. On environmentalist or strong animal welfare views it might be immoral to have a child, because of the environmental and animal welfare impact that additional people typically have. Finally, on anti-natalist views, the bads in life outweigh the goods, and it's almost always wrong to have a child.

This means, again, that we cannot present the decision of whether to have an abortion given moral uncertainty as a decision where one option involves some significant moral risk and the other involves almost no moral risk. We should have at least some credence in all the views listed in the previous paragraph; given this, in order to know what follows from consideration of moral uncertainty we need to undertake the tricky work of determining what credences we should have in those views. (Of course, we would also need to consider those views according to which it's a good thing to bring into existence a new person with a happy life, which might create an additional reason against having an abortion.)

Moreover, as with the case of vegetarianism, we must consider the issue of opportunity cost. Carrying a child to term and giving it up for adoption costs time and money (in addition, potentially, to psychological distress)

---

save a life, the strict vegetarian diet would only have to cost an additional $1.53 per week over a span of forty years. One might object that a vegetarian diet is cheaper than an omnivorous diet. This may, typically, be true. However, because one loses options by being vegetarian, a vegetarian diet must be at least as costly as the diet one has if one acts on the maxim 'eat whatever's cheapest', and it seems unlikely that such a maxim would *never* involve eating meat.

that could be used to improve the lives of others. According to a pro-choice view that endorses Singerian duties of beneficence, one may be required to have an abortion in order to spend more time or money on improving the lives of others. Again, what seems appropriate under moral uncertainty is critically dependent on what exactly the decision-maker's credences across different moral theories are.

In the above examples, we have just looked at the interaction effects between vegetarianism and abortion and duties of beneficence and population ethics. But, as noted in the previous section, there are *very many* implications of taking moral uncertainty into account. The interactions between these various implications may be quite subtle; a full analysis of the implications of moral uncertainty for any particular topic in practical ethics would need to take *all* of these implications into account. Applications of moral uncertainty may thus create *more* work for those working in practical ethics, not less.

III. Intertheoretic Comparisons

Interaction effects are one way in which the alleged implications of moral uncertainty might not follow, and choice of intertheoretic comparisons is another.

Consider vegetarianism again. Let's (simplistically) suppose that on the Ordinary Morality view, the welfare of (non-human) animals has 1/10,000th the moral weight of the welfare of humans, and that on the 'all animals are equal' view, the welfare of humans and animals are of equal moral worth. When philosophers have argued from moral uncertainty to vegetarianism, they've implicitly invoked one specific way of making intertheoretic comparisons between the Ordinary Morality view and the 'animal welfare' view. But that isn't the only way of making the comparison. Here are two different ways of making the intertheoretic comparison (see Table 8.6).

Table 8.6

Option	Ordinary Morality	All-Animals-Are-Equal-1	All-Animals-Are-Equal-2
1 unit of human welfare	10,000	10,000	1
1 unit of animal welfare	1	10,000	1
0 units of welfare	0	0	0

There are in fact two natural ways of revising the Ordinary Morality view in order to make the welfare of all animals equal. On the first view, All-Animals-Are-Equal-1, the revision is that animal welfare is much more valuable than the Ordinary Morality view supposes. On the second view, All-Animals-Are-Equal-2, the revision is that human welfare is much less valuable than the Ordinary Morality view supposes.

We believe that both ways of making the intertheoretic comparison are 'permissible': they represent different theories, one may have credence in either, and the question of what credence one ought to have in the different comparisons is largely a question for first-order moral theorizing. But whether or not the moral uncertainty-based argument for vegetarianism goes through depends to a large extent on which of these two intertheoretic comparisons we invoke. If Harry (in the original example) is unsure between Ordinary Morality and All-Animals-Are-Equal-1, then it is indeed true that he risks a grave wrong by eating meat. If, however, he is unsure between Ordinary Morality and All-Animals-Are-Equal-2, then he does not risk a grave wrong by eating meat—the badness of eating meat is the same size on the All-Animals-Are-Equal-2 view as it is on the Ordinary Morality view, and it remains plausible that the prudential reason in favour of eating meat, on the Ordinary Morality view, outweighs the reasons against eating meat on both the Ordinary Morality view and the All-Animals-Are-Equal-2 view.

To illustrate, consider the following two tables. Suppose (again very simplistically) that the prudential reason is 0.01 units in favour of chicken and 0.001 in favour of vegetarian; the reason against eating animals is 1 unit against chicken, not at all against vegetarian. The Ordinary Morality view regards units of prudential reason as 10,000 times as valuable as the units of moral reason not to eat animals.

If Harry has credence in All-Animals-Are-Equal-1 then it's clear that the moral risk of eating chicken is grave and that, unless Harry's credence in All-Animals-Are-Equal-1 were tiny, it would be inappropriate to eat chicken (see Table 8.7).

In contrast, if Harry has credence in All-Animals-Are-Equal-2, then the potential moral downside of eating chicken is much smaller. Indeed, the biggest potential loss of value is to fail to eat chicken if Ordinary Morality is correct. Harry would need to have a very low credence in Ordinary Morality in order for eating vegetarian to be the appropriate option (see Table 8.8).

Because there are two distinct and seemingly natural ways of making the intertheoretic comparison, we again see that the moral uncertainty-based

Table 8.7

Option	Ordinary Morality	All-Animals-Are-Equal-1
Eat chicken	99	−9,900
Eat vegetarian	10	10
Don't eat	0	0

Table 8.8

Option	Ordinary Morality	All-Animals-Are-Equal-2
Eat chicken	99	−0.99
Eat vegetarian	10	0.001
Don't eat	0	0

Table 8.9

Option	Ordinary Morality	No-Acts/ Omissions-1	No-Acts/ Omissions-2
Kill 1 person	−1,000	−1,000	−1
Let 1 person die	−1	−1,000	−1
No change	0	0	0

argument for vegetarianism doesn't straightforwardly go through. We need to make a controversial decision about which of these two ways of making the intertheoretic comparison is correct.

A similar issue is relevant to the moral uncertainty argument against abortion. As we noted above, we cannot say that there's no serious moral downside to keeping the child, because having a child costs resources that could be used to prevent suffering and death due to extreme poverty. This argument becomes stronger when we consider the issue of intertheoretic comparisons.

Let us assume that Isobel has some credence in the view that there's no morally relevant distinction between acts and omissions. Again, there are two distinct but natural ways of doing the intertheoretic comparison. Let us suppose that Ordinary Morality regards killing as 1,000 times as bad as letting die. Columns 2 and 3 in Table 8.9 represents the two ways of normalizing the view that rejects the acts/omissions distinction.

On No-Acts/Omissions-1, letting die is far worse than Ordinary Morality supposes; it's as wrong as killing. On No-Acts/Omissions-2, killing is much less bad than Ordinary Morality supposes; it's merely as wrong as letting die.

If Isobel only has some credence in No-Acts/Omissions-2, then her credence in the idea that there is no acts/omissions distinction is not going to have a big impact on the appropriateness ordering of her options. If, in contrast, she has some credence in No-Acts/Omissions-1, then the biggest moral consideration in her decision whether to have an abortion is not the potential killing of an innocent person, but is the opportunity cost of the resources that she would spend on the child, which could be used to prevent the deaths of others.

Once again, therefore, one cannot claim that the implications of MEC follow straightforwardly whatever set of reasonable credences one has. In addition to making (potentially controversial) claims about what credences one ought to have across different moral views, in order to come to a conclusion about what moral uncertainty considerations entail in a particular case one also must often make (potentially controversial) claims about what is the correct way of making intertheoretic comparisons across the views in which the decision-maker has credence.[19]

Note that none of what we've said so far is an argument for the conclusion that vegetarianism or anti-abortion views *don't* follow from consideration of moral uncertainty. All we've argued is that invoking moral uncertainty alone is not sufficient to conclude that vegetarianism is appropriate or that abortion is inappropriate. Instead, one must also invoke substantive and probably controversial assumptions about what credences one ought to have across a wide array of moral views, and across different choices of intertheoretic comparisons.

Nor are we arguing that moral uncertainty does not have concrete implications for real-life decision-makers. Once a decision-maker has determined at least approximately what her credences across different theories and across different intertheoretic comparisons are, maximizing expected

[19] One might claim that (i) one ought to have credence in both possible normalizations and that (ii) given this, the theory with the higher-stakes normalization will still be the primary determiner of different options' expected choice-worthiness. We find this plausible to some extent, but believe it still depends on what exactly one's credences are; if one has a very small credence in the high-stakes normalization, then one might worry that one is entering 'fanaticism' territory if one thinks that the recommendation of MEC in this instance is correct.

choice-worthiness will recommend some courses of action as appropriate and not others. We strongly suspect that the resulting recommendations will look quite different from the typical positions in debates on these issues, or from the view that one would come to if one simply followed one's favoured moral view.

Conclusion

In this chapter, we've argued that the moral uncertainty-based arguments that philosophers have given in the literature for the rightness of vegetarianism and the wrongness of abortion are too simple. The precise implications of maximizing expected choice-worthiness under moral uncertainty depend on controversial assumptions about what credences one ought to have across different moral views, and about how to make intertheoretic comparisons across theories.

We do believe, however, that consideration of moral uncertainty should have major impacts for how practical ethics is conducted. Currently, a central focus of practical ethicists is on determining what the most plausible view on a given issue is, by arguing in favour of that view, or by arguing against competing views. If moral uncertainty were taken into account, then an additional vital activity for practical ethicists to engage in, before any recommendations about how to act were made, would be to consider the implications of a variety of different moral views on this issue, to argue for what credences to assign to those views and for what the most plausible intertheoretic comparisons are, and then to work out which options have highest expected choice-worthiness. Insofar as taking moral uncertainty into account offers a very new perspective on our moral decision-making, however, it would be surprising if the conclusions of this were the same as those that practical ethicists typically draw.

9
Moral Information

Introduction

In this chapter, we turn to a final implication of moral uncertainty: the reason, in terms of expected choice-worthiness, it gives to gain new moral information. In what follows, we introduce a framework for understanding this.

In section I, we explain how we should assess the expected utility of new empirical information, and how we could use an analogous framework to work out the expected choice-worthiness of new moral information. In section II, we apply this framework to two examples: the choice of how a large foundation should spend its resources, and the choice of career for an individual. In section III, we consider to what extent the lessons from this framework change when we consider 'imperfect' information.

Before we begin, we should highlight that we use the unusual term 'moral information'. We use this term in the hope of remaining almost entirely non-committal on the issues of moral epistemology and moral metaphysics: as we understand it, something is a piece of moral information iff coming to possess it should, epistemically, make one alter one's beliefs or one's degrees of belief about at least one fundamental moral proposition. So, the term 'moral information' could apply to experiences, arguments, intuitions, or knowledge of moral facts themselves.

I. Assessing Gains in Information

In this section, we'll explain how one should calculate the expected utility of gaining empirical information (understanding 'utility' as the numerical representation of the agent's preference ordering). One can work out the expected utility of *perfect* information—that is, the expected utility of coming to know some particular proposition for certain—and the expected utility of *imperfect* information, which is the expected utility of improving one's

Moral Uncertainty. William MacAskill, Krister Bykvist, and Toby Ord, Oxford University Press (2020).
© William MacAskill, Krister Bykvist and Toby Ord.
DOI: 10.1093/oso/9780198722274.001.0001

evidence base but not coming to know any additional proposition for certain. We'll begin by discussing the simpler concept of the expected utility of perfect information, discussing imperfect information in section III. We'll illustrate the idea of perfect information with recourse to the following example,[1] before discussing the idea in general.

Salesman

Jonny sells ice-cream cones. He has fifty ice-cream cones and he makes $1 profit for each ice-cream cone he sells. He has the option of reserving a market stall by the beach for a day for $10. If the weather is sunny, then he will sell all his ice-cream cones; if it is raining, he will sell none. He has the option to purchase access to a new incredibly reliable meteorological service, which can tell him for certain whether it will rain or be sunny tomorrow. How much, rationally, should Jonny be willing to pay in order to know for certain how many ice-cream cones he'll be able to sell if he tries?[2]

According to the standard decision-theoretical analysis,[3] he should answer this question as follows. First, he should work out how many ice-cream cones he expects to sell, given his current evidence. Let's suppose that he thinks there is a 50/50 chance of rain. Second, he should work out the expected utility of his options, given his current evidence. In this case, the expected utility of not-reserving a market stall is 0. The expected utility of reserving the stall is $0.5 \times (\$50 - \$10) + 0.5 \times -\$10 = \$15$. The expected utility of reserving the stall is higher than the expected utility of not reserving the stall. So, given his current evidence, he should reserve the stall.

Third, he should work out the additional utility of gaining the new information. If he finds out that it will be sunny, then the additional information has no utility for him: he would not change his behavior with this new information, and so he would have made the same amount of money even without the new information. However, if he were to find out that it will rain, he would change his behavior: he would decide against reserving the stall. So, if it is the case that it will rain, the utility for Jonny of finding that out is $10.

---

[1] This version is adapted from the 'newsboy' example given in Louis Eeckhoudt and Philippe Godfroid, 'Risk Aversion and the Value of Information', *The Journal of Economic Education*, vol. 31, no. 4 (Autumn 2000), p. 382–8.

[2] We'll also make some simplifying assumptions: that Jonny doesn't value his time at all, that this is a one-time opportunity, and that the value of additional dollars for Jonny is linear over this range.

[3] See, for example, Howard Raiffa, *Decision Analysis: Introductory Lectures on Choices Under Uncertainty*, Reading, MA: Addison-Wesley, 1968.

Now, Jonny thinks there is a 50% chance that he will find out that it will be sunny (which would have no utility for him), and a 50% chance that he will find out that it will rain (which would be worth $10). So the expected utility of gaining that new piece of information is $0.5 \times \$0 + 0.5 \times \$10 = \$5$. This gives the amount up to which he should be willing to pay for the meteorological report.

In general, the expected utility of gaining new information is given by the expected utility of one's decision given that new information (in this case, $20 ($0.5 \times (\$50 - \$10) + 0.5 \times \$0$)) minus the expected utility of one's decision without that information (in this case, $15 (calculation given above)).

When dealing with the expected utility of information, there are some important points to note. First, as one might have noticed from the above, on our analysis, gaining new information has positive expected utility *only* if there is some chance that one will change one's behavior. If Jonny thinks that he would sell forty ice-cream cones even if it were raining, then there is no expected utility for him in gaining additional information, because he would reserve the stall either way. Similarly, if Jonny knows that he is very lazy, and will fail to reserve the stall no matter how rational it is for him to do so, then, again, gaining new information will have no expected utility for him. In reality, factors such as peace of mind can make it rational to gain new evidence even if one will not change one's behavior. But for simplicity, we leave these details to the side.

Second, note that the expected utility of information is very different from how much one actually has to pay for that information. Perhaps Jonny could find out whether it will rain tomorrow simply by checking online, costing him nothing. In which case, he simply had a bargain—but the amount he had to pay does not change the fact that the information had an expected utility of $5 (and that, if he had no better option, he should have been willing to pay up to $5 to receive it).

Third, the higher stakes a decision is, the greater the expected utility of information. To illustrate, suppose in the case above that we multiplied all the monetary values by 10: each ice-cream cone sells for $10, but Jonny has to pay $100 in order to reserve the stall. In which case, the expected utility of information for Jonny would have the same proportional change, increasing to $50.

The above method for calculating the expected utility of additional information is intuitively appealing and widely accepted within decision analysis. But, to our knowledge, it has only ever been used to work out the expected utility of gaining new empirical information: that is, information about how the world will pan out. One unique evaluation of all possible states of the world is always presupposed.

Improving our epistemic state with respect to the moral facts is something we can do, and something that could potentially change which actions we take and believe it's appropriate to take. If our argument in this book so far is correct, then it seems plausible that we should assess the expected choice-worthiness of gaining more information about moral facts in just the same way that we should assess the expected utility of gaining more information about empirical facts.

Given this, the expected choice-worthiness of gaining new information is given by the expected choice-worthiness of one's decision given that new information minus the expected choice-worthiness of one's decision without that information.[4]

In what follows, we'll give two examples to illustrate some applications of this analysis to moral information.

II. Two Examples

A Philanthropic Foundation

Our first example provides the simplest illustration of the expected choice-worthiness of moral information.[5] Let us suppose that the leader of a major philanthropic foundation is deciding how to allocate $10 million of her resources. She is deciding between two possible grants. The first would go to the Against Malaria Foundation (AMF), which she believes would provide, on average, one extra year of very high-quality life (one 'Quality Adjusted Life Year' or 'QALY') to the extreme poor for every $100 it receives.[6] The

---

[4] Formally, for some piece of information I and different ways j that the information could turn out, the expected choice-worthiness of gaining that piece of information I is: $\sum_{j=1}^{n}[C(I_j)(\max_A \sum_{i=1}^{n'} C(T_i \mid I_j)CW_i(A) - \max_A \sum_{i=1}^{n'} C(T_i)CW_i(A))]$. Note that this assumes a perfectly rational and enkratic agent.

[5] We give this example as a hypothetical, but it is relevant to real-life cases, in particular to the foundation Good Ventures, advised by the Open Philanthropy Project and its sister organization GiveWell. For a discussion of their uncertainty concerning different 'worldviews' (which includes moral uncertainty), see Holden Karnofsky, 'Worldview Diversification', *Open Philanthropy Project*, 13 December 2016, http://www.openphilanthropy.org/blog/worldview-diversification; Holden Karnofsky, 'Update on Cause Prioritization at Open Philanthropy', *Open Philanthropy Project*, 26 January 2018, https://www.openphilanthropy.org/blog/update-cause-prioritization-open-philanthropy.

[6] GiveWell, 'Mass Distribution of Long-Lasting Insecticide-Treated Nets (LLINs)'.

second would be to support corporate cage-free egg campaigns. She believes that every \$100 received by this campaign will ultimately cause farms to raise 3,800 laying hens (each of which live for approximately one year[7]) in a cage-free environment rather than a cage.[8] For simplicity, we'll stipulate that the foundation leader is certain of consequentialism.

Let's further suppose that the leader of this foundation is certain of the moral value of one QALY (for a human), so the current expected choice-worthiness of the grant to the Against Malaria Foundation is 100,000 QALYs. However, she is extremely uncertain about the value of improving conditions in factory farms: she is 99% certain that there is no value to ensuring that chickens live in a cage-free environment; she has 1% credence that the value of ensuring that a single hen is brought up in a cage-free environment (rather than that a different hen is brought up in a caged environment) is 1/100th of the value of a QALY. She believes that, across these two moral views, the value of one QALY stays constant.

Given this, the grant to Against Malaria Foundation has an expected choice-worthiness of 100,000 human QALYs,[9] whereas the grant to the cage-free egg campaigns has an expected choice-worthiness equivalent to only 38,000 human QALYs, so the best decision, given the credences she has, is to give the grant to the Against Malaria Foundation.

Now, suppose that the decision-maker has the option of gaining perfect information about the relative value of improving the conditions of layer hens versus providing one QALY. What's the expected choice-worthiness of this information? We can work this out using the framework given above. She should think that there's a 99% chance of finding out that the cage-free reforms are of no value, so gaining this information is 99% likely not to change her behavior, and therefore have no value (at least, within the context of this decision). But she should think that there's a 1% chance that she will learn that the cage-free campaigns are of value: if this happened,

<hr>

[7] 'The Life of Laying Hens', *Compassion in World Farming*, March 2012, https://www.ciwf.org.uk/media/5235024/The-life-of-laying-hens.pdf.

[8] Lewis Bollard, 'Initial Grants to Support Corporate Cage-free Reforms', *Open Philanthropy Project*, 31 March 2016, http://www.openphilanthropy.org/blog/initial-grants-support-corporate-cage-free-reforms. Of course, the hens that are raised in a cage-free environment are not the same hens as those that would have been raised in a cage. And, though it is not realistic to suppose that farms will raise exactly as many chickens when they are raised in a cage-free environment, we make this assumption for simplicity.

[9] Strictly speaking, QALYs are a unit of goodness rather than choice-worthiness, so a more accurate (but more cumbersome) way of saying the above is that there is an expected choice-worthiness equivalent to the choice-worthiness that theories ascribe to producing 100,000 QALYs for humans.

then the expected choice-worthiness of the grant to the cage-free campaigns would become equivalent in size to providing 3.8 million human QALYs. The additional benefit she would produce given this outcome would therefore be of equivalent value to providing 3.7 million QALYs. Multiplying the value of this outcome by its probability of 1% gives us the expected choice-worthiness of gaining the information, which is equivalent to providing 37,000 QALYs. The cost to provide one QALY via a donation to AMF is $100. So she should be willing to pay up to $3.7 million (that is, $37,000 \times \$100$) in order to gain this information before making her decision about where to spend the $10 million.

In the above calculation, her starting budget was not relevant. It turned out that she should spend $3.7 million to help direct her $10 million. This means spending $3.7 million out of a total spend of $13.7 million, which is 27%. Given the other details, these percentages stay the same, so regardless of her budget size she should be willing to spend about 27% of her budget in order to know how she ought to spend the remaining 73%. Thus, if her total budget were fixed at $10 million, then she should be willing to spend $2.7 million in order to find out how to spend the remaining $7.3 million.

The above example is highly idealized, with invented numbers for the moral views and their credences, as well as a convenient restriction to just two possibilities for the value of a year of a chicken's life. But it's not completely unrealistic: we deliberately chose empirically accurate numbers, and we chose credences in moral views that could have (in a very simplified form) represented the views of the leadership of the Open Philanthropy Project at one time. The example shows, therefore, that it's at least possible for the expected choice-worthiness of moral information to be very high, such that a significant proportion of one's resources should be spent on gaining new moral information. (We'll discuss later to what extent the fact that moral information is almost always 'imperfect information' changes things.) In general, because information brings about a proportional change in the expected choice-worthiness of the options under consideration, if you're dealing with extremely high-stakes issues, then the expected choice-worthiness of gaining new information becomes extremely high as well.

This is notable given that philanthropists (and other similar actors, like governments) almost never spend resources on gaining new moral evidence. The typical method for a foundation, for example, is to pick a cause area to focus on (such as education, or climate change), and then use their resources to try to optimize within that cause area. However, they typically spend very few resources to improve their answer to the question of what cause area it is most important for them to spend their resources on, even though answering that question will necessarily require making ethical judgements.[10]

Career Choice

As well as spending money to gain new moral information, one can also spend time gaining new moral information. This is relevant, for example, to the question of how much time young people should be willing to spend studying ethics before choosing which career to pursue. Again, we'll give an idealized example to illustrate. Consider Sophie. She comes from a poor family in the UK, but is very bright and hardworking, and won a scholarship to a top university. She's undecided about what career to pursue. She could become an NGO worker, and through that save the lives of one hundred people in developing countries, but it would mean that she could not give back to her family at all. Or she could become a lawyer: this would not benefit those in developing countries at all, but would mean that she could pay for health insurance and better living conditions for her extended family, improving the overall lives of each of twenty-two of her family members by 30%. She therefore realizes that she can benefit those in developing countries much more than she can benefit her family. But she isn't sure how to weigh those respective benefits. We'll assume, for simplicity, that she's certain in consequentialism. She's 95% confident that it's one hundred times more important to benefit her family, but has 5% credence remaining that it's just as important to benefit those in developing countries as it is to benefit her family, and that the moral value of benefiting her family stays constant across these two possible moral views. Given this, how much time should she be willing to spend studying ethics if doing so could give her perfect information about how to value benefits to her family compared with benefits to those in the developing world?

In what follows, we'll stipulate that saving one life in a developing country, according to the partial view, is worth 1 unit of value, and that benefiting someone's life by 30% provides 0.3 times as much benefit as

---

[10] A notable exception is Good Ventures and the Open Philanthropy Project, which undertake significant investigation to try to make cross-cause comparisons.

saving someone's life. Given her current beliefs, it is appropriate for Sophie to choose to become a lawyer: the expected choice-worthiness of doing so is $0.3 \times 22 \times 100 = 660$ units of value, whereas the expected choice-worthiness of becoming a NGO worker is $0.95 \times 100 + 0.05 \times 100 \times 100 = 595$ units of value. But she also has the option of getting more moral information: she could take several years out before university in order to study moral philosophy. How many years should she be willing to spend studying in order to get perfect information about how to weigh benefits to her family against benefits to those in the developing world?

In this example, she should think it 95% likely that she wouldn't change her decision, as this is her credence that the partial view will turn out to be correct. But she should think it 5% likely that she would change her decision (as a result of discovering that she should be impartial between distant strangers and her family) and that by choosing to become the NGO worker she would increase the value of her career (by $100 \times 100 - 0.3 \times 22 \times 100 = 9340$). So the expected choice-worthiness of this information is $0.05 \times 9340 = 467$. So she should be willing to lose out on 467 units of value in order to gain perfect information about how to spend her forty-year career. Assuming that the benefit to her family were spread evenly over a 40-year career, she produces $0.3 \times 22 \times 100/40 = 16.5$ units per year. So she should be willing to spend $28.3/(28.3 + 40) = 41.4\%$ of her time to gain perfect information about how to spend the remaining 58.6%. So, if she only had those forty years to spend, she should be willing to spend a little over sixteen of them studying ethics if this would give her perfect information about what she should do with the remainder of her career.

Like the previous example, this example was illustrated with invented credences, out of necessity. But it at least shows that the expected choice-worthiness of additional moral information *can* be high. And the thought, at least, that it could be worth anyone spending a significant proportion of their life studying ethics just so that they make a better decision at the end of that time is surprising. Indeed, for most non-philosophers, the thought that one should spend *any* time studying ethics before making major life decisions might be surprising.

Of course, in the above case the conclusion is not that Sophie actually should spend sixteen years studying ethics. Again, we need to distinguish the expected choice-worthiness of gaining moral information from the 'price' of that information—how much time it would actually take to get that information. Perhaps Sophie would learn most of what she needs to after only a few years of study. In which case it might no longer be worth spending the remaining decade learning a bit more. But that does not diminish the expected choice-worthiness of those few years of study—it just means that, for those few years, she is getting a bargain, evaluatively speaking.

A second caveat, when it comes to how much time the typical person should spend studying ethics, is that the above assumption that the benefit Sophie would produce is linear over a forty-year career will likely often be inaccurate. It seems plausible that the benefit one produces in one's career increases dramatically over the course of one's life, as one gets promoted, and becomes more experienced and more influential. In which case, insofar as studying ethics pushes back one's career, thereby taking years off the end of one's career, the cost of studying ethics is higher than the above calcula-tion would suggest. And one can lose career options by studying ethics for too long, providing another reason against too many years of study. Rather than sacrificing 41.4% of her time to gain perfect information, she should be willing to sacrifice enough time to reduce her future earnings/impact by 41.4%, which may be somewhat less.

But even despite these caveats, as with the previous case it seems plaus-ible that the expected choice-worthiness of gaining new moral informa-tion is higher than one might expect. It seems perfectly plausible that being in a better epistemic state with respect to the moral facts can mean that one does ten times as much good in the rest of one's life as one would otherwise have done (e.g. perhaps one focuses on climate change mitiga-tion rather than a domestic policy issue because one comes to believe that future people are much more important than one had thought). In which case, it would be worth spending half one's working life studying ethics in order to improve how one uses the remaining half—even if 80% of the value that one contributes to the world typically occurs in the latter half of one's career.

III. Imperfect Information

In the above examples, we assumed for ease of presentation that we'd be able to achieve certainty in the moral facts of the matter. But that's unrealistic: we should never end up with certainty about some controversial moral view. So, in our decision-analytic language, we should be thinking about imperfect information—information that improves our epistemic state rather than giving us certainty—instead of perfect information.

That we will gain only imperfect information doesn't change the framework, but it does make the mathematics more difficult, and it does reduce the expected utility of gaining new information. To illustrate how the framework works for imperfect information, consider the *Salesman* example again, and suppose that rather than being able to gain perfect information about the weather, Jonny is able to gain only imperfect information by asking a semi-reliable market forecaster: if it will be sunny, the forecaster will say so 90% of the time; if it will rain, the forecaster will say so 90% of the time.

As with perfect information, the expected utility of gaining new information is given by the expected utility of one's decision given that new information minus the expected utility of one's decision without that information. In order to work this out, we first must work out what credences Jonny ought to have, depending on what the forecaster says. Using Bayes' theorem, if the forecaster says it will be sunny, then Jonny ought to believe with 90% certainty that it will be sunny; similarly, if the forecaster says it will rain, then Jonny ought to believe with 90% certainty that it will rain.[11]

The expected utility of Jonny hearing the forecaster's view is therefore:

Expected utility of best decision given new information – Expected utility of best decision given no new information

$$= (0.5(0.9 \times (\$50 - 10) + 0.1 \times -\$10) + 0.5 \times \$0) - (0.5 \times (\$50 - \$10) + 0.5 \times (-10))$$
$$= \$17.50 - \$15$$
$$= \$2.50$$

So Jonny should be willing to pay up to $2.50 to hear the forecaster's opinion.

That was an illustration of the expected utility of gaining imperfect empirical information. For an example of the expected choice-worthiness of gaining imperfect moral information, consider again the philanthropic foundation example. As before, the foundation's leader has 99% credence that improving conditions in factory farms is of no value, and 1% credence

---

[11] In what follows, we'll only use examples of imperfect information sources where there is an equal probability of Type-I and Type-II errors. Incorporating the idea that some information sources might be more likely to make a Type-I than a Type-II error again makes the math slightly more complicated but would not change the framework for estimating the value of imperfect information, so we leave it out for simplicity. It's an interesting question, beyond the scope of this chapter, whether philosophical argument is more likely to make Type-I or Type-II errors regarding the wrongness of an action.

that improving those conditions for one hen is 1/100th as good as providing one QALY. She does not know the philosophical literature on animal ethics, but could investigate it to decide what answer the weight of philosophical argument favours. Suppose that the foundation leader believes that the majority opinion of the philosophical community will correctly assess moral issues 90% of the time.

If so, then she should estimate that, upon investigating the philosophical literature, there is 10.8% chance[12] that the weight of philosophical argument will favour the idea that improving conditions on factory farms matters morally, and 89.2% chance that it will favour the idea that improving conditions on factory farms does not matter morally. In accordance with Bayes' theorem, if she investigates the philosophical literature and the arguments favour the idea that improving conditions on factory farms matters morally, she should come to have a credence of 8.3% that improving conditions on factory farms matters morally; if she investigates the philosophical literature and the arguments favour the idea that improving conditions on factory farms does not matter morally, she should come to have a credence 0.11% that improving conditions on factory farms matters morally. Providing the grant for cage-free hens only has the higher expected choice-worthiness if she finds that the philosophical arguments favour the idea that improving conditions on factory farms matters morally. So the expected choice-worthiness of gaining this imperfect information is equivalent to providing $10.8\% \times ((8.3\% \times 3,800,000) - 100,000)) = 23,263$ QALYs. Because she can provide a QALY for $100, the foundation leader should therefore be willing to spend $2.3 million to gain this imperfect information in order to have a better estimate of how to spend the $10 million. Or, alternatively, 18.5% of her budget, if that budget is fixed (down from 27% for perfect information).

The extent to which the fact that moral information is inevitably imperfect information reduces the expected choice-worthiness of new information depends on how reliable or unreliable we believe the information to be. If the information is fairly reliable—we believe that the weight of philosophical argument is correct 90% of the time—then the expected choice-worthiness of gaining imperfect moral information can still be high. In contrast, if the foundation leader believed philosophical argument to be only 75% reliable,

---

[12] A $1\% \times 90\%$ chance that the weight of philosophical argument favours the moral importance of improving conditions on factory farms and this is the correct view, and a $99\% \times 10\%$ chance of a false positive.

then the expected choice-worthiness of gaining that imperfect moral information would be only $298,860, or 2.9% of her budget.[13] If the foundation leader believed philosophical argument to be only 70% reliable, then, for the purposes of this decision, the expected choice-worthiness of gaining the new moral information would be nil, because no matter which answer the philosophical literature favoured, she would not change her decision to fund the Against Malaria Foundation.[14]

The expected choice-worthiness of gaining new moral information depends crucially, therefore, on how reliable one takes the information to be. If one believes that one will not learn very much from doing study, research or reflection on ethical matters, then the expected choice-worthiness of gaining that moral information will be low.

But, at least sometimes, ethical study and reflection can result in drastic changes to one's beliefs, in ways that seem epistemically warranted. Many people, for example, have on the basis of philosophical arguments moved from having high credence that donating a large proportion of one's resources to effective causes is merely supererogatory to having high credence that doing so is obligatory. For these people, the expected choice-worthiness of the imperfect information they gained from engaging with philosophical arguments and personal reflection was not very different from the expected choice-worthiness that perfect information would have had.

It is, of course, difficult to assess the reliability of studying or researching moral philosophy, or engaging in ethical reflection. To get a crude approximation of the expected choice-worthiness of imperfect information, however, one could ask oneself: after a certain time period of investigation,

---

[13] In this case:

P(Philosophy favours animals) $= 0.75 \times 0.01 + 0.25 \times 0.99 = 0.255$

So:

P(Animals matter|Philosophy favours animals)

= P(Philosophy favours animals|Animals matter) × P(Animals matter)/P(Philosophy favours animals)

$= 0.75 \times 0.01/0.255 = 0.0294$

Gaining this imperfect information, therefore, is worth $0.255 \times (0.0294 \times 3,800,000 - 100,000)$ $= 2988.6$ QALYs or $298,860.

[14] In this case:

P(Philosophy favours animals) $= 0.7 \times 0.01 + 0.3 \times 0.99 = 0.304$

P(Animals matter|Philosophy favours animals) = P(Philosophy favours animals|Animals matter) × P(Animals matter)/P(Philosophy favours animals) $= 0.7 \times 0.01/0.304 = 0.023$

Even in the situation where the foundation leader learns that the weight of philosophical argument favours animals mattering, the expected choice-worthiness of giving the grant to the cage-free campaign is only worth as much as $0.023 \times 3,800,000 = 87,400$ QALYs, which is less than could be gained from giving the grant to the Against Malaria Foundation.

how likely am I to have changed my moral view (in a way that is epistemically warranted)? And, given that I change my view, what is the difference in choice-worthiness between the decision I'd make then and the decision I'd make now? This procedure would approximate the value of information, but it wouldn't be quite satisfactory. Really, you'd want to provide a probability distribution over all the possible ways in which you could change your view, and the gain in value for all of those possibilities. The expected choice-worthiness of imperfect information would be the integral of the gains in choice-worthiness with respect to that probability distribution. This would be very hard to calculate exactly, but for most cases it suffices to point out that it is quite large rather than to calculate it accurately.

How could you even guess the likelihoods of changing one's view? A simple way would be to use induction from past experience: if one has already spent a fair bit of time doing ethical research, one could look at how many months one had spent doing the research, how many times one had changed one's view on the topic, and how big a difference to the expected value of one's decisions those changes made. This would give one some amount of data by which to make a guess about how likely it is for one to change one's view given additional research. And if one hasn't done research in the past, then one could use information about the likelihood of change from those who have.[15]

---

[15] One could construe such belief-changes in an alternative way: that they are evidence of *overconfidence*, rather than rational updates on the part of the decision-maker (we thank Christian Tarsney for this objection).

We agree (as argued in Chapter 1) that people are often morally overconfident, and that they probably often over-update on new moral considerations. This might sometimes attenuate the apparent impact of gaining new moral evidence from studying moral philosophy. However, overconfidence can also lead one *not* to change one's view even though one ought to have done so, and it seems that self-serving, conformity, and status quo biases all make people more resistant to changing their moral beliefs than they ought to be.

What's more, it's clear that one can gain significant moral information through either moral philosophy or lived experience or both. If one studies moral philosophy, then one is exposed to a strictly larger range of arguments, and therefore evidence, than one otherwise would have; if one has a larger and more diverse array of life-experiences then one is, again, exposed to a larger set of evidence than one would otherwise have been.

Further, there are some moral views that seem to be more common among philosophers. The proportion of philosophers who believe it is wrong to eat factory-farmed meat, for example, is much higher than the proportion of the general public who believe the same. The same is true, we believe, for the idea that those who live in rich countries have significant obligations to strangers.

Conclusion

In this chapter we provided a framework for assessing the expected choice-worthiness of gaining new moral information, and illustrated this framework with respect to the decisions facing a philanthropic foundation and a young altruistically minded person deciding what career to pursue. Though conclusions on these matters are necessarily tentative, depending crucially on the credences of the decision-maker, it seems to us that, in at least some situations, the expected choice-worthiness of engaging in further ethical reflection, study, or research can be very high.

Conclusion

This book has covered a lot of ground. In the first chapter, we gave the case for taking moral uncertainty seriously, and for thinking that there are non-trivial answers to our central question, 'Given that we are morally uncertain, how ought we to act in light of that uncertainty?'

In Chapters 2–6, we developed a general account that provided our answer to that question. We defended an information-sensitive account: the correct rule for making decisions under moral uncertainty depends crucially on the information provided by the moral theories in which one has credence. We showed how the resources from voting theory and social choice theory could be harnessed to help us develop such an account, arguing that in conditions of merely ordinal theories the Borda Rule was the correct account, in conditions of interval-scale measurability and intertheoretic incomparability variance voting was the correct theory, and in conditions of interval-scale measurability and intertheoretic comparability of choice-worthiness differences, *maximize expected choice-worthiness* (MEC) was the correct theory. We further argued that we can make sense of intertheoretic comparability, and that different moral theories are often comparable.

Finally, we showed how the Borda Rule, variance voting and MEC could be unified together in those situations (which will be the norm for real-life decision-makers) where the decision-maker faces different informational conditions all at once. We separate the theories into groups of theories that are mutually comparable with each other, and set the variance of choice-worthiness of each group to be equal (using Borda scores to represent the choice-worthiness of options on the ordinal theories) before taking an expectation. We suggested that this unified account could be thought of as an extension of *maximizing expected choice-worthiness*.

We then charted the implications of moral uncertainty for issues in metaethics and practical ethics. We argued that non-cognitivism has a very hard time providing a satisfactory account of moral uncertainty, and that the prospects of a positive solution look bleak. We argued that, though

Moral Uncertainty. William MacAskill, Krister Bykvist, and Toby Ord, Oxford University Press (2020).
© William MacAskill, Krister Bykvist and Toby Ord.
DOI: 10.1093/oso/9780198722274.001.0001

moral uncertainty certainly has implications for practical ethics, those implications are not as obvious as has so far been presumed, and require at least somewhat controversial assumptions about what credences one ought to have in different moral theories. Also, we showed how the theory of decision-making under moral uncertainty gives us the resources to assess the value of gaining new moral information.

Though this book has covered a lot of ground, there is still much more to do. The topic of decision-making under moral uncertainty is as important, we believe, as the topic of decision-making under empirical uncertainty, and we believe that it should receive a commensurate amount of research attention. Right now, we have barely scratched the surface.

We will therefore suggest some promising and underexplored further lines of enquiry. There are some important topics that we simply didn't get to cover. These include the following.

- How to axiomatize decision-making under moral uncertainty.[1]
- How we should assign deontic statuses, such as 'permissible' and 'impermissible', under moral uncertainty.
- What a reasonable credence distribution across different moral theories looks like.
- What the implications of moral uncertainty are for political philosophy, and in particular whether they can provide a justification for political liberalism.[2]

There are other topics that would certainly benefit from much greater study than we were able to give them. These include the following.

- How to make decisions under moral uncertainty given theories that posit incomparability between options.
- What grounds intertheoretic comparisons of value.
- What the most plausible intertheoretic comparison claims are between particular moral theories.
- The implications of moral uncertainty for practical ethics.

---

[1] In particular, building on the excellent work on evaluative uncertainty done by Riedener, 'Maximising Expected Value under Axiological Uncertainty'.

[2] For some work on this topic, see Evan Williams, 'Promoting Value as Such', *Philosophy and Phenomenological Research*, vol. 87, no. 2 (September 2013) pp. 392–416.

Finally, there are also promising lines of enquiry regarding other forms of normative uncertainty, in particular the following.

- Whether and how we ought to take decision-theoretic uncertainty into account in our decision-making.[3]
- Whether and how we ought to form beliefs in the face of epistemological uncertainty.[4]

We will end on a final, more speculative, note. In Chapter 9, we provided a framework for the value of gaining moral information. This framework can allow us to more clearly reflect on the value of moral philosophy as a whole.

What are the most important priorities that the world faces? When we ask that question, it's most natural to start comparing the magnitudes of some of the biggest known problems in the world—climate change, global poverty, disempowerment of women and minority groups—or to speculate on what might be major problems even if their status as such is still controversial, such as the suffering of wild animals, or the risk of human extinction. But it's plausible that the most important problem really lies on the meta-level: that the greatest priority for humanity, now, is to work out what matters most, in order to be able to truly know what are the most important problems we face.

The importance of doing this can hardly be overstated. Every generation in the past has committed tremendous moral wrongs on the basis of false moral views. Moral atrocities such as slavery, the subjection of women, the persecution of non-heterosexuals, and the Holocaust were, of course, driven in part by the self-interest of those who were in power. But they were also enabled and strengthened by the common-sense moral views of society at the time about what groups were worthy of moral concern. Given this dismal track record, it would be extremely surprising if we were the first generation in human history to have even broadly the correct moral worldview. It is of paramount importance, therefore, to figure out which actions society takes as common sensically permissible today we should really think of as

---

[3] The first explorations of this idea are in MacAskill, 'Smokers, Psychos, and Decision-Theoretic Uncertainty'; Andrew Sepielli, 'What to Do When You Don't Know What to Do When You Don't Know What to Do…', *Noûs*, vol. 48, no. 3 (September 2014), pp. 521–44; and Michael G. Titelbaum, 'Rationality's Fixed Point (or: In Defense of Right Reason)', *Oxford Studies in Epistemology*, vol. 5 (2015), pp. 253–94.

[4] To our knowledge there has been no sustained work on this topic, though the literature on peer disagreement and higher-order evidence sometimes veers into it.

barbaric. New moral information doesn't simply contribute some fixed amount of value to the world: insofar as it influences society's moral views, it has a multiplicative impact on all the value we might achieve into the future.

Given the importance of figuring out what morality requires of us, the amount of investment by society into this question is astonishingly small. The world currently has an annual purchasing-power-adjusted gross product of about $127 trillion.[5] Of that amount, a vanishingly small fraction—probably less than 0.05%[6]—goes to directly addressing the question: What ought we to do?

One might worry that, despite its importance and comparative neglectedness, we simply cannot make meaningful progress on ethical questions, or that, if we do, our conclusions would have no influence anyway. But this, in our view, would be far too hasty. The impact of the median moral philosopher might be close to zero, but the mean is very high: on average, and over the long term, moral and political philosophy has made a huge difference to the world. Even just over the last few hundred years, Locke influenced the American Revolution and constitution, Mill influenced the woman's suffrage movement, Marx helped birth socialism and communism, and Singer helped spark the animal rights movement. If we broaden our horizons, and include Aristotle, Confucius, and Gautama Buddha in our comparison class, then it's hard to deny that the work of moral philosophy has shaped millennia of human history. And, simply by looking at the work in ethics done over the last few hundred years—by what is, globally speaking, a tiny number of people—it's hard not to believe that we have made significant progress.

---

[5] International Monetary Fund, 'Report for Selected Country Groups and Subjects (PPP Valuation of Country GDP)', 2017, https://goo.gl/RPV2Aw.

[6] 0.05% of annual gross world product is roughly $60 billion, which we can regard as an upper bound estimate of the (very difficult to quantify) amount of investment that goes toward fundamentally normative questions. As a comparison, the total UK government expenditure in 2016 was £772 billion (David Gauke, *Budget 2016*, London: Stationery Office, 2016, p. 5), of which £300 million, or 0.04%, was spent on funding for the humanities and economic and social sciences through their research councils (Department for Business Innovation & Skills, *The Allocation of Science and Research Funding 2015/16*, May 2014, pp. 17, 23). Insofar as we should expect governments to spend more on normative research than the private sector, and rich countries to spend more than poor ones, and that the vast majority of humanities and social sciences funding goes to empirical research, it would be very surprising if the world as a whole invested a larger proportion of its resources into addressing normative questions than this.

We think, therefore, that considerations of moral uncertainty and the value of moral information should lead us to conclude that further normative research is one of the most important moral priorities of our time. Ideally, one day we will have resolved the deep moral questions that we face, and we will feel confident that we have found the moral truth. In the meantime, however, we need to do the best we can, given our uncertainty.

Bibliography

Adams, Fred C. 'Long-Term Astrophysical Processes', in Nick Bostrom and Milan M. Ćirković (eds), *Global Catastrophic Risks*. Oxford: Oxford University Press, 2008, pp. 33–47.

Adams, Pauline Austin and Joe K. Adams. 'Confidence in the Recognition and Reproduction of Words Difficult to Spell', *The American Journal of Psychology*, vol. 73, no. 4 (December 1960), pp. 544–52.

Allais, Maurice. 'Allais Paradox', in John Eatwell, Murray Milgate, and Peter Newman (eds), *The New Palgrave: A Dictionary of Economics*. London: Macmillan, 1987, vol. 1, pp. 78–80.

Arpaly, Nomy. 'On Acting Rationally against One's Best Judgement', *Ethics*, vol. 110, no. 3 (April 2000), pp. 488–513.

Arpaly, Nomy. *Unprincipled Virtue: An Inquiry into Moral Agency*, New York: Oxford University Press, 2013.

Barry, Christian and Patrick Tomlin. 'Moral Uncertainty and Permissibility: Evaluating Option Sets', *Canadian Journal of Philosophy*, vol. 46, no. 6 (2016), pp. 898–923.

Beckstead, Nick. 'On the Overwhelming Importance of Shaping the Far Future'. PhD thesis, Rutgers University, 2013.

Beckstead, Nick. 'Recklessness, Timidity and Fanaticism'. Unpublished MS.

Bergström, Lars. *Grundbok i värdeteori*. Stockholm: Thales, 1990.

Binmore, Ken. *Rational Decisions*. Princeton, NJ: Princeton University Press, 2009.

Blackburn, Simon. 'Dilemmas: Dithering, Plumping, and Grief', in H. E. Mason (ed.), *Moral Dilemmas and Moral Theory*. Oxford: Oxford University Press, 1996, pp. 127–39.

Blackburn, Simon. *Ruling Passions*, Oxford: Clarendon Press, 2001.

Blackorby, Charles, David Donaldson, and John A. Weymark. 'Social Choice with Interpersonal Utility Comparisons: A Diagrammatic Introduction', *International Economic Review*, vol. 25, no. 2 (1984), pp. 327–56.

Blackorby, Charles, Walter Bossert, and David Donaldson. *Population Issues in Social-Choice Theory, Welfare Economics and Ethics*. New York: Cambridge University Press, 2005.

Bollard, Lewis. 'Initial Grants to Support Corporate Cage-Free Reforms', Open Philanthropy Project, 31 March 2016. http://www.openphilanthropy.org/blog/initial-grants-support-corporate-cage-free-reforms

Bordes, Georges and Nicolaus Tideman. 'Independence of Irrelevant Alternatives in the Theory of Voting', *Theory and Decision*, vol. 30, no. 2 (March 1991), pp. 163–86.

Bostrom, Nick. 'Astronomical Waste: The Opportunity Cost of Delayed Technological Development', *Utilitas*, vol. 15, no. 3 (November 2003), pp. 308–14.

Bostrom, Nick. 'Pascal's Mugging', *Analysis*, vol. 69, no. 3 (July 2009), pp. 443–5.

Briggs, Rachael. 'Decision-Theoretic Paradoxes as Voting Paradoxes', *Philosophical Review*, vol. 119, no. 1 (January 2010), pp. 1–30.

Brink, David O. 'The Separateness of Persons, Distributive Norms, and Moral Theory', in R. G. Frey and Christopher W. Morris (eds), *Value, Welfare, and Morality*. Cambridge: Cambridge University Press, 1993, pp. 252–89.

Broome, John. *Weighing Goods: Equality, Uncertainty, and Time*, Cambridge, MA: Basil Blackwell, 1991.

Broome, John. 'The Most Important Thing about Climate Change', in Jonathan Boston, Andrew Bradstock, and David L. Eng (eds), *Public Policy: Why Ethics Matters*. Acton, ACT: Australia National University E Press, 2010, pp. 101–16.

Broome, John. *Climate Matters: Ethics in a Warming World*, New York: W. W. Norton, 2012.

Broome, John. *Rationality Through Reasoning*, Chichester, West Sussex: Wiley-Blackwell, 2013.

Buchak, Lara. *Risk and Rationality*. Oxford: Oxford University Press, 2013.

Bykvist, Krister. 'How to Do Wrong Knowingly and Get Away with It', in Sliwinski Rysiek and Svensson Frans (eds), *Neither/Nor: Philosophical Papers Dedicated to Erik Carlson on the Occasion of His Fiftieth Birthday*. Uppsala: Uppsala University, 2011.

Bykvist, Krister. 'Evaluative Uncertainty and Consequentialist Environmental Ethics', in Leonard Kahn and Avram Hiller (eds), *Environmental Ethics and Consequentialism*. London: Routledge, 2014, pp. 122–35.

Bykvist, Krister and Jonas Olson. 'Expressivism and Moral Certitude', *Philosophical Quarterly*, vol. 59, no. 235 (April 2009), pp. 202–15.

Bykvist, Krister and Jonas Olson. 'Against the *Being for* Account of Normative Certitude', *Journal of Ethics and Social Philosophy*, vol. 6, no. 2 (July 2013).

Calhoun, Cheshire. 'Responsibility and Reproach', *Ethics*, vol. 99, no. 1 (January 1989), pp. 389–406.

Carlson, Erik. 'Extensive Measurement with Incomparability', *Journal of Mathematical Psychology*, vol. 52, no. 4 (June 2008), pp. 250–9.

Chang, Ruth. 'Voluntarist Reasons and the Sources of Normativity', in David Sobel and Steven Wall (eds), *Reasons for Action*. Cambridge: Cambridge University Press, 2009, pp. 243–71.

Christensen, David. 'Disagreement as Evidence: The Epistemology of Controversy', *Philosophy Compass*, vol. 4, no. 5 (September 2009), pp. 756–67.

Connell, F. J. 'Probabilism', in Thomas Carson (ed.), *The New Catholic Encyclopedia*, 2nd edn. Detroit, MI: Thomson/Gale, 2002.

Cotra, Ajeya. 'AMF and Population Ethics', The GiveWell Blog, 12 December 2016. http://blog.givewell.org/2016/12/12/amf-population-ethics/

Cotton-Barratt, Owen. 'Geometric Reasons for Normalising Variance to Aggregate Preferences'. Unpublished MS. http://users.ox.ac.uk/~ball1714/Variance%20normalisation.pdf

Danielsson, Sven and Jonas Olson. 'Brentano and the Buck-Passers', *Mind*, vol. 116, no. 463 (July 2007), pp. 511–22.

Dasgupta, Shamik. 'Absolutism vs Comparativism about Quantity', *Oxford Studies in Metaphysics*, vol. 8 (2013), pp. 105–48.

Department for Business Innovation & Skills. *The Allocation of Science and Research Funding 2015/16*. May 2014.

Dreier, James. 'Dispositions and Fetishes: Externalist Models of Moral Motivation', *Philosophy and Phenomenological Research*, vol. 61, no. 3 (November 2000), pp. 619–38.

Easwaran, Kenny. 'Regularity and Hyperreal Credences', *The Philosophical Review*, vol. 123, no. 1 (January 2014), pp. 1–41.

Eeckhoudt, Louis and Philippe Godfroid. 'Risk Aversion and the Value of Information', *The Journal of Economic Education*, vol. 31, no. 4 (Autumn 2000), pp. 382–8.

Eriksson, John. 'Moved by Morality: An Essay on the Practicality of Moral Thought and Talk'. Dissertation, Uppsala University, 2006.

Eriksson, Lina and Alan Hájek. 'What are Degrees of Belief?', *Studia Logica*, vol. 86, no. 2 (July 2007), pp. 185–215.

Fine, Kit. 'Guide to Ground', in Fabrice Correia and Benjamin Schnieder (eds), *Metaphysical Grounding: Understanding the Structure of Reality*. Cambridge: Cambridge University Press, 2012, pp. 37–80.

Fricker, Miranda. 'The Relativism of Blame and Williams's Relativism of Distance', *The Aristotelian Society Supplementary Volume*, vol. 84, no. 1 (June 2010), pp. 151–77.

Gauke, David. *Budget 2016*. London: Stationery Office, 2016.

Gibbard, Allan. *Thinking How to Live*. Cambridge, MA: Harvard University Press, 2003.

GiveWell. 'Against Malaria Foundation', November 2016. http://www.givewell.org/charities/against-malaria-foundation/November-2016-version

Gracely, Edward J. 'On the Noncomparability of Judgments Made by Different Ethical Theories', *Metaphilosophy*, vol. 27, no. 3 (July 1996), pp. 327–32.

Graham, Peter. 'In Defense of Objectivism about Moral Obligation', *Ethics*, vol. 121, no. 1 (October 2010), pp. 88–115.

Greaves, Hilary and Toby Ord. 'Moral Uncertainty about Population Axiology', *Journal of Ethics and Social Philosophy*, vol. 12, no. 2 (November 2017), pp. 135–67.

Greenwell, James R. 'Abortion and Moral Safety', *Crítica*, vol. 9, no. 27 (December 1977), pp. 35–48.

Guerrero, Alexander A. 'Don't Know, Don't Kill: Moral Ignorance, Culpability, and Caution', *Philosophical Studies*, vol. 136, no. 1 (October 2007), pp. 59–97.

Gustafsson, Johan E. and Olle Torpman. 'In Defence of My Favourite Theory', *Pacific Philosophical Quarterly*, vol. 95, no. 2 (June 2014), pp. 159–74.

Hájek, Alan. 'Waging War on Pascal's Wager', *The Philosophical Review*, vol. 112, no. 1 (January 2003), pp. 27–56.

Hájek, Alan. 'What Conditional Probability Could Not Be', *Synthese*, vol. 137, no. 3 (December 2003), pp. 273–323.

Hansson, Sven Ove. *The Structure of Values and Norms*. Cambridge: Cambridge University Press, 2001.

Hare, Caspar. 'Take the Sugar', *Analysis*, vol. 70, no. 2 (April 2010), pp. 237–47.

Hare, R. M. *The Language of Morals*. Oxford: Clarendon Press, 1952.

Harman, Elizabeth. 'Does Moral Ignorance Exculpate?', *Ratio*, vol. 24, no. 4 (December 2011), pp. 443–68.

Harman, Elizabeth. 'The Irrelevance of Moral Uncertainty', *Oxford Studies in Metaethics*, vol. 10 (2015), pp. 53–79.

Harman, Elizabeth. 'Ethics is Hard! What Follows?'. Unpublished MS.

Hedden, Brian. 'Does MITE Make Right? On Decision-Making under Normative Uncertainty', *Oxford Studies in Metaethics*, vol. 11 (2016), pp. 102–28.

Hicks, Amelia. 'Moral Uncertainty and Value Comparison', *Oxford Studies in Metaethics*, vol. 13 (2018), pp. 161–83.

Hillinger, Claude. 'The Case for Utilitarian Voting', *Homo Oeconomicus*, vol. 22, no. 3 (2005), pp. 295–321.

Holton, Richard. 'Partial Belief, Partial Intention,' *Mind*, vol. 117 (2008), pp. 27–58.

Hudson, James L. 'Subjectivization in Ethics', *American Philosophical Quarterly*, vol. 26, no. 3 (July 1989), pp. 221–9.

Hurka, Thomas. 'Asymmetries in Value', *Noûs*, vol. 44, no. 2 (June 2010): pp. 199–223.

International Monetary Fund. 'Report for Selected Country Groups and Subjects (PPP valuation of country GDP)', 2017. https://goo.gl/RPV2Aw

Jackson, Frank. 'Decision-Theoretic Consequentialism and the Nearest and Dearest Objection', *Ethics*, vol. 101, no. 3 (April 1991), pp. 461–82.

John Paul II. 'Encyclical Letter *Evangelium Vitae*'. *Acta Apostolicae Sedis*, no. 87 (1995), pp. 401–522.

Kagan, Shelly. *The Limits of Morality*. Oxford: Oxford University Press, 1989.

Kamm, Frances. 'Non-Consequentialism, the Person as an End-in-Itself, and the Significance of Status', *Philosophy & Public Affairs*, vol. 21, no. 4 (Autumn 1992), pp. 354–89.

Karnofsky, Holden. 'Worldview Diversification', Open Philanthropy Project, 13 December 2016. http://www.openphilanthropy.org/blog/worldview-diversification

Karnofsky, Holden. 'Update on Cause Prioritization at Open Philanthropy', Open Philanthropy Project, 26 January 2018. https://www.openphilanthropy.org/blog/update-cause-prioritization-open-philanthropy

Kelly, Thomas. 'The Epistemic Significance of Disagreement', *Oxford Studies in Epistemology*, vol. 1 (2005), pp. 167–96.

Kolodny, Niko. 'State of Process Requirements?', *Mind*, vol. 116, no. 462 (April 2007), pp. 371–85.

Krantz, David H., R. Duncan Luce, Patrick Suppes, and Amos Tversky. *Foundations of Measurement*, vol. 1: *Additive and Polynonial Representations*. New York: Academic Press, 1971.

Lang, Gerard. 'The Right Kind of Solution to the Wrong Kind of Reason Problem', *Utilitas*, vol. 20, no. 4 (December 2008), pp. 472–89.

Lenman, James. 'Non-Cognitivism and the Dimensions of Evaluative Judgement', Brown Electronic Article Review Service, 15 March 2003. http://www.brown.edu/Departments/Philosophy/bears/homepage.html

Leslie, John. *The End of the World: The Science and Ethics of Human Extinction*. London: Routledge, 1998.

Lichtenstein, Sarah and Baruch Fischhoff. 'Do Those Who Know More Also Know More about How Much They Know?', *Organizational Behavior and Human Performance*, vol. 20, no. 2 (December 1977), pp. 159–83.

Lichtenstein, Sarah, Baruch Fischhoff, and Lawrence D. Phillips. 'Calibration of Probabilities: The State of the Art to 1980', in Daniel Kahneman, Paul Slovic, and Amos Tversky (eds), *Judgment Under Uncertainty: Heuristics and Biases*. Cambridge: Cambridge University Press, 1982, pp. 306–34.

Liguori, Alphonsus. *Theologia Moralis*, 2nd edn, 1755.

Lockhart, Ted. 'Another Moral Standard', *Mind*, vol. 86, no. 344 (October 1977), pp. 582–6.

Lockhart, Ted. *Moral Uncertainty and Its Consequences*. New York: Oxford University Press, 2000.

MacAskill, William. 'How to Act Appropriately in the Face of Moral Uncertainty'. BPhil thesis, University of Oxford, 2010.

MacAskill, William. 'The Infectiousness of Nihilism', *Ethics*, vol. 123, no. 3 (April 2013), pp. 508–20.

MacAskill, William. 'Normative Uncertainty'. DPhil thesis, University of Oxford, 2014.

MacAskill, William. 'Smokers, Psychos, and Decision-Theoretic Uncertainty', *The Journal of Philosophy*, vol. 113, no. 9 (September 2016), pp. 1–21.

MacAskill, William. 'Normative Uncertainty as a Voting Problem', *Mind*, vol. 125, no. 500 (October 2016), pp. 967–1004.

MacAskill, William and Toby Ord. 'Why Maximize Expected Choice-Worthiness', *Noûs* (July 2018).

Markovits, Julia. 'Acting for the Right Reasons', *The Philosophical Review*, vol. 119, no. 2 (April 2010), pp. 201–42.

Matheny, Jason Gaverick. 'Reducing the Risk of Human Extinction', *Risk Analysis*, vol. 27, no. 5 (October 2007), pp. 1335–44.

Medina, Bartolomé de. *Expositio in primam secundae angelici doctoris D. Thomæ Aquinatis*, 1577.

Moller, Dan. 'Abortion and Moral Risk', *Philosophy*, vol. 86, no. 3 (July 2011), pp. 425–43.

Moore, G. E. *Principia Ethica*. Cambridge: Cambridge University Press, 1903.

Moulin, Hervé. 'Condorcet's Principle Implies the No Show Paradox', *Journal of Economic Theory*, vol. 45, no. 1 (June 1988), pp. 53–64.

Nagel, Thomas. 'The Value of Inviolability', in Paul Bloomfield (ed.), *Morality and Self-Interest*. New York: Oxford University Press, 2008, pp. 102–16.

Nissan-Rozen, Ittay. 'Against Moral Hedging', *Economics and Philosophy*, vol. 31, no. 3 (November 2015), pp. 349–69.

Norwood, F. Bailey and Jayson L. Lusk. *Compassion, by the Pound: The Economics of Farm Animal Welfare*. New York: Oxford University, 2011.

Oddie, Graham. 'Moral Uncertainty and Human Embryo Experimentation', in K. W. M. Fulford, Grant Gillett, and Janet Martin Soskice (eds), *Medicine and Moral Reasoning*. Cambridge: Cambridge University Press, 1994, pp. 144–61.

Okasha, Samir. 'Theory Choice and Social Choice: Kuhn versus Arrow', *Mind*, vol. 120, no. 477 (January 2011), pp. 83–115.

Pascal, Blaise. *Lettres Provinciales*, 1657.

Peterson, Martin. 'From Outcomes to Acts: A Non-Standard Axiomatization of the Expected Utility Principle', *Journal of Philosophical Logic*, vol. 33, no. 4 (August 2004), pp. 361–78.

Pfeiffer, Raymond S. 'Abortion Policy and the Argument from Uncertainty', *Social Theory and Practice*, vol. 11, no. 3 (Fall 1985), pp. 371–86.

Portmore, Douglas W. 'Position-Relative Consequentialism, Agent-Centered Options, and Supererogation', *Ethics*, vol. 113, no. 2 (January 2003), pp. 303–32.

Posner, Richard A. *Catastrophe: Risk and Response*. Oxford: Oxford University Press, 2004.

Pronin, Emily. 'How We See Ourselves and How We See Others', *Science*, vol. 320, no. 5880 (30 May 2008), pp. 1177–80.

Pronin, Emily, Daniel Lin, and Lee Ross. 'The Bias Blind Spot: Perceptions of Bias in Self Versus Others', *Personality and Social Psychology Bulletin*, vol. 28, no. 3 (March 2002), pp. 369–81.

Rabinowicz, Włodek and Toni Rønnow-Rasmussen. 'The Strike of the Demon: On Fitting Pro-Attitudes and Value', *Ethics*, vol. 114, no. 3 (April 2004), pp. 391–423.

Raiffa, Howard. *Decision Analysis: Introductory Lectures on Choices Under Uncertainty*. Reading, MA: Addison-Wesley, 1968.

Raz, Joseph. 'Permissions and Supererogation', *American Philosophical Quarterly*, vol. 12, no. 2 (April 1975), pp. 161–8.

Raz, Joseph. *The Morality of Freedom*. Oxford: Clarendon Press, 1986.

Rees, Martin J. *Our Final Century: A Scientist's Warning: How Terror, Error, and Environmental Disaster Threaten Humankind's Future in this Century—on Earth and Beyond*. London: Heinemann, 2003.

Regan, Donald. *Utilitarianism and Cooperation*. Oxford: Clarendon Press, 1980.

Rhodes, Richard. *The Making of the Atomic Bomb*. London: Simon & Schuster, 1986.

Ridge, Michael. 'Certitude, Robustness, and Importance for Non-Cognitivists', Brown Electronic Article Review Service, 15 March 2003. http://www.brown.edu/Departments/Philosophy/bears/homepage.html

Ridge, Michael. 'Ecumenical Expressivism: The Best of Both Worlds?', *Oxford Studies in Metaethics*, vol. 2 (2007), pp. 51–77.

Riedener, Stefan. 'Maximising Expected Value under Axiological Uncertainty'. BPhil thesis, University of Oxford, 2013.

Rosen, Gideon. 'Culpability and Ignorance', *Proceedings of the Aristotelian Society*, vol. 103, no. 1 (June 2003), pp. 61–84.

Rosen, Gideon. 'Skepticism about Moral Responsibility', *Philosophical Perspectives*, vol. 18, no. 1 (December 2004), pp. 295–313.

Ross, Jacob. 'Rejecting Ethical Deflationism', *Ethics*, vol. 116, no. 4 (July 2006), pp. 742–68.

Scanlon, T. M. *What We Owe to Each Other*. Cambridge, MA: Harvard University Press, 1998, 238–41.

Schroeder, Mark. *Being For*. Oxford: Oxford University Press, 2008.

Schroeder, Mark. 'Value and the Right Kind of Reason', *Oxford Studies in Metaethics*, vol. 5 (2010), pp. 25–55.

Schulze, Markus. 'A New Monotonic, Clone-Independent, Reversal Symmetric, and Condorcet-Consistent Single-Winner Election Method', *Social Choice and Welfare*, vol. 36, no. 2 (February 2011), pp. 267–303.

Sen, Amartya. *Collective Choice and Social Welfare*. San Francisco: Holden-Day, 1970.

Sen, Amartya. *Choice, Welfare, and Measurement*. Cambridge, MA: MIT Press, 1982.

Sen, Amartya. 'Internal Consistency of Choice', *Econometrica*, vol. 61, no. 3 (May 1993), pp. 495–521.

Sepielli, Andrew. 'What to Do When You Don't Know What to Do', *Oxford Studies in Metaethics*, vol. 4 (2009), pp. 5–28.

Sepielli, Andrew. ' "Along an Imperfectly Lighted Path": Practical Rationality and Normative Uncertainty'. PhD thesis, Rutgers University, 2010.

Sepielli, Andrew. 'Normative Uncertainty for Non-Cognitivists', *Philosophical Studies*, vol. 160, no. 2 (September 2012), pp. 191–207.

Sepielli, Andrew. 'Moral Uncertainty and the Principle of Equity among Moral Theories', *Philosophy and Phenomenological Research*, vol. 86, no. 3 (2013), pp. 580–9.

Sepielli, Andrew. 'What to Do When You Don't Know What to Do When You Don't Know What to Do…', *Noûs*, vol. 48, no. 3 (September 2014), pp. 521–44.

Sepielli, Andrew. 'Moral Uncertainty and Fetishistic Motivation', *Philosophical Studies*, vol. 173, no. 11 (2016), pp. 2951–68.

Sepielli, Andrew. 'How Moral Uncertaintism Can Be Both True and Interesting', *Oxford Studies in Normative Ethics*, vol. 7 (2017), pp. 98–116. https://www.oxford-scholarship.com/view/10.1093/oso/9780198808930.001.0001/oso-9780198808930-chapter-6

Singer, Peter. 'Famine, Affluence, and Morality', *Philosophy & Public Affairs*, vol. 1, no. 3 (Spring 1972), pp. 229–43.

Sliwa, Paulina. 'Moral Worth and Moral Knowledge', *Philosophy and Phenomenological Research*, vol. 93, no. 2 (September 2016), pp. 393–418.

Slovic, Paul, Baruch Fischhoff, and Sarah Lichtenstein. 'Facts Versus Fears: Understanding Perceived Risk', in Daniel Kahneman, Paul Slovic, and Amos Tversky (eds), *Judgment Under Uncertainty: Heuristics and Biases*, Cambridge: Cambridge University Press, 1982, pp. 463–90.

Smith, Michael. *The Moral Problem*. London: Wiley-Blackwell, 1994.

Smith, Michael. 'Evaluation, Uncertainty, and Motivation', *Ethical Theory and Moral Practice*, vol. 5 no. 3 (September 2002), pp. 305–20.

Suppes, Patrick and Joseph Zinnes. 'Basic Measurement Theory', in R. Duncan Luce, Robert R. Bush, and Eugene Galanter (eds), *Handbook of Mathematical Psychology*, vol. 1, New York: John Wiley & Sons, 1963, pp. 3–76.

Svavarsdóttir, Sigrún. 'Moral Cognitivism and Motivation', *The Philosophical Review*, vol. 108, no. 2 (April 1999), pp. 161–219.

Taber, Charles S. and Milton Lodge. 'Motivated Skepticism in the Evaluation of Political Beliefs', *American Journal of Political Science*, vol. 50, no. 3 (July 2006), pp. 755–69.

Tarsney, Christian. 'Rationality and Moral Risk: A Defense of Moderate Hedging'. PhD thesis, University of Maryland, 2017.

Tarsney, Christian. 'Moral Uncertainty for Deontologists', *Ethical Theory and Moral Practice*, vol. 21, no. 3 (2018), pp. 505–20.

Tarsney, Christian. 'Rejecting Supererogationism', *Pacific Philosophical Quarterly*, vol. 100, no. 2 (June 2019), pp. 599–623.

Tarsney, Christian. 'Intertheoretic Value Comparison: A Modest Proposal', *Journal of Moral Philosophy*, vol. 15, no. 3 (2018), pp. 324–44.

Tideman, T. N. 'Independence of Clones as a Criterion for Voting Rules', *Social Choice and Welfare*, vol. 4, no. 3 (September 1987), pp. 185–206.

Tideman, T. N. *Collective Decisions and Voting: The Potential for Public Choice.* Aldershot: Ashgate, 2006, pp. 123–42.

Titelbaum, Michael G. *Quitting Certainties: A Bayesian Framework Modeling Degrees of Belief.* Oxford: Oxford University Press, 2012.

Titelbaum, Michael G. 'Rationality's Fixed Point (or: In Defense of Right Reason)', *Oxford Studies in Epistemology*, vol. 5 (2015), pp. 253–94.

Tversky, Amos and Daniel Kahneman. 'Judgement under Uncertainty: Heuristics and Biases', *Science*, vol. 185, no. 4157 (27 September 1974), pp. 1124–31.

Von Neumann, John and Oskar Morgenstern. *Theory of Games and Economic Behavior.* Princeton, NJ: Princeton University Press, 1953.

Weatherson, Brian. 'Review of Ted Lockhart, *Moral Uncertainty and Its Consequences*', *Mind*, vol. 111, no. 443 (July 2002), pp. 693–6.

Weatherson, Brian. 'Running Risks Morally', *Philosophical Studies*, vol. 167, no. 1 (January 2014), pp. 141–63.

Williams, Bernard. 'Persons, Character, and Morality', in Amélie Oksenberg Rorty (ed.), *The Identities of Persons*, Los Angeles: University of California Press, 1977, pp. 197–216.

Williams, Evan. 'Promoting Value as Such', *Philosophy and Phenomenological Research*, vol. 87, no. 2 (September 2013) pp. 392–416.

Wolf, Susan. 'Moral Obligations and Social Commands', in Samuel Newlands and Larry M. Jorgensen (eds), *Metaphysics and the Good: Themes from the Philosophy of Robert Merrihew Adams*, Oxford: Oxford University Press, 2009, pp. 343–67.

Young, H. P. 'An Axiomatization of Borda's Rule', *Journal of Economic Theory*, vol. 9, no. 1 (September 1974), pp. 43–52.

Zimmerman, Michael. 'Is Moral Obligation Objective or Subjective?', *Utilitas*, vol. 18, no. 4 (December 2006), pp. 329–61.

Zimmerman, Michael. *Living with Uncertainty: The Moral Significance of Ignorance.* Cambridge: Cambridge University Press, 2008.

Zimmerman, Michael. *Ignorance and Moral Obligation.* Oxford: Oxford University Press, 2014.

Index